American
the Belgiar

To Ambassador Baver,

This is a story that exemplifies
the shared values that are at
the core of the American - Belgian
relationship. Thank you for
your leadership in strengthening
that relationship.

Jon W. ____

American Airman in the Belgian Resistance

Gerald E. Sorensen and the Transatlantic Alliance

JEROME W. SHERIDAN

McFarland & Company, Inc., Publishers

Jefferson, North Carolina

LIBRARY OF CONGRESS CATALOGUING-IN-PUBLICATION DATA

Sheridan, Jerome W., 1961–
    American airman in the Belgian Resistance : Gerald E. Sorensen
and the Transatlantic Alliance / Jerome W. Sheridan.
        p.   cm.
    Includes bibliographical references and index.

    ISBN 978-0-7864-9497-2 (softcover : acid free paper) ∞
    ISBN 978-1-4766-1687-2 (ebook)

    1. Sorensen, Gerald E., 1919–1944. 2. World War, 1939–1945—
Underground movements—Belgium—Biography. 3. Belgium—
History—German occupation, 1940–1945. 4. United States. Army
Air Forces. Bomb Squadron, 339th—Biography. 5. United States.
Army Air Forces.—Aerial gunners—Biography. 6. World War,
1929–1945—Aerial operations. I. Title. II. Title: Gerald E.
Sorensen and the Transatlantic Alliance.
D802.B4S46 2014
940.53'493092—dc23
[B]   2014035020

BRITISH LIBRARY CATALOGUING DATA ARE AVAILABLE

Front cover image: Gerald E. Sorensen (courtesy of DeLoy Larson)

Printed in the United States of America

McFarland & Company, Inc., Publishers
    Box 611, Jefferson, North Carolina 28640
    www.mcfarlandpub.com

For
Jenny Abeels
and
Nora Lee Morton

Contents

Acknowledgments   ix

Preface   1

Introduction   5

1 • Family, Faith and Fatherland   11

2 • Aviation Cadet   29

3 • A Wartime Romance   49

4 • Jerry's Air War   67

5 • The Underground   88

6 • King, Law and Liberty   106

7 • The Summer of 1944   128

8 • Brothers in Arms   150

9 • Farewell   169

10 • The Legacy   191

Epilogue   215

Appendix: AOMDA Belgium   221

Chapter Notes   223

Bibliography   233

Index   237

Acknowledgments

This author is deeply grateful to the many individuals in both America and Belgium who so kindly assisted with the research and preparation of this book. Thanks to the enthusiastic support of so many people, I acquired a wealth of factual detail and a comprehensive understanding of the broader context of the times in which Gerald E. (Jerry) Sorensen and the people that knew him lived. However, it must be made clear that if any factual errors or omissions have crept into the final version of the book, the responsibility for those errors and omissions rests solely with me. I likewise apologize in advance to any individuals who deserved to be thanked in these pages but whose contributions were inadvertently overlooked.

Most of the information about Jerry's family, faith, and upbringing came from his family members. Darwin Sorensen, Jerry's cousin and childhood best friend, gave me a crystal clear view of what Jerry's childhood and upbringing were like. Evelyn (Sorensen) Whyte, Jerry's cousin and the maid of honor at his wedding, likewise provided an excellent perspective on his personality. Jerry's nephew DeLoy Larsen and his niece Claudette (Larsen) Lundt generously shared a considerable amount of family history. They also showed me around Rose, Idaho, brought me to the family cemetery in Groveland, and helped me locate the relevant places in Tyhee where Jerry spent his teenage years. I was touched by the hospitality, generosity, and helpfulness of Jerry's relatives, all of whom made me feel genuinely at home. Moreover, their insights into the Latter-day Saints (LDS) faith and what it meant for Jerry's character were indispensible to the story. Jerry's surviving family members and their descendants are remarkable and, in many ways, inspiring people. I am honored to have gotten to know them.

I would like to thank Caspar Van Haalen of Pocatello High School for providing invaluable access to information about Jerry's primary and secondary education in a journey that took me on a deep exploration of Old Poky's architecture and archives. Jenny Johnson and Julie Monroe of the University of Idaho helped with information about Jerry's university experience. In Belgium, Robyn Keesling provided important access to information about the Idaho House that otherwise would not have been available. In the early stages of the writing of this book, Kent Jamison shared insights into the LDS faith that were important for understanding Jerry's character and the decisions that he took, insights that led me to pursue the understanding of Jerry's faith in more detail.

To understand Jerry's military service, I had the distinct honor and privilege of talking with three veterans of the United States Army Air Forces during World War II. Judge Maurice Braswell was a B-17 tail gunner during the war. General Robert Brazley (ret.) and Major General Charles Wilson (ret.) were both veterans of the Aviation Cadet program. All three gave me excellent personal perspectives about life in the USAAF and what service on a bomber was really like. They are testaments to why journalist Tom Brokaw called those who fought the Second World War the "Greatest Generation."

Similarly, the Commemorative Air Force Airbase Arizona enabled me to experience first-hand a ride in one of the world's last remaining airworthy B-17s. It is one thing to read a book or talk with someone about what flying in a B-17 was like. It is a qualitatively different experience to actually fly in one. Experiencing a Flying Fortress in the air gave me a much deeper perspective on the life and service of the brave men who flew during the war. It was an experience that will never be forgotten.

I thank Lowell Hoffman for the introductions to Judge Braswell and General Brazley. His editorial commentary on an early draft of the book was also very helpful. Lowell and Ruth Hoffman's graciousness in permitting me to take over their office and use their equipment in a last minute push to complete the manuscript was greatly appreciated. Bruce Hoffman went above and beyond the call of duty in assisting me with the preparation of the photographs that are included in this book. Jerry's great nephew Pete Larsen was helpful with some legal matters, and he provided me with some additional insight into the Larsen family.

Chris Dickon encouraged me to complete this project. Chris' book, *The Foreign Burial of American War Dead: A History* and his ongoing work on Americans who served in British and Commonwealth armed forces demonstrate an admirable commitment to remembrance. In addition, his insights into publishing and his little "pats on the back" along the way were more encouraging to me than Chris realizes.

In Belgium, I extend a very special thank you to Sandrin Coorevits. Sandrin was there at the beginning of this project when we "discovered"

Jerry's grave together. At critical points along the way, Sandrin helped me stay focused on what the project is really all about. She is a shining example of the true meaning of remembrance and the transatlantic relationship.

Although he had nothing to do with the research and writing of this book, I would like to thank USAF Master Sergeant Chris Almeria for his commitment to the annual Memorial Day ceremony at Jerry's grave, as well as the ceremonies at the other isolated graves in Belgium. In a similar spirit, I would very much like to thank all of the past and present leaders, volunteers, and supporters of the American Overseas Memorial Day Association (AOMDA) in Belgium for helping to keep Jerry's memory alive. Likewise, the employees of the American Battle Monuments Commission at the Ardennes, Henri-Chapelle, and Flanders Field American Cemeteries deserve a special recognition. For them, each day is Memorial Day.

Brian Dick from the United States Embassy to the Kingdom of Belgium is the embodiment of American-Belgian relations. In addition to everything else he does in support of AOMDA's mission, Brian provides invaluable support to the ceremony at Jerry's grave and the other isolated grave ceremonies. I am also grateful for the useful feedback Brian gave on an early draft of this manuscript.

Monsieur Louis Darbé of the village of Marcq shared with me some valuable information that was contained in his private files. Some of this information proved to be a valuable first step in helping me to locate subsequent authoritative sources of information. Monsieur Darbé also organized an expedition for me to Lanquesait in which we found traces of the *Wolverine,* and in which he introduced me to Madame Madeleine Petit. I am especially grateful to Monsieur Darbé for introducing me to the surviving members of the *Refuge Tarin* of the Secret Army.

Getting to know these *maquisards* was a special treat. Cesar Van Herreweghen, Max Robert, Maurice Leclerq, Maurice Husson, Léon Allard, and Roger Duquennoy all made the reality of what life was like in the Secret Army come alive. Their memories of the war, Jerry, Roger and Mac shed light on how truly remarkable this story really is. Similarly, members and friends of the *Fraternelle du Maquis de Saint-Marcoult,* like Marie-Christine Chevalier and Lea De Vos, provided additional valuable leads for information on Jerry's life in the Secret Army. Bernard Deherder, the president of the *Fraternelle,* provided some missing facts in the story, and he kindly keeps me in the loop about activities to commemorate Jerry.

Anne Ghiste of the community of Silly provided some key facts concerning the Secret Army. Christie Bell made it possible for me to acquire a wealth of clandestine press materials and other documents that belonged to her grandfather who was active in the Resistance. These documents enhanced my understanding of the Belgian Resistance in general and filled in an interesting missing detail in the story.

Rob Troubleyn of the Belgian Royal Military Museum was very helpful in locating and providing information on the military service of Arthur Abeels. It was comforting that the documentary support he provided corroborated Jenny's stories about her father and his service in the military.

Edouard Renière helped clarify the individuals in the Comet Line who sheltered Jerry before he entered the Abeels' home. Victor Schutters was likewise very helpful in providing information about the Comet Line and the role his grandfather played in sheltering Jerry. I am also grateful to Mr. Schutters for putting me in touch with Mac's daughter, Janine Park, who graciously met me for a lunch in Pennsylvania. Janine shared stories about her family and her father that she had learned from her mother and grandmother. She also shared files and photographs that she inherited from her father, whom she never knew. I would like to thank Janine for opening up her family history to me, which again filled in a key piece of the story.

I give a profound posthumous thank you to Jim Ed Morton. It must not be easy when a stranger from Belgium walks into your home to dredge up the distant past about your wife's first husband, especially when you have been married to her for sixty years. However, Jim Ed's tolerance of the intrusion and his hospitality were amazing. Even more amazing was meeting Nora Lee Morton. Although her health was already beginning to fail at the time we met, Nora Lee provided a unique and intimate insight into Jerry's character. She is an exceptional woman. Nora Lee's son Jones Morton continued to be very helpful in sending follow-up information. Jones and I have gotten together a few times subsequent to that first meeting, and each time I have learned something new. I consider him a friend. As a whole, the Morton family are fine people, patriotic Americans, and justifiably quite proud of their mother. It is a privilege to know them, and I am grateful for all of the support that they have given to this project.

Ultimately, this book is due to my friendship with Jenny Abeels. My initial conversations with Jenny are what gave me the impetus to write this book. I spent hours and hours in memorable conversations with Jenny over several years, and she graciously gave me copies of her documents, photographs, and other records to use in this book. All of this information has given this book its richness of detail about life in the Abeels household, about Jerry's experiences in Belgium, and about life in Belgium under the occupation. Jenny kept the memory of Roger, Jerry and Mac alive, and her home was a virtual museum in their honor. When she passed away on November 5, 2011, Belgium and America lost part of their shared history, as well as one of the most committed believers in the transatlantic alliance. One of my greatest regrets in life is that Jenny never saw the final version of this book. Without her, it would not have been possible.

Finally, I owe a very special thank you to Laura and Austin for providing the support and personal space that were required to make this book a reality. Their patience while I was engaged in untold hours of research and writing was a testament to their own commitment to remembrance. They supported me through this project because both believe that stories like this must be told to ensure that the torch of remembrance is passed to the next generation. Although the research for this book led them to some unusual vacation destinations, both Laura and Austin embraced the travel to learn more about parts of America that they would have otherwise never seen.

Laura took a personal interest in this story from the beginning and helped me with the research along the way. Her outstanding proofreading and editing skills were essential in preparing drafts of the book for publication. However, her talents go well beyond writing and editing. Laura is an entrepreneur who has overcome personal tragedy and professional setbacks to get to where she is today with a successful business and a loving family. Like Nora Lee, she is a woman who bounces back and a woman who stays true to her values. She continues to inspire me on a daily basis. On top of everything else, she is an extremely talented musician. This author is a lucky man.

Preface

A simple stone cross marks a grave in the silence of an old cemetery in Ganshoren, Belgium. The inscription on the cross reads:

Gerald Sorensen (USA)
Mort Pour La Belgique
1919–1944

The cross poses more questions than it answers. Who was this Gerald Sorensen from America? Why did he die for Belgium? The date implies that he died in Belgium during the Second World War, so why is he not buried alongside his countrymen in the hallowed grounds of an immaculately maintained American military cemetery in Belgium? Why is he here? Why is he so far from home in a neglected and overgrown cemetery, surrounded by Belgian Resistance fighters? Was his contribution to Belgium's liberation significant? Why does no one know his story? In May of 2004, the author vowed to answer these questions.

This book tells the true story of Staff Sergeant Gerald E. (Jerry) Sorensen. Jerry Sorensen was acting as the ball turret gunner on an American B-17 bomber when it was shot down over Nazi-occupied Belgium in May of 1944. The Belgian Resistance recovered Jerry and led him to the home of Arthur and Clémy Abeels, who sheltered him in Ganshoren under the noses of the Nazi occupiers. During the summer of 1944, Jerry grew very close to the Belgian family. Arthur and Clémy came to consider Jerry a son, while their children, Roger and Janine (Jenny), came to consider him as a brother. Jerry in turn called Arthur and Clémy "Pop" and "Ma." He thought of Roger as the brother he always wanted, and he regarded Jenny as his youngest sister. Roger was active in the Secret Army of the Belgian Resistance. As the friendship between Jerry and Roger blossomed, Jerry decided that he, too, would join the Secret Army and fight alongside his Belgian brother for the liberation of the country. On the day of the liberation, they were killed in combat with the Nazis, fighting together side-by-side.

This book is in part the biography of Jerry Sorensen's brief life. It

describes his childhood growing up in rural Idaho, his university experience, and his decision to volunteer for the United States Army Air Forces
(USAAF). It explains the ups and downs of his training in the USAAF, and
how he met the woman who would become his wife. It reviews his deployment to Europe, his experience in combat and how he came into the Abeels
home thanks to the actions of the Belgian Resistance. It delves into how
the bonds of friendship and love bloomed between him and the Abeels
family over the summer of 1944. It recounts the story of his underground
war service in the Belgian Resistance and the fateful day on which he was
killed. It discusses the impact that his life and the war had on those who
knew him.

Then, this book is more than just the biography of Jerry Sorensen.
It paints a picture of the circumstances and times in which Jerry, his family,
and his young widow lived in America. It describes what life was like for
ordinary citizens in occupied Belgium as well as what life was like in the
Belgian Resistance movements that arose to fight the Nazis. It recounts the
extraordinary sacrifices of the Belgians who literally risked their lives to
save Allied airmen and to combat the Nazi occupation of their country.

Perhaps more importantly, the book explains the values that the American Jerry Sorensen and the Belgian Roger Abeels shared, and why those
values led them to make the decisions that they did. Jerry and Roger truly
believed in the cause that America and Belgium fought for, and they will-
ingly laid down their lives for that cause. In doing so, Jerry Sorensen and
Roger Abeels became symbols of the transatlantic relationship and of the
enduring ties that bind America and Europe together in an alliance of values. They help us to understand the core nature of the transatlantic alliance
of today embodied in the North Atlantic Treaty Organization (NATO).

After the war, Jerry and Roger were posthumously honored for their
sacrifice. However, with the passage of time, memories began to fade. Belgian politicians and government officials who promised to keep the memory
alive left office. Family members and friends of the Abeels faded into retirement and passed away. Members of the American military, diplomatic, and
civilian communities in Belgium who knew what happened to Jerry rotated
home, taking the story with them. As the world continued to evolve, fewer
and fewer stories about the war were passed on to the next generation. Outside of family members in America, a handful of veterans of the Belgian
Resistance, and an aging woman in Ganshoren, Jerry's story was forgotten,
and his grave was largely ignored. That began to change sixty years after
Jerry had died.

In 2004, this author, together with Sandrin Coorevits, "rediscovered" Jerry's grave in a neglected section of an old civilian cemetery in Ganshoren that is closed to new burials. As members of the American Overseas Memorial Day Association (AOMDA) in Belgium, we placed American and Belgian flags on the grave in Jerry's honor. At that time, nothing was known about Jerry or why he was buried there. We only knew from the headstone that he was an American serviceman lying in an isolated grave outside of the three American cemeteries in Belgium. We also noticed that very intriguing inscription under his name on the headstone, "*Mort pour la Belgique*," and that the grave bore a plaque left by what we assumed to be a widow and a mother.

On Memorial Day of the following year, our tiny ceremony at the grave grew a little when we brought flowers to accompany the flags, and played the American and Belgian national anthems on a CD. As time passed, the ceremony began to attract other attendees, and it continued to evolve and to grow. By 2006, the author had made contact with Roger's sister, Jenny, who participated in the ceremony for five years until she passed away. By 2010, a small delegation of United States Air Force personnel from the Supreme Headquarters Allied Powers Europe (SHAPE) joined the ceremonies. They now participate each year to salute a fallen colleague from an earlier era. Members of the Secret Army Veterans Association are present, and the anthem of the Belgian Resistance is played. Scouts and children from local and international schools come to the ceremony to learn about Jerry and Roger's story. The ceremony has even been honored by the presence of the ambassador of the United States of America to the Kingdom of Belgium, and when the ambassador cannot attend, a high-ranking official of the embassy represents the ambassador. This ceremony is now a tradition for AOMDA Belgium, and it has attracted as many as a hundred attendees. It takes place each year on the morning of Memorial Day.

As this tradition took root, the author began to research Jerry's story to find out why an American airman was buried in a neglected civilian cemetery in Belgium. The search started with nothing to go on. No one from the American Battle Monuments Commission or the United States Embassy knew that the grave was even there. The first step was a Freedom of Information Act request to the relevant government department for official records. A perusal of the official records revealed a clue that led to contact with Jenny Abeels. That in turn led to Dumas, Texas, where the author met Jerry's widow. Additional research turned up relatives in Idaho, Utah, and Arizona who graciously opened up their homes. A chance encounter in the village of

Marcq-lez-Enghien led to contact with men in Belgium who served with Jerry in the Secret Army, as well as several others who shared information about the Belgian Resistance.

While researching this story, the author discovered that some highly inaccurate and misleading information about Jerry's story was published in some newspapers in America immediately after the war. It appears that a couple of American newspaper reporters got wind of the story shortly after the events occurred and wrote about it. However, they were clearly more interested in telling a good story than they were in investigating the truth of what had happened. The result was that a couple of interesting works of fiction based on the bare details of the story appeared in the press. Unfortunately, these works of fiction have resurfaced on the Internet and are today retold by people who do not know any better.

Therefore, at the beginning, one of the author's principal goals in writing this book was to set the historical record straight. Every effort has been made to ensure that the facts presented in the book are documented. Although the book relies in places quite heavily on personal interviews with people who knew Jerry, like Jenny Abeels, the author has tried wherever possible to verify the information gathered from personal interviews with documentary evidence. The endnotes explain the places where the sole source of evidence is personal interviews, as well as any discrepancies or unanswered questions resulting from the use of interviews. Where there is any doubt in a fact presented in the story, that doubt is noted either in the text or in the endnotes. This book is a work of history.

However, this book is also a call to action. The author is a professor who studies and teaches about the European Union, NATO, and the transatlantic relationship. Treaties created these institutions that structure transatlantic relations today, but the institutions themselves are actually rooted in values, not treaties. Common values bind America and Europe together today, just as they bound Jerry and Roger together in 1944. The defense of those values is just as relevant today as it was in 1944. That lesson must be taught to future generations, and that is why the deaths of Jerry and Roger must not be forgotten.

Introduction

It was a split-second decision. For weeks, Jerry and Roger had harassed the Nazis as members of the Secret Army, an armed Belgian Resistance organization. They had collected intelligence, engaged in acts of sabotage, and gathered arms in preparation for this day. Now, rolling slowly past them was an open-top car filled with SS officers. Should they open fire? They did not deliberate the question. This was the opportunity that they had been waiting, training, and hoping for. It was their chance to strike back at the hated Nazis and to bring Belgium one step closer to its liberation. The target was too tempting. Jerry and Roger simply took aim and fired.

Immediately, things went disastrously wrong. A company of SS (*Schütz-staffel*, the armed wing of the Nazi party) men appeared from around the corner. Badly outnumbered, Jerry and Roger took off down the country lane from which they had just come. Bullets pockmarked the ground around them as the Nazis gave chase. Jerry and Roger darted into a side road, temporarily evading the deadly fire. They knew that the Nazis would pursue them and that they would be shot in the back if they continued to run. Surrender was not an option, since they also knew that the Nazis would show no mercy. They were like a pair of rabbits hunted by a pack of dogs.

Jerry and Roger decided to make a stand, and they spotted a nearby rabbit hutch that would provide some cover. They jumped to the ground, and using the wall of the hutch to protect their backs, they positioned themselves for their final defense. As the SS men rounded the corner, Jerry and Roger opened fire. The battle-hardened Nazis instinctively dived to the ground and returned the fire. Bullets flew in both directions as the home of the bewildered and terrified rabbits became a battleground. If Jerry and Roger felt the same way, they did not show it. They remained calm and cool as they fired their submachine guns, determined to defend themselves as long as their ammunition lasted. The Nazis encircled the position, and one of them got close enough to throw a grenade into Jerry and Roger's defensive position. As it exploded, shrapnel tore through the bodies of both young men as they fought together side-by-side. Jerry and Roger had become part of history.[1]

Gerald E. (Jerry) Sorensen did not want to become part of history, at least not in that fashion. He certainly did not want to die. He was a twenty-four-year-old American with a newlywed wife and plans of raising a family on his farm. Likewise, Roger Abeels did not want to die. He was a highly intelligent and serious twenty-year-old Belgian, with dreams of raising a family and a bright future ahead of him. Both Jerry and Roger wanted to live, and both had a lot to live for.

As individuals, they were quite different from each other. They came from different cultures, practiced different religions, and spoke different languages. However, both were men who held deep values and who lived by their principles. Both wanted to live, but both wanted to live according to their values, and not in any other way. The choices that they made reflected that.

Jerry's values were rooted in his faith, in his family, and in the United States of America. After Pearl Harbor, he could not sit back and do nothing while everything that he believed in was threatened. That is why he volunteered for the United States Army Air Forces (USAAF) while he was still in university. That decision ultimately led him to the home of Roger Abeels, after the bomber on which Jerry was serving was shot down in the skies over Belgium. Roger's values were rooted in the deep sense of patriotism and personal responsibility that his parents had instilled in him. He fervently believed in his family, his country, and his king. That is why Roger chose to join the Belgian Resistance and fight against the Nazis in the shadows of the occupation.

In the summer of 1944, Belgium was still occupied but liberation was on its way as the Allied armies fought their way out the hedgerows in Normandy. All that duty required Jerry to do was to stay in hiding in the Abeels' home and wait for the Allied armies to reach him. That is what almost all of the other Allied airmen who were sheltered by the Belgian Resistance did. All that duty required Roger to do was to keep a low profile, avoid the labor draft, and wait for the liberation to come. That is what almost all of the other Belgian young men his age did. Yet the principles that Jerry and Roger held dear made them decide to go beyond what duty required.

Rather than stay in the relative safety of his family's home, Roger chose to fight in the Secret Army against the Nazis. At the beginning of August, he left to carry on the struggle in the forests of southern Belgium. Jerry gladly went with him and volunteered to take up arms in the Secret Army.

He, too, became a registered member of the Secret Army. Neither young man thought of these decisions as choices. Rather, they simply acted according to what their principles required them to do. Both young men believed that all people should live in a world of freedom and democracy, where human rights and the rule of law are protected. Both knew that these values transcend national borders. Both felt a responsibility to defend their values. Ultimately, both were willing to die for those values despite the fact that they had so much to live for.

Today, the values that Jerry and Roger died for are so deeply entrenched in the cultures of North America and Europe, and so deeply embedded in the institutions of Western government, that people take them for granted. The average American and the average European of today has only known a life of freedom. They have no doubt that their children will continue to live in freedom, nor do they doubt that their grandchildren, great-grandchildren, and great-great-grandchildren will continue to do so.

Jerry and Roger lived in a time, not all that long ago, when that state of affairs could not be taken for granted, either in Europe or in America. Twice in the twentieth century, a powerful and ruthless neighbor invaded Belgium. On both occasions, Belgians suffered occupation, starvation, dictatorship, deportations, executions, torture, deprivation, and unspeakable atrocities. Violations of human rights were the norm, not the exception. On both occasions, Belgium resisted. However, resistance alone was not enough to restore freedom in the face of an enemy that was far more numerous and powerful. Belgium needed allies to regain its freedom.

While Belgium was suffering under the jackboot of the Nazis, the United States was at war with two totalitarian empires on opposite sides of the world. Both empires shared a contempt for America and the values that it represented. Both empires posed a direct threat to the American way of life. Today it seems so obvious that America and its allies would win the Second World War. In 1942, that fact was not at all evident. In the Western Theater, Pearl Harbor had been bombed, the Philippines had been lost, and Japan controlled large swaths of China, Southeast Asia and the Pacific. Japan even occupied two of the Aleutian islands of Alaska. In Europe, Hitler's *diktat* was law from the coast of the Atlantic to the gates of Stalingrad. German U-boats were cruising up and down the East Coast of the United States, sinking American ships within the sight of private American citizens on shore.[2] America was threatened, and Americans knew it. America, too, needed allies to maintain its freedom.

In both world wars, the United States and free democratic nations in

Europe and Asia rose to the challenge that the authoritarian empires facing them posed. Together they stopped the advance of their enemies. Together they resisted the occupation. Together they rolled back the occupation and defeated the enemies of freedom.[3] However, the aftermath of the struggle to vanquish the evil that their enemies had unleashed was truly horrific. In the space of one generation, ninety-five million people had lost their lives as a consequence of two truly global wars.[4]

Emerging from the ashes of the Second World War, leaders from across the political spectrum in both Europe and America vowed that this must never, ever, happen again. To ensure that it would not, they created institutions to spread, support, protect, and defend Western values. They created the organization that would become the European Union (EU) to rebuild Europe economically based on free markets, and to rebuild it politically based on human rights and the rule of law. They created the North Atlantic Treaty Organization (NATO) to protect and defend Europe's newly regained liberty against the totalitarian menace that the Soviet Union had become after the war.

In the days of the Cold War, both institutions embraced West Germany, the former enemy, and turned it into a genuine democracy and a Western ally. When the Cold War ended, both institutions did the same for the nations of Central and Eastern Europe as they liberated themselves from Soviet control. Together, the EU and NATO today unite almost the entire European continent under the umbrella of freedom and democracy. That is why today, with only a few exceptions, the nations of Europe live in a degree of peace, prosperity, and freedom that was unimaginable at the end of the Second World War.

However, like the values they nurture and defend, the EU and NATO themselves are taken for granted today. Both institutions continue to do their work of keeping Europe and America free and secure. In fact, because of the complexity of the threats Europe and America face today, the work of these institutions has become even more important since the end of the Cold War. Yet most Americans and most Europeans neither notice nor care. Such apathy is dangerous. It is neither comfortable nor diplomatic to admit, but anti-democratic ideologies and autocratic leaders do exist. Transatlantic values are threatened. History gives every reason to believe that if Europeans and Americans do not stand together in defending their shared values today, the freedoms that they take for granted will be swept away tomorrow.

In 1944, Jerry and Roger did not know that they and their generation were paving the way for the transatlantic institutions that keep us safe today.

They only knew that a peaceful world in which freedom was secure was the type of world that they wanted their children to live in. They also knew that they shared a mutual responsibility to create that world, and they knew that they had to defend their common values together, despite their many cultural differences. In a very personal way, they embodied the commitment that lies at the basis of NATO today. Put differently, in 1944 Jerry and Roger were then what the transatlantic alliance is now. That is why they deserve a place in history.

Seventy years after his death, there are still people alive who knew Jerry Sorensen. Everyone who knew Jerry says the same things about him. Jerry was the perfect gentleman. He was kind, considerate and respectful. He was intelligent and inquisitive. He was attractive. He was friendly and outgoing. He was cheerful and blessed with a wonderful sense of humor. He never shirked from duty and was always the first to volunteer to serve others. He was a natural born leader and a dedicated family man. Most importantly, he was a man of faith and values. This book is the story of those values, and that story begins in the village of Rose, Idaho.

• 1 •

Family, Faith and Fatherland

Rose, Idaho, is nestled in a setting that is so typical of the American West. The Sawtooth Range of the Rocky Mountains towers in the distant northwestern horizon. In between Rose and those mountains lie the great lava fields of the Snake River Plain, remnants of the violent geological events that created today's Yellowstone National Park. To the east and south of Rose, the Blackfoot River winds its way west to join the Snake River. The Caribou and Teton Mountains stand on the other side of that river, as does the town of Blackfoot just to the south of Rose. The word "Blackfoot" comes from the earliest settlers of the region. In those days, prairie fires would sweep through the high grass and sagebrush of the area, leaving soot and ash which would turn boots black as the settlers walked through.[1] The Shoshone Native American tribe still inhabits the Fort Hall Indian Reservation, which lies 10 miles (16 kilometers) farther to the south between Blackfoot and Pocatello. Rose itself is not even a village. Rather, it is little more than a hamlet of a couple of dozen farms eking out a living from the semi-arid land. The most prominent structure in Rose was and is the church, to which nearly all of the local farmers belonged. With its mountains, plains, farms, and nearby Indians and geographic wonders, Rose could well have been the setting for a movie about the pioneer farmers who settled the American West.

In 1915, Ephraim and Louella Sorensen started their farm together in Rose on forty acres of land that they purchased from the Chapman family. A few months later, Nephi and Arlinda Sorensen started a farm next door. This was not a coincidence. Ephraim and Nephi were brothers. Louella and Arlinda were sisters. Both couples started families as soon as they could. Within a few years, Nephi and Arlinda had two sons, Darwin and Harold, and two daughters, Veliene and Evelyn. Ephraim and Louella had two daughters, Aletta, born in 1915, and Thora, born in 1917. Ephraim and Louella's third child was their one and only son, Gerald Ephraim Sorensen, who was born on Friday, October 31, 1919. Gerald pronounced his given name with a hard "G" sound, but his friends and family usually called him Jerry, which he wrote with a "J."

The two Sorensen families managed their farms together and raised their families together. In fact, the families cooperated so closely that the children used to joke that they did not really know whose parents were whose. This cooperation started right at the beginning when the families moved to Rose. There was no house on the property Nephi and Arlinda bought, so they stayed on Ephraim and Louella's farm until Nephi could construct his own home. Ephraim and some of the neighbors helped Nephi build his home.

As they became more experienced farmers and as their families grew, Ephraim and Nephi moved to the business of sheep farming. By the late 1920s, each owned about one thousand head of sheep, and they together managed an additional one thousand head that belonged to the Johnston Sheep Company. To feed those sheep, as well as to feed and support their own families, they raised crops and maintained half a dozen dairy cows. They grew beets mostly for feeding the sheep in the winters. Beans, carrots, hay and, of course, Idaho potatoes provided food for the family and additional income when the surplus was sold. Between the two farms was a small orchard and garden, where trees provided fruit like apples.

In the summer months, Nephi and Ephraim developed a division of labor with each other. Nephi took the sheep along the Blackfoot River into the foothills of the Caribou Mountains to graze in the high meadows, and he remained there for most of the summer. He built a small cabin in the mountains over a spring, near Brockman Creek. Arlinda and the children would join him there for part of the summer. While Nephi was busy with the sheep in the mountains, Ephraim took care of the crops in the fields. The Sorensen brothers' farms ran alongside the Lavaside and Peoples twin canals, from which Ephraim could divert some water to irrigate the fields. Without that source of water, crop farming would have been impossible in the dry summer months. Meanwhile, Louella and Arlinda spent a lot of time in the summers making clothes for the children to wear to school in the autumn.

At harvest time, all of the farmers in Rose worked together, particularly when equipment needed to be rented. Grain threshing machines were expensive, and it made no sense for each farmer to own one to use just once a year. So, the farmers in Rose hired a threshing machine to come to each farm in turn. They would all meet at one neighbor's fields to harvest and load hay and shocks of grain on to wagons that teams of horses would pull to the thresher. Meanwhile, the women would get together and prepare a big meal or pick wild fruit. When the harvesting was done on one farm, they would move on to the next farm and do the same. This continued until all of the crops of the farmers in Rose were harvested. The relationship among all of the families in Rose was close, cooperative, and mutually beneficial.

As soon as Jerry and his cousin Darwin were old enough to help, Ephraim and Nephi put them to work on the farms. When they were old enough to distinguish between a weed and a crop, they got the job of pulling the weeds in the fields. When they were a bit older and stronger, they got the additional job of milking the cows. When they were old enough to use tools safely, repairing the fences and other things around the farm that broke were added to their chores. Working on the farms was just a natural part of their childhoods.

During the summers, Darwin joined his father tending sheep in the mountains while Jerry helped his father tend and irrigate the crops. During the rest of the year, they did these tasks together. There was no time for either of them to "play" with other children in the sense that children know that term today. Something always needed to be done around the farm or in the mountain meadow. There was always a weed to be pulled, a fence to be mended, a cow to milk, an animal to find or feed, or some other chore to do. The thought of wandering off to go play at a neighbor's house never crossed their minds. The same was true for the neighbors' kids; it was a farming community. Still, Jerry and Darwin were boys and they sometimes managed to turn the chores that needed to be done into little games like who could pull a given set of weeds the fastest, or who could find the lost cow first. That is the way Jerry grew up. Outside of church and school, he and Darwin spent their time working with each other on the farms. They were farmhands and best friends as well as cousins.

Jerry and the other children attended the Lavaside Grade School, which was along the Lavaside canal, about 1.5 miles (2.4 kilometers) from the Sorensen farms. Jerry usually rode a horse to school in the morning; it had a small corral in the back to accommodate the children's horses. However, when his horse was needed for a job on the farm, Jerry walked the distance. Getting to school in the winter months was more of a challenge. Winters in Rose were very severe with substantial snowfalls. The Lavaside canal that ran along the road to the school was elevated, and the wind would blow the snow off of the canal and onto the road below. As a result, the snow on the road to school would often pile up higher than Jerry's head.

In those days, this was not an excuse for cancelling school. So, Jerry, Darwin, and the other children would climb with their horses up to the top of the canal bank and ride along the frozen canal to get to school. Sometimes they would hitch a horse to a sleigh, and the kids would ride together to school through the snow and ice.

The Lavaside School was a two-room schoolhouse. Grades one through four met together in one room, and grades five through eight met together in the other. The teachers were a husband and wife team with the surname Ison. Mrs. Ison taught the younger children while Mr. Ison taught the older ones. The Isons lived in the basement of the school, where there was also a small gym-playroom for the cold winter months. At recess, the children from grades 1 though 8 would all play together. Recess did not last long, and there was no hanging around to play after school. The children had work to do on the farms. Sometimes, the children entered spelling bees and geography competitions in Blackfoot. However, those activities were usually just for the girls, since the boys had chores to do on the farm.[2]

Growing up on a farm in an isolated rural community shaped Jerry's work ethic. However, the truly defining influence on his character was the church in the middle of the hamlet. The Sorensen families, and everyone else in Rose at the time, were devout members of the Church of Jesus Christ of Latter-day Saints. To the rest of the world, members of this church are known as Mormons. The faithful refer to themselves as Latter-day Saints or LDS. Members of this church are Christians, but some of the doctrines of their faith put them at odds with other Christian faiths. The differences stem from the fact that the LDS have a third sacred scripture, the Book of Mormon, in addition to the Old and New Testaments of the Bible.

The Book of Mormon is a spiritual history that explains how the LDS believe the Christian faith came to America. To very briefly summarize, the Book of Mormon teaches that 600 years before the birth of Christ, God directed the Prophet Lehi, his family, and a small group of followers on a journey from Jerusalem to America. They brought the Old Testament to America, and established a community that became a great civilization called the Nephites. Like the Israelis from whom they descended, the Nephites waited for the arrival of the Messiah. Following Jesus Christ's life, death, and ascension into heaven, he returned to Earth in America to reveal the New Testament to the peoples who lived on that continent. In the Book of Mormon, Christ taught the centrality of family to faith, and he revealed America to be the new Promised Land. In this Promised Land, God can make anything possible for families who are faithful, and who are

The original LDS Church in Rose, Idaho, that Jerry attended (courtesy Evelyn Whyte).

willing to work hard to realize the opportunities that God has given them. Although overly simplistic, this summary of LDS beliefs reveals three fundamental ways that Jerry's faith shaped the type of person he became.

In the first place, Jerry's faith shaped his views toward community life, family, and marriage. Family and community are central to the LDS. The faithful meet not only for prayer and religious instruction on Sundays, but they also meet regularly throughout the week in activities devoted to such things as poor relief and youth activities. The LDS church is the center of community life for the faithful, who refer to each other as brothers and sisters. The LDS have a moral obligation to assist each other when it is required. They also have a financial obligation to donate to the church, which in turn supports a wide array of social, cultural, educational and, of course, religious activities. Mormons abstain from the use of alcohol, illicit drugs, tobacco, and other stimulants, and sexual relations outside of marriage are forbidden. Such prohibitions serve to preserve the harmony of the community. Jerry took these prohibitions to heart and abided by them.

Most importantly, the family unit is the basic building block of the LDS religion, and the cornerstone of LDS religious practice. For the LDS, marriage is an eternal commitment. Raising a family is a core responsibility, and devotion to family is a divine commandment. The Book of Mormon teaches that marriage and family relationships outlive death itself and continue into the afterlife. Therefore, spending time with one's family is much more than something one does for pleasure or out of a sense of responsibility. It is an act of religious practice and devotion. From a very early age, Jerry absorbed these principles. He grew up in an environment where clean living was the norm, and he recognized that he had a responsibility to the community. He did not use or think about the concepts of "marriage" or "family" lightly. When the time would come for Jerry to marry, he knew that this was a decision that would literally last forever. Moreover, for Jerry no sacrifice was too great for his parents, children, family, or brothers and sisters in the community. God commanded it.

The second way that Jerry's faith shaped his character was in his devotion to country. For Mormons, America is the new Promised Land where everything is possible for those who are willing to hard work for it. The mission of the LDS was to restore the faith in this new Promised Land, or Zion. This included restoring the faith among the Lamanites, the LDS term for Native Americans who the LDS believe descended from the followers of Lehi, but had fallen away from the faith. Later revelations hold that God's hand lay behind the founding of the United States of America itself, and that God inspired the founding fathers to write the Declaration of Independence and the Constitution. In the Church's *Doctrine and Covenants*, God reveals that "it is not right that any man should be in bondage one to another. And for this purpose have I established the Constitution of this land, by the hands of wise men whom I raised up unto this very purpose, and redeemed the land by the shedding of blood."[3] Later the same scripture states,

> We believe that governments were instituted of God for the benefit of man…. We believe that no government can exist in peace, except such laws are framed and held inviolate as will secure to each individual the free exercise of conscience, the right and control of property, and the protection of life. We believe that all governments necessarily require civil officers and magistrates to enforce the laws of the same; and that such as will administer the law in equity and justice should be sought for and upheld by the voice of the people … we do not believe that human law has a right to interfere in prescribing the rules of worship to bind the consciences of men, nor dictate forms for public or private devotion; that the civil magistrate should restrain crime, but never control conscience; should punish guilt, but never suppress the freedom of the soul.[4]

In this passage, fundamental rights that are enshrined in the Declaration of Independence and the Constitution are enshrined in the doctrine of the LDS church as God's will. The LDS know that God gave them the freedom and economic opportunities that they enjoy in America, and that it is their duty to defend that political and economic freedom. Simply stated, for the LDS, duty to country is duty to God. Jerry internalized that value. It was a value passed on to him from his father.[5]

The third way that Jerry's faith shaped his character was that it taught him that adherence to his values requires struggle against persecution and hardship. The LDS faith is rooted in such struggle. The early adherents of the faith suffered both officially sanctioned and unofficial populist persecution. Shortly after they established the church, they were forced to leave their homes in Palmyra, New York, and build new homes in Kirkland, Ohio. They were forced to do the same again when they moved from Kirkland to Nauvoo, Illinois. While the faithful were living there, the founder of the faith, Joseph Smith, was jailed and murdered by a lynch mob. The Mormons then fled across the Mississippi River to the Iowa territory. From there, the church's new leader, Brigham Young, led them on a long and perilous journey to Salt Lake City, Utah, where the church was able to permanently establish itself. Even then, tensions between the early LDS church and the federal government were always present until the church abandoned its tolerance of polygamy.

However, despite the persecution and scorn that Mormons faced, the church leadership always drew a distinction between the principles upon which the United States was founded and the actions of individual political leaders. They taught that one should always be loyal to the former, even when the actions of the latter were threatening. For example, at the same time that the Mormons were living as refugees in the Iowa territory, they raised a battalion of volunteers to fight for the United States in the Mexican-American War of 1846–1848. To this day, the story of that Mormon Battalion occupies an important place in the education of young men in the LDS Church. Like all Mormons, Jerry was taught this history of struggle in the face of persecution. Like his forefathers in the faith, Jerry was a man who would stick to his beliefs despite what people may think or do to him.

Jerry's family history, too, was rooted in struggle against persecution and hardship. It was Jerry's grandparents who converted to the LDS. His paternal grandparents, Niels Sorensen and Mette Marie Larsen, were from Denmark. His maternal grandparents, John Cope Dean and Elizabeth Howard, were from England. In the nineteenth century, it was not easy to be a European Mormon. Because of their unique twist on the story of the resurrection of Jesus and their emphasis on America as the new Zion, Mormonism did not resonate well with the leaders of European society. The emerging middle classes and the intelligentsia heaped nothing but contempt upon the religion's converts in Europe. However, the LDS did appeal to workers and farmers like Jerry's grandparents, who were seeking meaning in life during Europe's industrial revolution.

For those living under harsh industrial conditions or in economically depressed rural areas, Mormonism offered a Promised Land of unlimited opportunity, replete with modern day apostles, prophets, personal revelations, and spiritual gifts from God for those who worked hard and prayed. Therefore, despite the official scorn, Europeans did convert to the LDS Church, particularly in the Protestant countries of the north where its values of hard work and clean living were already well established. For its part, the LDS Church encouraged its European converts to immigrate to Utah, and it helped them financially to do so. It was this "Gathering to Zion" that brought Jerry's grandparents to America.[6]

Niels and Mette Sorensen married in 1882, and they immigrated to America from Aalborg, Denmark, in 1884 with two infant sons. By 1888, they had settled down to a life of sheep farming in Chesterfield, Idaho, and raised a family of seven sons: Jans, Soren, Niels, John, Nephi, and Marion, and Jerry's father, Ephraim. Over twenty years earlier, Jerry's maternal grandparents had immigrated to America as children. John Cope Dean was from Audley, England, and was eight years old when his family immigrated. Elizabeth Howard was five when her family emigrated from Birmingham. When Jerry's maternal grandparents immigrated to Utah, there was no transatlantic railroad. Their families travelled to Utah by wagon train, a trek that was notorious for its hardships and dangers. Indeed, Jerry's great-grandmother died en route, leaving his grandmother to be raised by her father working on the family farm. John and Elizabeth Howard met and married in Woodruff, Utah, in 1877. They spent over twenty years as farmers, growing wheat and raising some cattle and horses. They also were the proud parents of one boy and ten girls, spaced nearly evenly at two years apart: Mary, Matilda, Lucy, Julia, Sarah, Eliza, Emma, Arlinda, John, Agnes and Jerry's mother, Louella. In 1905, John gave up farming. The family moved to Groveland, which is outside of Blackfoot near Rose. John took up carpentry and worked in the real estate business. He and Elizabeth both devoted much of their time to the church.

It is not clear how, but while the Sorensens were living in Chesterfield, Idaho, and the Deans were living in Woodruff, Utah, the two families met, or at least a son and a daughter did. Jens Sorensen married Matilda Dean in 1902. However, the marriage came to a tragic end when Matilda passed away in childbirth two years later at the age of twenty-three. After her death, the Sorensen and the Dean families clearly stayed in contact with each other, since Ephraim Sorensen married Louella Dean and Nephi Sorensen married Arlinda Dean. Thus, three of the Sorensen boys married three of the Dean girls. All three marriages took place in the Temple at Salt Lake City, a source of pride for both sets of parents.[7]

If one could summarize Jerry's childhood in Rose, it was rather Spartan by modern standards, and it was certainly not easy. However, it was a rather typical upbringing in rural America at the time, and farm boys across the country experienced many of the same things that Jerry did. By the standards of the day, it was a happy childhood in a loving extended family. What set Jerry apart from the mainstream of the boys in American society at the time was his LDS faith. Jerry believed that by doing his duty to his family, he was doing his duty to God. By doing his duty to country, he was doing his duty to God. By doing his duty to family, he was doing his duty to both God and country. For Jerry, duty to God, duty to family, and duty to country were all the same thing. Struggle, hard work, clean living, and devotion were simply the way that God intended Jerry to do his duty to all three.

Everyone who lived in Rose at the time were Mormons and shared these beliefs. People in Rose did not lie, and they did not steal. They greeted each other with a smile, and they helped each other out when needed. They did not drink nor swear. They abstained from sexual contact outside of marriage, and illicit drugs simply did not exist. At the very least, if any of these things were going on in Rose, Jerry was blissfully unaware of them. He was sheltered from the problems and moral dilemmas that face young people of today, even in rural communities. The Mormon lifestyle was the only lifestyle that Jerry knew. However, economics soon changed his world.[8]

The Great Depression hit rural communities hard, as the price of all agricultural products plummeted. By 1932, the price of sheep in Idaho had fallen to $2.25 per head, the lowest price in the century.[9] Sheep farming was the core business of Ephraim and Nephi, and the brothers were finding it harder and harder to make ends meet. On top of that, Louella gave birth to a baby daughter, Shirley, on October 1 of that year. Although it was a joyous event, it did give Ephraim an extra mouth to feed. Compounding these economic problems was the fact that the health of the father of Louella and Arlinda began to fail, and he needed some help getting by in Groveland. Ephraim and Nephi faced a truly difficult economic situation. They made the decision to leave the sheep business and to give up their farms in Rose.

Nephi and Arlinda decided that they would move to Groveland to help out Arlinda's father. However, they agreed to wait a year before doing so in order to wrap up the brothers' farm businesses. In the meantime, Ephraim would take up dairy farming in another location. Although the prices of all agricultural products remained below their 1929 levels throughout the Depression, dairy farmers in Idaho at least were a little better off than other types of farmers. Feed costs for dairy cows in Idaho were 23 percent less than the national average, and dairy farmers managed to reduce costs by working through cooperatives that engaged in activities like owning bulls together or producing butter together.[10] For Ephraim, dairy farming must have looked like the least worse alternative in a world of poor choices as a farmer. However, to make a dairy farm successful, he would have to move to a place with a larger market and more developed farmer cooperatives than what existed in Rose. He found such a place in Tyhee, Idaho.

Tyhee lies immediately south of the Fort Hall Indian Reservation and about 6 miles (10 kilometers) north of Pocatello. Like Rose, it was a hamlet rather than a village. However, it did offer two advantages for Ephraim and his family. The first was economic, since its proximity to Pocatello offered Ephraim a larger market and infrastructure of agricultural cooperatives to support his dairy business. The second was the fact that it was an active and growing Mormon community, where Bishop Sam Dunn would soon be building a new LDS church.[11] It was obvious to Ephraim that he and his family would feel at home there.

Ephraim and Louella Sorensen with their daughter Shirley (courtesy Jenny Abeels).

Ephraim and Louella moved to Tyhee with their baby girl, Shirley, at the beginning of 1933, but they waited a year before moving Jerry and his other two sisters. There were two reasons for that. First, there was no house on the property that Ephraim bought, and he would have to build one to make room for them.[12] Secondly, it made sense for his eldest daughter, Aletta, to stay put since she was a senior at the Firth Rural High School. Thora was in her freshman year at Firth, and Jerry was finishing up his eighth grade at Lavaside. The year that the three eldest children spent with Uncle Nephi and Aunt Arlinda proved to be an eventful one. For Jerry, it was the year that he graduated from Lavaside and entered high school at Firth. For Aletta, it was not only the year that she graduated from high school, but it was also the year that she fell in love with and married Leo Larsen. So by the time the new family home in Tyhee was ready in the summer of 1934, Jerry and Thora moved there without their sister. Aletta and her new husband had moved to Groveland where Leo had just bought a farm. Meanwhile, Nephi sold the farms in Rose and moved to Groveland to be near Arlinda and Louella's parents. Nephi left farming and got a job with the Idaho Potato Starch Company, where he would work for the rest of his life.

Ephraim did his best to provide for his family during the Depression.

However, times were tough and every penny counted. Jerry was fourteen when he moved to Tyhee, and he was now fully capable of doing anything that needed to be done on the farm. His main job was to take care of the crops, and these were primarily used to feed the dairy cows. He planted the fields with a horse and plow, weeded them by hand, and hauled in the harvest when the time came. Jerry helped out with the cows, too, of course, and began to develop an interest in how to raise dairy cattle better. The Sorensen family was by no means wealthy, or even middle class. They were poor farmers, living on the edge of subsistence. However, as the 1930s went on, Ephraim began to do well enough that he could actually begin to save some money. He even reached a stage where he could afford to buy a tractor. Although he resisted the idea of doing so at first, his son-in-law Leo proved on his own farm the value of a tractor, and that convinced Ephraim to buy one. That tractor was the first motorized vehicle that Jerry ever drove, and may well have been the only motorized vehicle he drove before he joined the United States Army Air Forces.[13]

Jerry transferred to the Pocatello High School from Firth as a sophomore. His sister Thora was originally a year ahead of him. However, she had to take some time off from school during her junior year, so she ended up in Jerry's class. Jerry and Thora took a bus to get from Tyhee to Pocatello High School, and it probably took them an hour to make the 7.5 mile (12 kilometer) one-way commute each day. Jerry was a solid student, and he scored high on IQ tests. However, he did not have time for extracurricular activities. He was expected and needed to work on the farm before he left for school in the morning and as soon as he got back from school in the afternoon. Only the city boys from Pocatello had the time to participate in sports and other outside activities. However, Jerry was beginning to develop an appreciation for the application of science to farming, and he did join the high school Science Club. Thora was not as good of a student as Jerry was, but this was not considered so important in that community in those days. Thora's self-accepted role in life was to become a wife and a mother. She joined the J.U.G. Club in high school, which stood for "Just Us Girls." It was a club dedicated to teaching girls about homemaking and to "further their knowledge of the domestic arts." They also learned about etiquette, and the J.U.G. club sponsored a tea for the faculty each spring.[14]

As was the case in Rose, Jerry's main activity outside of the farm in Tyhee was his participation in the church. Since 1913, the LDS have incorporated the Boy Scouts of America program as an integral part of their youth activities. The youth activities themselves are considered an important part of the religious life of the church. Jerry initially belonged to the LDS Boy Scout troop in Rose. He then switched to the Boy Scout troop in Tyhee. Neither troop put a lot of emphasis upon earning merit badges and rank advancement. The scouts were all farm boys whose time and energy were needed at home. There is no record of what scouting rank Jerry ultimately earned. However, it is possible that there is one remnant of Jerry's scouting activities that remains. In 1932, the Eastern Idaho Area Boy Scout Council erected a historical marker at the spot of the Fort Hall Indian Trading Post. Each scout from the council that participated brought a stone for use in the construction of the marker. There is no record of whether Jerry participated in this activity, but it is probable that he did so. The marker still stands today and is made of the stones that the scouts brought. What is certainly known is that Jerry participated in the other youth activities of the LDS in both Rose and Tyhee. He belonged to the Aaronic Priesthood, a youth organization within the church. He participated in the church's religious instruction programs, and he graduated from his LDS Seminary training on May 21, 1937.[15]

Pocatello High School was and is affectionately known as "Old Poky" to its students, alumni, and faculty. It was at Old Poky that Jerry received his first real exposure to teenagers who were not raised in the LDS faith. In Rose, the church dominated the hamlet, life at its school, and its public life in general. Pocatello was much different. It was a city, and Old Poky was a distinctly secular institution. The building itself was large and architecturally impressive. Coming from a two-room schoolhouse in Rose and a high school in Firth that was not much larger, Jerry must have been astonished to think that it was a school when he saw Old Poky for the first time. Old Poky also had its own traditions and a proud forty-year history when Jerry started school there. Two United States presidents had spoken on its grounds, Theodore Roosevelt in 1902 and William Howard Taft in 1908. Although a large number of the 256 students in Jerry's class were LDS, there was also a large number who were not. In fact, ministers from the Methodist, Congregationalist, Baptist, and Center Christian churches, as well as bishops from the LDS church, participated in Jerry's baccalaureate and commencement ceremonies. It appears that the majority of the student body leaders when Jerry went to school there, and the boys who were active in sports, were not LDS. The contact with a large number of non–Mormon youth must have also made an impression on Jerry. Although the 1930s were a much more innocent age than today, Jerry undoubtedly saw and heard things coming from teenagers at Old Poky that he had never seen or heard before in his life.

On May 26, 1937, Jerry and Thora graduated from Old Poky. Jerry was ranked 135th in his class, placing him solidly in the middle. However, his IQ was listed at 116, which is considered at the high end of the superior intelligence range. It appears that work on the farm got in the way of homework, because, given his native intelligence, he probably could have finished higher in his class ranking if he would have had more time for his studies. However, the academic side of his character would only blossom after high school, and this was foreshadowed in his class yearbook, *The Pocatellian*.

Graduating seniors were asked what they wanted in life, and their answers were included in the yearbook. Some answered with a career plan, like "Chemical Engineer," "Secretary," "Shoemaker" or "Nursing," as Thora did. Others answered the question philosophically, with comments like "Be Dignified." Others joked about it, answering with "Casanova the Second" or "I'll Leave It Up to You." Jerry answered the question with one word: "Education." He was now thoroughly convinced that he still had a lot to learn about the world and that education would be the key to his future.[16]

Jerry knew that he wanted to be a farmer and follow in his father's footsteps. Given his father's experience, he also knew that dairy farming was the branch of farming that he wanted to go into. However, Ephraim was a self-taught farmer who had to be convinced by his son-in-law to invest in a tractor. Jerry was going to do things differently. In the 1930s, the University of Idaho was one of the country's leading institutions in dairy farming. The university had helped rid Idaho of bovine tuberculosis, and the cows that its College of Agriculture owned gained national recognition for their record-breaking production of milk and butter. The university's dairy barn incorporated innovative technologies like fully automatic feed grinders and electrical ventilation systems. It even broadcast radio programs about advancements in agriculture and home economics through local radio stations throughout the state, including the one in Pocatello that Jerry listened to. Jerry knew that the University of Idaho was where he needed to be.[17]

In the autumn of 1938, Jerry enrolled in the University of Idaho's Southern Branch in Pocatello. In this way, he could attend classes while living at home, both to save costs and to continue to help his father on the farm. He took some business classes, as well as forestry, zoology, and psychology. In his second semester he earned a Sears and Roebuck Freshman Scholarship, which paid a handsome reward of $100 toward his education. For someone like Jerry growing up on a farm in the Great Depression, $100 was a small fortune. It is probably that scholarship that enabled Jerry financially to make his next move, transferring to the University of Idaho's main campus in Moscow. After all, the advances in dairy science that Jerry wanted to learn and see were at the main campus in Moscow, not at the Southern Branch in Pocatello. With his scholarship in hand, Jerry matriculated on the main campus in the fall semester of 1939, and he declared a major in dairy health.[18]

Since Jerry was now living far away from home, he had to worry about paying for room and board. Jerry was a poor farmer. He did not have the money to live in a standard dormitory or fraternity, or to buy a meal plan in a dining hall. Renting an apartment was completely out of the question. Jerry solved the problem of his living expenses in the same way that his father and the other farmers of Rose and Tyhee had solved the problem of high fixed costs in farming. That is, he joined a cooperative.

The Idaho House was a cooperative dormitory that provided affordable housing for 118 male students, primarily from lower income backgrounds. For that reason, it was nicknamed "Poverty Flat" on campus. However, the Idaho House was not a charity. The students paid for the rent of their rooms, but they brought their living costs down by working together to support themselves and the building. The students themselves ran the Idaho House.

Jerry at the University of Idaho (courtesy DeLoy Larsen).

Although a young faculty couple lived in the building and served as the "proctor" and the "hostess," their job was simply to keep an eye on what the young men in the building were doing. The students did everything themselves.

A student menu committee decided what the men would eat in consultation with the university's dieticians. The students bought the food in large quantities and cooked it themselves under the direction of an elderly woman who lived in the Idaho House for free. The students did their laundry together, and they took care of the building's maintenance. A student scholarship committee helped the members keep their academic grades up. The students also ran a commissary that purchased things like snacks, candy, and toiletries in large quantities to achieve cost savings. The commissary resold these things to the members at a small profit. All profits from this commissary were invested in things needed for the house, like washing machines, irons, radios, games, magazines, and other items that the members voted to spend the money on. The students paid for everything in advance. At the end of the year, the difference between what the students paid and what the actual costs were was reimbursed to the students. The total cost of Jerry's room and board was about $18 a month. By comparison, students who lived in the university's fraternities paid twice that amount.

Jerry's University of Idaho graduation portrait (courtesy Evelyn Whyte).

The Idaho House was an initiative of the LDS Church, and more specifically of George S. Tanner, who directed the LDS Institute at the university. He founded four such cooperatives at the university, one of which was for women. The Idaho House and the other cooperatives were run according to Mormon principles and values. They provided students like Jerry with a homelike atmosphere, comfort, and a sense of cooperation and belonging. However, only about 25 percent of the students who lived in the

university's cooperatives were actually Mormon. Through these cooperatives, the LDS church was helping hundreds of non–Mormons achieve a
university education.[19]

Living in this type of atmosphere afforded Jerry the opportunity to
focus on what had become the two pillars of his life: his education and his
faith. For the first time in his life, he was freed of the daily chores of the
farm, and the tasks he was assigned at the Idaho House were not demanding. Jerry could devote himself fully to his university experience. At first,
the change in lifestyle involved a bit of an adjustment. His first semester at
Moscow was a bit rocky academically. However, after that semester his
grades improved remarkably. Jerry did particularly well in his dairy health
and agriculture classes, which is clearly what he cared most about. He took
business classes, which would be important for running a farm. He also
took a couple of non-required and non-credit classes on Christianity,
including a course entitled "The Christian Home." Subjects like sports, the
liberal arts, and social studies did not seem to interest him.[20]

Unlike when he was in high school, the absence of farm duties meant
that Jerry was free to pursue extracurricular activities at Moscow. He joined
the university's Agriculture Club, and became very active in the university's
4-H Club. The 4-H Club was a youth based organization devoted to experimenting with new ideas in agriculture and applying them to farm life. During Jerry's time at the university, the 4-H Club was literally a way for youth
who were going in to farming to experiment in scientific farming practices
that they would apply in later life. It enjoyed the support of the U.S. Department of Agriculture and, to this day, it encourages youth through hands-
on learning. At the time that Jerry belonged, the pledge of the 4-H Club
was: "I pledge my head to clearer thinking, my heart to greater loyalty, my
hands to larger service, and my health to better living for my community
and my country." It is hard to imagine a better summary of Jerry's secular
beliefs. Jerry became the president of the University of Idaho's 4-H Club in
his senior year.

Jerry was also an active member of Lambda Delta Sigma. Today,
Lambda Delta Sigma is a Mormon sorority for university women. At the
time that Jerry was a member, it was a Mormon student association for
both men and women. It offered social activities on campus organized on
Mormon principles, thereby providing an alternative to activities involving
the consumption of alcohol, or worse. Lambda Delta Sigma was Jerry's primary social outlet, and he also became president of the University of Idaho's
Lambda Delta Sigma chapter during his senior year. Thus, from a high

school boy who had no time for frivolities like extracurricular activities, in his senior year at the university he was the president of two student associations, and he was an active member of a third.[21]

On June 1, 1942, Jerry graduated from the University of Idaho with a bachelor of science degree in agriculture, with a major in dairy health science. Had world events not intervened, he would have spent the following year in missionary work for the LDS church. Following that missionary service, he would have joined his father in the dairy business and become the modern dairy farmer that he wanted to be and had trained to be. Of course, meeting "Miss Right" and starting a family was also high on his priority list. However, the circumstances of Jerry's graduation were anything but ordinary.

During the first semester of his senior year, the Japanese attacked Pearl Harbor, and four days later, Germany and Italy declared war on the United States. America found itself at war with two powerful and ruthless enemies, one across the Atlantic in Europe, the other across the Pacific in Asia. Like all Americans, Jerry was shocked by the barbarity of the surprise attack on Pearl Harbor. He was convinced that Germany and Japan were dead set on annihilating America and its way of life. Jerry's patriotism ran deep, and duty called. Going off on missionary work, finding a wife, and starting a career as a farmer could wait. Jerry vowed to defend his country, his family, and his faith against the enemies of freedom.

• 2 •

Aviation Cadet

By Jerry's last semester at the University of Idaho, the United States was engaged in the largest military aircraft production program ever undertaken by any country in history. The United States Army Air Forces (USAAF) would need tens of thousands of qualified pilots, navigators, and bombardiers to fly those aircraft and deliver their deadly payloads to the enemy. Recruiters fanned out on college and university campuses across the country to find young men who were willing to do the job. After the surprise attack on Pearl Harbor, Jerry had already decided that he was going to defend his family, faith, and country against the totalitarian empires that threatened them. Perhaps it was because of one of those USAAF recruiters that he decided to do so as a pilot. He volunteered for the USAAF's Aviation Cadet program even before he graduated from the University of Idaho.[1]

It is not obvious why Jerry wanted to be a pilot. Growing up on the farm, he had probably never driven anything more complicated than a tractor. He had certainly never been inside of an airplane, even as a passenger, let alone tried to fly one. However, he knew that he wanted to be a pilot all the same. If this sounds odd, one must remember that most young American men in the Depression era simply did not have the opportunity to fly, or to drive cars, or to travel, or to do many of the other things that young men today take for granted. For those young men, the allure of flying planes was magical, as it must have been for Jerry. As a farmer, Jerry knew the earth. The USAAF promised to take him to the sky.

In fact, Jerry's lack of experience with airplanes and complicated vehicles was the norm for the overwhelming majority of young men who would fly for the USAAF during the war. Therefore, the USAAF created the Aviation Cadet program to turn land-bound young men like Jerry into qualified pilots, navigators, and bombardiers. The key word in that statement is "qualified." Pilots, navigators, and bombardiers were highly skilled positions. In the modern U.S. Air Force, it normally takes four years to become an officer, and well over a year of flight training after that to become a qualified fighter pilot. In 1942, the USAAF did not have that kind of time. The Aviation Cadet program was designed to produce qualified pilots, navigators, and bombardiers quickly.

The program was very rigorous, and the training normally lasted for thirty-nine weeks. The first three weeks were spent at a Classification Center where the cadet was tested to determine in what specialization he would be trained. The second stage was a nine-week Preflight School where the cadets learned military life and the basic academic skills necessary to be a pilot. These first two stages were spent entirely on the ground. The third stage was a nine-week Primary Flight School in which the cadets would actually learn how to fly an airplane. The fourth stage was a nine-week Basic Flight School in which the cadets learned the basics of military flying and maneuvers. The fifth and final nine weeks were devoted to Advanced Flight School. In this stage, the cadets learned mission-related skills for the aircraft that they would fly in combat, like formation flying for bomber pilots and pursuit flying for fighter pilots.

If an aviation cadet successfully completed this program, he would receive a commission as a second lieutenant, and the prized silver wings of a U.S. Army Air Forces pilot, navigator or bombardier. If at any point along the way he failed or "washed-out" of the program, he would become an enlisted man and would end up serving either as an aerial gunner or on the ground in a supporting role for the military aircraft that others would fly. The Aviation Cadet program was so rigorous that the majority of the young men who signed up for it washed out. For that reason, washing out was considered neither a disgrace, nor a dishonor. Everyone knew what the USAAF was testing for. Success required a natural innate ability to fly. Only the best of the best of potential pilots who entered the program actually became pilots.

One morning in early May of 1942, Jerry went to the local office of the Aviation Cadet Examining Board with a copy of his birth certificate, copies of his school transcripts, and three letters of recommendation. He was handed a test booklet and answer sheets for the Aviation Cadet Qualifying Examination. This was a multiple choice and short answer test that would measure his knowledge and intellectual abilities in six areas: mathematics, vocabulary, reading comprehension, knowledge of recent developments, judgment, and mechanical comprehension. Essentially, the point of the test was to determine if he possessed the minimum intellectual and common sense skills needed to become a pilot. The test took about two hours. Jerry and the other would-be cadets who took the test with him waited while the examining board graded it.[2]

Jerry passed and was given a physical examination in the afternoon. This tested his eyesight, hearing, and general physical fitness and health. Interestingly enough, Jerry's official high school and university photographs show him wearing eyeglasses, as does one other photograph of him with a cow that was taken while he was in university. At this early stage in the development of the USAAF's Aviation Cadet program, the need to wear glasses would have automatically disqualified him from the program. However, those three are the only photographs that exist of Jerry wearing glasses. His family and friends have no memory of Jerry ever wearing glasses, of him ever needing to wear glasses, or of him ever having any problems with his eyesight. Moreover, his eyesight was periodically tested throughout his service in the USAAF, and it never disqualified him for any flying position. Whatever the reason was that Jerry wore the eyeglasses in those three high school and university photos, the correction must have been so slight that it did not really matter. He certainly did not wear them when he visited the examining board that day. Jerry passed the physical exam, and the examining board gave him a letter certifying his eligibility for the Aviation Cadet program. He was told to go home and wait for his notification to take the oath of enlistment. Jerry had just cleared a significant obstacle on his way to becoming a pilot. Forty-nine percent of the young men who took the examination during the same month that Jerry did failed the test and were refused entry into the Aviation Cadet program.[3]

On May 18, 1942, Jerry appeared before the local Selective Service Board. At that time, the Aviation Cadet program was open only to volunteers, and the Selective Service Board needed to first verify that Jerry had not yet been drafted. Once that was verified, the board immediately inducted him into the USAAF Enlisted Reserve. Jerry was now officially a member of the USAAF and ready for the Aviation Cadet program. However, the program was not yet ready for Jerry. His first order was to return home and wait for the call to active duty. This would take a few months, and in the meantime, Jerry attended his graduation ceremony from the University of Idaho on June 1. He spent the summer and early autumn helping his father on the farm in Tyhee.

At the end of October, the call finally came. Jerry reported for duty at the Ninth Service Command's Induction Center at Fort Douglas, Utah, where he presented the letter that certified his eligibility for the Aviation Cadet program. The Induction Center administered some simple tests to see if there was any change in his physical or mental status since he had signed up in May. Everything was fine. The Induction Center sent him to the Santa Ana Army Air Base in California, home of the West Coast Training Command. At Santa Ana, Jerry would undergo classification and, if he passed classification, preflight training.

The Santa Ana Army Air Base had neither an airport nor a runway. No airplanes were anywhere in sight. Instead it was a training facility consisting of three principal units: the Army Air Forces Classification Center, the Army Air Forces Preflight School for Pilots, and the Army Air Forces School for Bombardiers-Navigators. It also included a much smaller Santa Ana Branch School of Aviation Medicine for training medical corps officers. In effect, the Santa Ana Army Air Base was a makeshift town covering an area of over 1,337 acres (5.5 square kilometers) where over 23,000 men lived and worked.

When Jerry arrived there either on or shortly after November 11, the experience must have made quite an impression on him. The farm boy from rural Idaho had never seen anything like Santa Ana before in his life. He and the recruits who arrived with him were shepherded to the Classification Center. He was assigned to a barracks and shown his bunk. He was told to leave his bag next to his bunk, and he and the other cadets were assembled outside of the barracks. He was then given his first uniform issue: six pairs of pants, six shirts, six pairs of boxer shorts, six T-shirts, eleven pairs of socks, two pairs of shoes, two ties, one military jacket, one overcoat, one raincoat, two coveralls (known as zoot suits), five caps, towels, a shaving kit, bedding and other items. It was probably the most clothing that Jerry had ever owned at one time in his life.

It was now that the reality of life as an Aviation Cadet began to set in, because the process of washing out cadets from the program began immediately. Before Jerry and the cadets could put on their new uniforms, they were required to remove their civilian clothes and line up naked to undergo a public and therefore embarrassing physical examination to verify the state of their health. It would be the first of many humiliating experiences that the cadets would undergo during their training. Sometimes would-be cadets did not even make it through this first test. Jerry took it in stride. Following that medical examination, he and his fellow inductees were told to don their new uniforms and report for inspection. Jerry was then ordered to bundle up his civilian clothes for shipment home. He was told that he would not need civilian clothes again for the duration of the war.

For the next three weeks, Jerry underwent the process of classification. He was not yet officially an aviation cadet. Classification would determine if he would become one. If he passed, it would also determine if he was best suited to become a pilot, a bombardier, or a navigator. Although Jerry wanted to be a pilot, the choice was not his. He would be trained in whatever specialization the USAAF decided was best. Classification involved a variety of tests covering the would-be cadet's intellectual aptitude, sensory and motor abilities, and psychological well-being. On the intellectual side, it involved a series of written and oral examinations testing candidates' abilities in mathematics, science, comprehension, judgment, leadership, alertness, map reading, understanding of mechanics, ability to synthesize technical information, and other skills that were needed in the USAAF. The sensory and motor tests measured sensory performance such as eyesight, peripheral vision, depth perception, and hearing. They pitted man against machines in tests of coordination, dexterity, reaction time, and ability to perform under pressure. The psychological tests were designed to determine a would-be cadet's social and leadership skills as well as his overall fitness as an officer and a gentleman. The psychological tests involved one-on-one sessions with trained psychologists in which would-be cadets had to respond to embarrassing questions like "do you like boys," "when was the last time you wet the bed," and "what do you see in this ink spot." Most would-be cadets, and probably Jerry, resented such questions as implying things about their character that were not true. Based on their performance on each of these tests, the would-be cadets were awarded a score on a nine-point scale that was popularly called the "stanine," a contraction for Standard Nine. The stanine determined if a Cadet would move on to pilot training.

Thanksgiving came on November 23 while Jerry was at the Classification Center. Although the USAAF tried as best as it could, Thanksgiving fare was a far cry from the dinners that Jerry had known growing up. The would-be cadets marched to dinner as they did every day of the week. Jerry stood in line and picked up the tray. He went down the serving line, as various barely recognizable Thanksgiving items were plopped upon his tray: turkey, dressing, potatoes, gravy, green vegetables, and cauliflower, with pumpkin pie for dessert. He was even allowed to go back through the line for seconds. However, it was all very cold and military. After dinner, it was back to the barracks. There was no radio, no football games, no leftovers, and most importantly, no family. It was just an ordinary day of the year, with a different menu.[4]

Five days later, the moment of truth came. Jerry and his fellow would-be cadets were marched to the classification headquarters to learn how their stanines had placed them. One by one they were called forward in alphabetical order, and since his name was Sorensen that involved a long wait for Jerry. When his turn came, he marched up before the officers who were seated behind a table. They had a sheet of paper in front of them with his name and serial number. They asked Jerry to verify that this information was correct, and then they turned it over. The paper said "pilot." To say that Jerry was elated would be an understatement. This was everything he wanted. He was now officially an aviation cadet and on his way to becoming a pilot.

The fact that Jerry had already made it to becoming a pilot aviation cadet was something to be proud of. Based on their performance, about one quarter of the cadets in Jerry's class were redirected toward training as bombardiers and navigators. They would remain aviation cadets, but they would not be trained as pilots. The overwhelming majority of the young men chosen for navigator and bombardier training would have preferred to be pilots, and they regarded their selection for bombardier or navigator training as a disappointment. However, the choice was not theirs. The USAAF needed bombardiers and navigators as well as pilots, and the needs of the USAAF preempted the desires of an aviation cadet. In fact, those selected as navigators were usually more natively intelligent than those selected as pilots. Navigators required mathematics skills that went beyond those needed to be a pilot, and the stanine needed to become a navigator was therefore higher. Navigator and bombardier cadets were also more fortunate than they realized at the time. If they successfully completed their training, navigators and bombardiers would become officers with the same rank and pay as the pilots. The same is not true for the one-quarter of the cadets who simply washed out at this stage for failing to pass the classification tests. They became enlisted men, and served during the war as either aerial gunners or in supporting roles on the ground. Jerry, and the remaining one-half of the men who entered Santa Ana with him, went on to Preflight School as potential pilots.

Each Aviation Cadet belonged to a class that was designated by a number and a letter. The number indicated the year that the cadet would graduate if he competed his training. The letter indicated the month. Jerry was in class 43-I, which meant that, if he completed his training, he would become a pilot in October of 1943. The class in turn was divided into "squadrons" of about 180 men. The squadrons were the primary unit of organization for the cadet's training and life in general. A commissioned USAAF officer, normally a captain, commanded each squadron. Another commissioned USAAF officer, normally a first lieutenant, served as the

Squadron 62 at the Santa Ana Army Air Base. Jerry is in the second row from the bottom, the second airmen to the left of the emblem in the middle of the photograph (courtesy DeLoy Larsen).

commander's adjutant and "right hand man." Each squadron was in turn divided into "flights" under the responsibility of an enlisted first sergeant. Each flight was divided into "squads." The first sergeant and the other non-commissioned officers (NCOs) who assisted the squadron commander and his adjutant did not have formal command over the cadets. However, they were responsible for the cadets and the cadets did have to obey their instructions.

Formal direct command of the cadets was in the hands of fellow cadets who were appointed by the squadron commander. A cadet captain and cadet adjutant assisted the squadron commander. A cadet flight lieutenant assisted the squadron commander's adjutant. A cadet flight sergeant commanded each flight, while a cadet first sergeant was responsible for how the flights formed and drilled together. Cadet corporals commanded each squad. These cadet officers and cadet NCOs played a very important role in the life of the ordinary cadets. The regular officers and NCOs issued their orders through the cadet officers and NCOs. It was the cadet officers and NCOs who were responsible for ensuring that those orders were carried out under the watchful eyes of the regular officers and NCOs.[5]

On the first anniversary of the attack of Pearl Harbor, Jerry and other members of class 43-I moved from the Classification Center to the Preflight School. He was assigned to Squadron 62, under the command of Captain J.T. Ansberry.[6] Captain Ansberry had a difficult job. He and the men in his squadron were ready for Preflight School, but Preflight School was not ready for them. In December of 1943, the USAAF was absorbing aviation cadets at a higher rate than it could train them. Class 43-G had not yet graduated at the Santa Ana Air Base, as Class 43-H entered Preflight School. Jerry's class of 43-I had to wait until 43-G moved on before they could enter Preflight School. What would Captain Ansberry do with his squadron? He had to fill five and a half days of his men's time each week, and, in order to do so, he tried everything he could think of. He drilled them. He introduced them to firearms. He taught them how to do guard duty. He put them on "mess maintenance" duty, which was exactly the same thing that enlisted personnel knew as "KP." He and the base organized some makeshift classes on the military and rudimentary military skills. However, the classes were intended to keep the cadets busy more than anything else. Squadron 62, and Class 43-I in general, was basically marking time. Jerry was experiencing all of the trappings of the life of an aviation cadet, without actually being in training.

Christmas came to Santa Ana during this period, and suddenly the USAAF seemed to develop a heart. All cadets were given a three-day pass for the holiday. However, they were not allowed to travel more than 100 miles from the Santa Ana Air Base. There is no record of what Jerry did with his Christmas pass. However, two things are almost certain. Given the depth of his faith, there is no doubt that Jerry sought out a local LDS ward, and that he stayed during the holiday with a local Mormon family. There is also little doubt that he was in a reflective rather than a festive mood during the holiday season. Jerry was far away from his family in Pocatello. Moreover, America was at war, and the news that reached America in 1942 from the battlefields around the world was mostly bad. In Asia, the Japanese had taken the Philippines, and American Marines were locked in bitter conflict on the island of Guadalcanal. In Europe, the Nazis occupied or controlled nearly the entire continent and their forces had reached as far east as Stalingrad and Moscow. Americans were fighting and dying to stop the advance of both empires. It was not at all evident that America would succeed. Jerry knew that the time was coming for him to be pulled into this maelstrom of death and destruction. "Peace on Earth" and "Goodwill Toward Men" must have taken on a special meaning for him that Christmas Day.

Jerry returned to Santa Ana after the holiday, and life quickly returned to normal. However, a new holiday soon arrived that would mark the beginning of another challenge that would follow Jerry throughout his military career. Officially, alcohol was banned on the Santa Ana Air Base. The same was true of gambling, and smoking was strictly confined to certain areas and times. There were no special passes given for the New Year's holiday and the squadrons were mostly confined to barracks on New Year's Eve. Given the rules in place, it should have been a quiet evening. However, alcohol found its way into the barracks that evening, and the rules were not as strictly enforced as they normally would be. Apparently, the "powers that be" on base looked the other way for this particular holiday. Cadets in nearly all of the squadrons enjoyed toast after toast of forbidden drink that evening. They played craps and poker, and they smoked. As a Mormon, Jerry was not about to participate in any such activities. He and the small minority of non-drinking aviation cadets like himself spent the evening playing games with each other and enjoying soft drinks. The other cadets mocked them as they continuously tried to get them to drink and join in what they regarded as fun. Friendships were rearranged, as Jerry and the other non-drinking cadets became social outcasts in the eyes of those who did drink. The experience did not bother Jerry. His faith had prepared him for such events. However, it was something that he would encounter again and again throughout his time in the military. At least he and his friends did not have hangovers when the squadron fell in for inspection early on the morning of New Year's Day.[7]

On Monday, January 4, Class 43-I finally entered Preflight School. This training involved three key elements, two of which were official parts of the program, and one of which was unofficial. The first official part was basic physical and military training. In principle, this training was similar to what took place at West Point. In practice, it was more similar to what enlisted men in the Army received. Aviation cadets underwent a strenuous program of physical training. They learned to march and drill like soldiers.

They learned to fire weapons. They were assigned to work details. They did mess management. They did latrine duty and barracks maintenance. Uniforms were always to be kept neat. Clothes were to be hung in a specific order, with shirts and coats buttoned and trousers underneath. Shoes were to be laced, tied and in their proper place. All buttons had to be polished. Beds were made tight. There were assigned places for books, caps, luggage, laundry bags, and the meager personal possessions that cadets were allowed to keep. The barracks were to be kept spotless, and were inspected with white gloves to ensure that they were. Failure to perform, inadequate performance, or indiscipline in any of these duties would lead to a cadet receiving a certain number of "demerits" depending upon the severity of the offense. The cadets called the demerits "gigs" and the process of receiving them as being "gigged." Cadets who accumulated more than eight gigs in any week were assigned to walk "punishment tours" on Saturday afternoons and Sundays while their classmates usually enjoyed free time or passes to go off base. If a cadet earned more than seventy-five gigs during his stay at the Santa Ana Air Base, he would be washed out of the program.

The second official part of the training was classroom instruction. The aviation cadets took classes that would prepare them to be officers, and that would lay the basis for the knowledge that they would need to acquire to become a pilot. Military courses included things like army organization, military customs and courtesies, chemical warfare defense, safeguarding military information, pistols, guard duty, and drill. Pilot courses included classes like theory of flight, radio code, mathematics, meteorology, physics, recognition of aircraft, communications, and first aid. The latter set of classes was more important than the former in determining whether or not a cadet would be washed out. What the USAAF really needed were pilots who could dead reckon, read weather patterns, distinguish friends from foe, and generally get their airplanes from point A to point B. Tests occurred weekly, and the results of each cadet were posted in public for all to see. Cadets were required to achieve a cumulative grade average of 85 percent across all of the courses, and the grade average in no one course could be below 70 percent. Failure to make these grades would likewise lead to a Cadet being washed out of the program.

Then there was the unofficial but very real part of the process. Aviation cadets were neither officers nor enlisted men. They wore a distinctive uniform that was similar to an officer's uniform, but without a recognized rank. In fact, they were at the bottom of the army hierarchy on base. They were bossed around and hazed by officers and enlisted NCOs alike. Cadets were addressed simply as "Mister," usually in a derogatory tone of voice. Many of their instructors and immediate supervisors in tasks were second lieutenants who had graduated from officer training school. Dubbed ninety-day-wonders, officer training school graduates themselves had never endured the rigors or suffered the indignities that they subjected the aviation cadets to, nor would they ever become pilots unless they themselves joined the Aviation Cadet program. Some of these ninety-day-wonders were resentful of the Aviation cadets, who would go on to lead the "glamorous" life of a pilot. The cadet officers and cadet NCOs could be just as bad. Those who were so inclined could behave as dictatorial tyrants, constantly seeking to put their fellow cadets in their place. Meanwhile, although the regular NCOs could not haze the cadets, they did treat them as they would treat enlisted men in basic training, pushing them through the rigorous physical and military training with a fair share of verbal abuse. Some cadets simply could not handle the hazing and resigned from the program, imagining that enlisted life would be better. Others allowed the hazing to get to them, and were washed out of the program for disciplinary reasons. Officially, hazing was forbidden at Santa Ana. In practice, it was a reality, particularly at the time period that Jerry was there. It is not known if Jerry was personally hazed or not. However, given the fact that he was a Mormon who did not drink, smoke, or gamble, he would have been a prime target for hazing, particularly after New Year's Eve.

Jerry survived this ordeal, and he graduated from Preflight Training on March 11, 1943. Altogether, 3,217 aviation cadets graduated with him. Only sixty-two had washed out since classification, one of the lowest class washout rates in Santa Ana's history.[8] Even so, by now over one-half of the men who entered the Aviation Cadet program with him in November had either washed out of the program or had been tracked as navigators and bombardiers. Forty percent of those who remained as pilot aviation cadets would wash out in the six months to come. It was now time for Jerry to learn to fly an airplane in Primary Flight School. Jerry must have impressed his superiors at Santa Ana because he was given what was a plum assignment for Primary Flight School: the Ontario Army Air Base in Ontario, California.

The Ontario Army Air Base was actually not a USAAF facility at all. The USAAF needed skilled pilots for combat, and there were few to spare for training. So, the USAAF contracted out the job of teaching its aviation cadets to fly to private companies. The private companies provided the airfields, instructors, planes, and maintenance. The USAAF provided a skeletal crew of officers and NCOs to oversee the training and to verify officially if the cadets had or had not succeeded in the training. It was the private companies that actually ran the show at this stage in a cadet's training. In fact, the Ontario Army Air Base was just the USAAF's name for a private training facility. Its civilian name was the Cal-Aero Flight Academy.[9]

The president and owner of Cal-Aero was Major Corliss C. (C.C.) Moseley. Moseley was a combat pilot in the U.S. Army Air Corps during the First World War. After the war, he served as an Air Corps test pilot and training officer. He also commanded the California Air National Guard for a time at the Griffith Park Aerodrome. After he retired from the service, Major Moseley became an aviation entrepreneur. He went into the commercial airline business and was a co-founder of the company that would become Western Airlines. Eventually, Western Airlines merged into today's Delta Airlines. In addition to founding Cal-Aero, Moseley founded the Mira Loma and Polaris Flight Academies.

When Jerry entered Cal-Aero over the weekend of May 13–14, he must have thought that he was entering a luxury resort. The cadets at Cal-Aero slept two to a room in motel-like buildings, as opposed to the stark, open, and crowded barracks that Jerry had known at Santa Ana. Everything was new and well maintained. The behavior of his superiors was likewise quite different. Little or no hazing took place at Cal-Aero. It was a civilian airfield that was run by civilians. They had little time for or interest in engaging in such antics. The training, too, was different since the sole point of Jerry's presence at Cal-Aero was to teach him how to fly.

Upon his arrival, Jerry was assigned to a squadron and a room. The next day, he was issued his flight gear: a leather helmet, goggles, a blue gabardine flight suit and leather gloves. He donned his flight gear for his official photograph for the class book, which he would receive if he passed Primary Flight Training. He was also issued twelve Army technical field manuals for use in his ground classes. The next step was assignment to an instructor. Jerry's squadron was marched to the flight line and assigned to instructors in groups of four. The group of four would become Jerry's squad during his time at Cal-Aero. The instructor for Jerry's squad was a Mr. Hall. The other members of the squad were Aviation Cadets H. Ramey, E. Lloyd, L.M. Bean, and Lt. Singletary. Lt. Singletary was already a commissioned USAAF officer when he joined the aviation cadet program to become a pilot. Officers like Singletary kept their rank and privileges while training as a cadet, and they received much better treatment than the "Misters" they were training with.[10]

Jerry and the other cadets spent one-half of each day on the ground with classes, along with some physical training and drill. The second half of the day was spent in the air. Evenings were free for recreation and study until 10:00 p.m. Weekends were normally free for the cadets who were free of "gigs" and who kept up their grades. Long Beach, California, was not far away and was a popular weekend destination for Jerry and the other cadets.

The classes at Cal-Aero were all directly related to teaching Jerry how to fly an aircraft. The most important class was considered to be aircraft engines and operating systems. The next most important was navigation. Other classes included subjects like meteorology, aircraft identification, and theory of flight. Cadets were required to maintain a grade average of at least 75 percent in each of their classes.

The flying part of the training began almost immediately. Jerry was now considered a "Dodo," or a pilot who had not yet soloed. His flying took place in a Stearman PT-13B, a two-seat biplane produced by the Boeing Corporation under license from Stearman. Mr. Hall sat in the front seat and Jerry sat behind him. There was no canopy, so Jerry and Mr. Hall flew in the open air with helmets and goggles. There was a hose connecting Mr. Hall's voice to Jerry's ears. This allowed communication to occur in the open air when the plane was in flight. However, the communication was one-way, from Mr. Hall to Jerry. Mr. Hall would often use hand signals because of the noise of the engine. For the first couple of weeks, Jerry flew dual with Mr. Hall, but with each session, Mr. Hall yielded more and more control of the aircraft to Jerry. At some point in the first two or three weeks, Jerry had to prove to Mr. Hall that he could fly the airplane solo. At a minimum, this would occur after six hours of flying time. At a maximum it would take twelve hours, and on average it took ten. If a cadet was unable to solo after twelve hours, the cadet was washed out of the program.

At some point within the required time frame, Jerry and Mr. Hall were flying dual. It seemed like a typical day and flight to Jerry. They landed, and the Stearman came to a stop. Mr. Hall told Jerry to stay seated as he jumped out of the aircraft. He then leaned over the side of the aircraft and told Jerry to take the Stearman up and land it a couple of times on his own. Jerry was astonished, nervous, and probably scared. But he successfully did what he was told. Having soloed, Jerry was no longer a Dodo. He was now a pilot. His flying training then turned to maneuvering the plane in flight, and procedures to follow in emergency situations. He would initially learn how to do these maneuvers with Mr. Hall in the plane, and then he practiced them solo when Mr. Hall felt that Jerry was ready.

Jerry's squadron at graduation from Primary Flight School (courtesy DeLoy Larsen).

Jerry descends from his plane after a solo flight at the Ontario Army Air Base/Cal-Aero Air Flight Academy. His instructor, Mr. Hall, is next to the plane (courtesy William Jones Morton).

Precision maneuvers were added first, like pylon eights, elementary eights, chandelles, and lazy eights. The attention of the training then turned to accuracy, with practice in precision landings and approaches, how to land with power off, and how to deal with short runway fields. Finally, the training turned to more complicated aerial acrobatics like loops, Immelmann turns, slow rolls, half rolls, snap rolls, and split S's. With each passing day, Jerry was becoming a better and better pilot.

Cadets would make all kinds of mistakes in Primary Flight School, particularly in the

Jerry in his pilot flight suit (courtesy DeLoy Larsen).

early days after they first soloed. The most common mistake was the "ground loop." A ground loop occurred when a plane was not properly aligned with the runway while it came in for a landing. If the plane landed at an angle, even a slight angle, the momentum of the plane as the brakes were applied would cause the front of the plane to slow but not the back of the plane. Coming at an angle, the back of the plane would move either to the right or to the left, depending on the angle of the misalignment. As it did so, the momentum would force the tip of the wing that was opposite of the angle to dig into the dirt runway, causing the plane to pivot on the wing tip. When the motion stopped, the plane would have completed a 180 degree turn, and the pilot would find himself facing the direction from which he came.

Although wind could cause a ground loop, it was usually due to inattentiveness of a pilot who failed to notice the drift in the tail section of the plane as it came in to land. The cadets used to joke that the Stearman had a built in ground loop, because its narrow landing gear made a drift in the tail harder to detect. Other common errors that cadets would make included standing an airplane on its nose by applying the brakes too tightly, and damaging wings on the ground while the plane was moving or parking too close to other airplanes. If any of these errors occurred early in the Preliminary Flight Training, the cadet was normally forgiven, provided that he learned from his mistake. Besides, the Stearman was relatively easy to repair. It was cloth covered, and its wings were made of spruce wood. However, if errors of control were persistent or if they occurred at the final stages of Primary Flight School, a cadet would be washed out. By the time that Primary Flight Training was finished, a cadet had to demonstrate absolute control of an aircraft at all times.

Jerry not only succeeded at this stage, but he did so with an outstanding record. His graduation ceremony from Cal-Aero was on May 20, 1943. In addition to the usual certificate testifying that he had succeeded, he received a few special things. First was the class book with the photograph of him that was taken when he entered Cal-Aero. Jerry was very proud of that photograph, and to this day nearly all of his surviving friends and direct relatives own a copy. He was also awarded the Gold Star Flying Award for a perfect flying record. Jerry never experienced an accident or mistake of any kind at Cal-Aero. His name was inscribed in a special plaque on the academy's Hall of Fame. Major Moseley gave him a credit-card sized gold-colored plastic certificate in a wallet engraved with Jerry's name. This was an extremely promising beginning for Jerry's career as a pilot. He had not only proven that he could fly an airplane, he had proven that he could fly one very well.[11]

However, that fact was not good enough to make him a military pilot. Turning civilian pilots, like Jerry now was, into military pilots was what the next two stages of the Aviation Cadet program were all about. Around May 27, Jerry reported for duty at the Merced Army Airfield in California for his Basic Flight School. Unlike Cal-Aero, Merced was a genuine military base, and it was back to the reality of military life. The instructors and personnel were all military, and some were quite resentful of the "country club" life that the aviation cadets had experienced in Preflight School. The hazing began immediately, as the message for the cadets became very clear: you are back in the army now.

On the surface, Basic Flight School had the same structure as Primary Flight School. Upon arrival, Jerry was assigned to a squadron, which determined his sleeping location and the order of everyday life. He and three other cadets were assigned to a squad with an instructor. One-half of each day was spent in classes, physical training, and drills. The other half was spent in flying. However, that is where the similarities ended. In addition to the reinforced military discipline and training, the classes were more difficult. The volume of material that the cadets were required to learn increased dramatically. Classes in subjects like flight instruments and radio navigation, as well as night classes, were thrown into the mix.

The flying, too, was more complicated. The cadets now practiced in a Vultee "Valiant" BT-13, which the cadets nicknamed the "Vibrator." It was an all-metal, low-winged, single engine aircraft with a glass canopy. It was much more sophisticated than the Stearman that Jerry flew at Primary Flight School, and much larger. It looked and felt like a military plane. It included features like landing flaps and radio equipment for air to ground communication. Unlike the Stearman, the cadet sat in the front, with the instructor behind him. Also, because it was metal and more sophisticated, it was more difficult to repair than the Stearman. The flight training itself involved perfecting the skills of aerial maneuver learned in Primary Flight School, and adding new ones such as spins. It also introduced the cadets to cross-country navigation, formation flying, and night flying, skills that would be indispensible as military pilots. Underlying all of this was instrument flying, which was probably the most fundamental skill taught in Basic Flight Training.[12]

About one-third of the way into his training, on either Thursday, June 15, or Thursday, June 22, Jerry was on a solo training flight practicing his maneuvers when it was time to come in for the landing. Perhaps his mind was still on the maneuvers that he had just completed. Perhaps his mind was on the classroom work. Perhaps he was angry with his instructor or thought that his instructor would be angry with him. Perhaps his eyesight really was not perfect. Perhaps he was thinking about dinner. For whatever reason, his mind was not 100 percent concentrated on the landing that day, and he failed to notice the slight drift in the tail section of his Valiant as he came in for the landing. As the plane touched the ground, the tail began to turn. The wing tip dug into the dirt airfield, and the plane pivoted on the fixed point. The Valiant came to an abrupt stop. Jerry was sitting on the airfield, facing the direction that he had just come from, and his plane was damaged. Jerry had ground looped.

In the early stages of Primary Flight School, this mistake would have been forgiven. However, Jerry was now in Basic Flight School. At this stage in his training, a basic failure to control an airplane was unforgiveable. He was supposed to have absolute control of his aircraft at all times. Jerry's fate was in his instructor's hands. If the instructor referred the incident to the base's examining board, Jerry would almost certainly be washed out. Sometimes, instructors forgave mistakes like this at this stage of training because of circumstances like wind that were beyond the control of the cadet. Sometimes, a cadet made a genuine lapse of judgment or error that warranted an instructor washing the cadet out. Personalities and prejudices could also enter into the instructor's opinion as much as performance. It is possible that Jerry's instructor simply did not like Jerry or that he did not like Mormons. For whatever reason, the instructor told Jerry that he was referring the incident to the examining board and that he would recommend that he be washed out of the program. Jerry, who had a perfect flying record at Cal-Aero, was now almost certainly going to be washed out for making one mistake in Basic Flight School. The incident occurred on a Thursday. The examining board would meet again on Monday. The writing was on the wall.

Merced, California, was known as the Gateway to the Yosemites because it was not far from Yosemite National Park. Knowing that this was probably his last weekend as an aviation cadet, Jerry decided to make the most of the circumstances. One of his classmates and friends, Otto Zach from Oregon, was in a similar situation. Like Jerry, he was a farmer before the war, and his family raised cattle. Like Jerry, he knew that he would probably be washed out on Monday when the examining board met. Jerry and Otto asked the base commander, Col. Harvey F. Dyer, for a three-day pass. Col.

Dyer was sympathetic to their plight and granted the request. They left on Friday morning to enjoy the weekend.

There is no doubt that Jerry truly enjoyed his weekend at Yosemite. He sent pictures back to his family and friends showing him enjoying the natural wonders of the park. He also encountered a different kind of natural wonder. Jerry and Otto, farm boys from Idaho and Oregon, met a couple of city girls from Los Angeles who were also staying at the park. Jerry took an interest in Beverly Maechelson, while Otto hung out with Betty Binger. The weather was beautiful, and the swimming pool was inviting. Beverly wore a rather daring bathing suit for the times, and Jerry had probably never met anyone quite like her before. He was clearly impressed, as the captions that he wrote on his photos demonstrate. However, he also clearly remained true to his faith and his values. The weekend gave Jerry what was probably a much needed innocent moment of carefree youth, in the midst of the war and the pending personal disaster that would soon meet him when the examining board convened on Monday.

Jerry returned to the base on Sunday evening. As expected, the examining board confirmed his instructor's recommendation the next day. Jerry had washed out of the Aviation Cadet program. Mister Gerald Sorensen was now Private Gerald Sorensen. By this point in the war, the USAAF had decided that leaving wash-outs among surviving aviation cadets was bad for the morale of the latter. So, Jerry was ordered to immediately evacuate his place in the barracks. He did not even have the chance to say goodbye to the other members of his squad or the friends that he made. He was ordered to the Amarillo Air Force Base in Texas for basic training as an enlisted man.[13]

Washing out of the Aviation Cadet program did not mean that Jerry was a failure. In 1943, the Army Air Force needed tens of thousands of skilled and trained pilots very quickly. The Aviation Cadet program was designed to ensure that only those who could learn to fly very quickly would succeed. Those who did succeed had an almost innate ability to pilot an aircraft. Jerry was intelligent, fit, and very motivated to become a pilot. Because of his performance at Cal-Aero, he had already proven that he was an excellent civilian pilot. There is no doubt that Jerry would have become an excellent military pilot if he had been able to spend more time in training. However, the USAAF did not have time for training. There was a war on and they needed to produce tens of thousands of excellent military pilots quickly. Although the numbers vary according to the source, it appears that about seventy-five percent of the young men who entered the Aviation

Cadet program washed out, normally at the Preflight, Primary or Basic stage. All of these men, including Jerry, had volunteered for the USAAF. They were not drafted. These were men who wanted to serve.

Jerry joined the USAAF to defend his family and faith, as well as his country. Becoming a pilot was Jerry's preferred means of accomplishing that goal, but that avenue was now closed for him. However, Jerry was not going to let that fact stand in the way of his primary goal of defending his values. The vast majority of USAAF enlisted personnel served in mechanical or other ground-based support functions that were essential for keeping the Air Force's fighters and bombers in the air. These were (and are) extremely important jobs to be done, and Jerry could have chosen that route. However, Jerry did not want that kind of duty. Despite washing out of the Aviation Cadet program, Jerry was still determined to fight this war from the air. He decided that he would now try to become an aerial gunner, protecting a bomber in the air over enemy territory.

Of course, Jerry was more than disappointed about washing out of the Aviation Cadet program. He wanted to be a pilot and his path to becoming one had looked quite good prior to Merced. However, he accepted the outcome and, in spite of everything it meant for what he wanted to do, he was able to joke about his ground loop later on.[14] Within a few weeks, he even came to regard it as a terrific stroke of luck, and perhaps as an act of divine intervention. After all, if Jerry had not ground-looped his plane, he would not have washed out. If he had not washed out, he would never have been assigned to the Amarillo Army Air Force Base. If he had not been assigned to Amarillo, he would never have met Nora Lee Lewis.

· 3 ·

A Wartime Romance

Hardship, strength, and faith in God forged the character of Nora Lee Lewis. She grew up in a world of adversity and contradictions. She overcame that upbringing through the force of her inner strength, with her faith serving as guideposts in the direction of a better life. Nora Lee was a woman of integrity who took responsibility for her life and who lived by her principles. She chose to live that way. She did not inherit these values from her parents.[1]

Nora Lee's father was Clyde Sydney Lewis, who was born to a farming family near the town of Prairie Hill in Limestone County, Texas. His parents, Alfred and Sally, did their best to raise Clyde to be a decent young man. They taught him farming. They raised him as a Christian and inspired him to read and learn the Bible. They instilled in him a sense of patriotism, and a sense of pride to be both an American and a Texan. However, even in his youth, Clyde marched to the beat of a different drummer.

When America entered the First World War, Clyde volunteered for the United States Navy. After completing his basic training, he decided that a life at sea was not for him. So, Clyde took matters into his own hands and deserted. He did not desert out of cowardice, a lack of patriotism, or an unwillingness to serve. Rather, he simply did not like the Navy, and he decided to serve his country in a different way. Using his brother's name, Clyde then joined the United States Army.

Clyde became a private in the 19th Field Artillery Regiment of the 5th Field Artillery Brigade, which was constituted in Texas and primarily consisted of Texans. The regiment sailed for Europe on May 27, 1918, and after a brief stay in Liverpool, arrived at La Valdalion, France, on June 12 for training with the French Army. On August 8, the 5th Field Artillery Brigade took over responsibility for artillery in the St. Die sector in the Lorraine as a part of the 5th Infantry Division. It was there that Clyde first saw action in the American attack at Frapelle, where after seizing its objective, the division faced numerous German counterattacks and heavy shelling.

49

In September, the 5th Division was reassigned to the new American First Army, and it was transferred to the Villers-en-Haye Sector. From 12 to September 16, Clyde and his brigade participated in the Saint Mihiel offensive, again facing numerous counterattacks and intense artillery fire, often with gas shells. Although the 5th Division itself was withdrawn from the front lines on the 17th, Clyde's 5th Artillery Brigade remained in position in the Limey sector in support of the 78th Division until October 3. From October 4–10, the 5th Field Artillery Brigade was shifted to the Puvenelle Sector in support of the 90th Division, and it remained in place at Puvenelle in support of the 7th Division when the 7th relieved the 90th. During its time at Puvenelle, Clyde's artillery brigade was subject to incessant counter-artillery fire, including significant use of mustard gas.[2]

Although Clyde was never wounded seriously enough for the Army to consider him a casualty, the reality was that he had been exposed to heavy shelling for three months, including frequent poison gas attacks. Gas masks helped prevent immediate and obvious serious injury, but the technology that the gas masks relied upon was far from perfect. Clyde and the other men who endured the gas attacks still inhaled poison gases to the point where their senses of taste and smell were impaired, sometimes for life, even if they were not officially counted as casualties. Clyde likewise suffered from some shell shock, on account of the frequent artillery attacks and the sheer terror that haunted the men when they were exposed to gas.

Following the Armistice on November 11, the 5th Field Artillery Brigade rejoined the 5th Division, and the unit settled into occupation duty in Luxembourg. Clyde and his regiment returned to New York on July 21, 1919, and were demobilized at Camp Bragg. Armed with an honorable discharge from the Army, Clyde applied to straighten out his service record. The Navy could have pressed charges against him for desertion when his true identity became known. However, his service in the Army proved that Clyde was neither unpatriotic nor a coward, and the Navy decided not to pursue him. Ultimately, Clyde's Army records were changed to reflect his true identity, and he received a government veteran's pension for his service. He settled down to a life of cotton and corn farming on some land that was owned by his father near the town of Groesbeck in Limestone County, Texas.

Clyde had already met Nannie Mae Robinson before he entered the service. Like Clyde, Nannie Mae was born on a farm in Limestone County. Her parents were Texans, but her grandparents were Cajuns who had moved to Texas from Louisiana. However, Nannie Mae's parents died when she was only a child, and she never really knew them. Her older sister Dolly took Nannie Mae in and tried to raise her as best she could. Although Dolly was well-intentioned, she was ill-equipped for the task at hand.

Dolly was married to a man named Freeman, but Freeman apparently died at a young age, and Dolly never remarried. A diary records that Nannie Mae grew up in an environment of "old women and wayward girls," so it appears that Dolly raised Nannie Mae on her own. Although it is never easy for a single woman to raise a child on her own, it was even more difficult in those days than it is today. Dolly simply could not provide the kind of upbringing for Nannie Mae that she undoubtedly would have liked to. Nannie Mae never received a proper education, and her childhood was marked by extreme poverty.

The "old women and wayward girls" that Nannie Mae grew up around had a cynical attitude toward men, and they taught Nannie Mae not to trust them. Nannie Mae grew up believing that men were only interested in betraying young women and getting them into trouble. She never learned how to be a homemaker or to take care of domestic tasks. She did enjoy working at jobs outside of the home. In a later time and place, Nannie Mae probably would have made a good career woman, but there was no such thing as a career woman in the Limestone County of the 1920s, outside of the odd jobs that her sister did.

It is not clear how, but Clyde met Nannie Mae while she was still a child living with Dolly. Clyde impressed Nannie Mae as a man who was different from all of the other ones she had seen, and all of the other ones Dolly warned her about. Clyde and Nannie Mae struck up a friendship. They kept up the friendship when Clyde entered the service and corresponded when he was in the Army in France. Nannie Mae was only twelve at the time. Their letters to each other were formal rather than romantic, as was befitting for a relationship between a child and an adult. Nevertheless, the correspondence laid the basis for what would come later. Clyde and Nannie Mae were married after Clyde returned from the war. He was twenty-seven and she was just sixteen.

Clyde and Nannie Mae lived on Clyde's farm in Groesbeck, where Nora Lee Lewis was born on Thursday, January 11, 1923. Nora Lee was Clyde and Nannie Mae's first-born, and they would go on to have four sons after Nora Lee: Alfred, Clyde, Chester, and Tracy. Nora Lee's father enjoyed an outstanding reputation in the community of Groesbeck. Everyone knew him to be a devout Christian, and his neighbors considered him to be "the best darned farmer in the county." There is no doubt that Nannie Mae and Clyde loved each other. In Nannie Mae's eyes, Clyde could do no wrong, and he was the only man that she ever trusted. As a hardworking Christian farmer, Clyde was very different from the other men that the women in Nannie Mae's life had warned her about during her childhood. Or so it appeared.

The poison gas attacks that Clyde experienced during the war cast a long shadow over their marriage. By all outward physical appearances, Clyde had recovered from the war, and he seemed to be leading a stable and normal life. In reality, he was anything but stable and normal. The poison gases used on the Western Front had far more insidious and long-term effects than was realized at the time. They influenced Clyde in ways that went far beyond outward appearances, and in ways that changed the core of his personality. He developed an ungovernable temper, and he was gripped by a paranoia that the government or others would come to get him. He began sleeping with a butcher knife under his mattress.

Clyde became a man of contradictions. At one moment, he could be a kind and loving husband and father. In the next, something wouldn't go right or something would cross his mind that would cause him to fly into a rage. He wanted to provide so many things for his family, and he wanted to "get ahead" in life. However, things always seemed to go wrong with the farm. When things went wrong, he would take it out on Nannie Mae, blaming her for the problem or accusing her of making it worse. Clyde tried to and often did live as the Christian that he was in his youth. He and Nannie Mae raised their children to be devout members of the United Church of Christ. However, Clyde would sometimes drink heavily, swear with the worst, and get into trouble with the law. He bootlegged during Prohibition to make ends meet, at the same time that he was living an outward life of a good Christian farmer. Clyde would work very hard on the farm and in the home one day. On the next he could simply disappear, leaving crops unattended and unharvested in the field. Clyde's disappearances imposed a heavy burden on Nannie Mae and their children.

To a modern student of psychiatry, Clyde's behavior would be easily recognizable. Paranoia, irritability, outbursts of anger, exaggerated responses, detachment from others, emotional mood swings, hyper vigilance followed by abandonment of responsibility, etc., are all well-known symptoms of the psychological effects of shell shock and exposure to poison gas. The gas had become a part of Clyde's character. As one study of survivors of gas attacks put it:

> Unlike a bullet or piece of shrapnel, which could lodge in the body and be removed surgically, gas was systemic. A toxin could be drawn deep into the

lungs and spread through the viscera, akin to a pathogen from a plague. The visible damage caused by mustard gas to the skin and eyes offered tangible evidence of what a poison could do inside a body. For many veterans, the gas had become an integral element of themselves. In contrast to shrapnel, the chemical agent had no definite physical limits, and no operation could remove it.[3]

Today we would say that Clyde suffered from Post-Traumatic Stress Disorder, severely aggravated by the effects of the chemicals he was exposed to. However, in Clyde's time people did not know about such things. They just knew that Clyde wasn't quite right after the war, and no one knew what to do about it. Even if they had known, it would not have made Clyde any easier to deal with.

Nannie Mae's childhood did not equip her to cope with this situation. She, too, had her share of contradictions. On the one hand, Nannie Mae was a kind and affectionate individual who loved her husband and her children very much. On the other hand, her childhood haunted her with insecurity. Nannie Mae was embarrassed by her lack of education and the circumstances in which she grew up. She felt misunderstood, and she believed that her children regarded her with embarrassment. She lived with a feeling of loneliness and she was heartbroken because she believed that no one understood her. When Clyde would blame her and accuse her in his fits of rage, she simply took it and cried. She knew deep down inside that she wasn't responsible for the Great Depression, or the drought, or the new government regulation, or whatever else Clyde was really angry with. However, Nannie Mae's insecurity led her to internalize Clyde's anger, and his outbursts left her very sad.

It was particularly hard for Nannie Mae to take Clyde's disappearances. He would disappear for days, weeks, months, or even years at a time. He never explained where he went or what he did when he was gone. During Clyde's longer disappearances, Nannie Mae did not cope very well with running the farm or raising the family. Clyde's father would help her out with the farm. However, the ultimate responsibility for the business and the family still fell on her shoulders. On at least three occasions when Clyde disappeared for extended periods of time, she had to divorce him in order to take care of the farm's business. Each time this happened, Nannie Mae vowed that she would never forgive him. However, each time that Clyde walked back into the house, she forgave him for everything, running to him with outstretched arms, sobbing and kissing him. Clyde was the only man that Nannie Mae would ever love, and she remained convinced that he was better than any other man out there, despite everything that he did to her.

Nannie Mae had a pet nickname for her daughter Nora Lee, "Nody" (pronounced "no-dee"). Nannie Mae wanted her Nody to have a better life, and she wanted to protect her Nody from men who would betray her. Nannie Mae tried to drill into her Nody the idea that men would only be interested in ruining her, or getting her into trouble. She taught her Nody that if a girl stayed quiet, men would leave her alone, and that this was better than attracting attention. She also taught her Nody that that if a woman excelled in life, people would just expect more of her. So she told her daughter that a woman should not try to stand out or succeed in life. Nannie Mae's philosophy was that a woman should simply avoid men, be quiet, and try not to be noticed.

However, Nora Lee was not the Nody that her mother wanted her to be, and she completely rejected her mother's philosophy. As she was growing up, Nora Lee recognized what was going on her around her at a relatively early age. Her mother had never learned to be a homemaker, and her mother did not take care of her children as most mothers of the time would have done, even when Clyde was around. When Clyde was absent, Nannie Mae slipped into depression and ignored the children's needs even more. The children were forced to fend for themselves.

Nora Lee was the oldest, and from somewhere deep inside of herself, she knew that her brothers needed more parenting than what her mother was capable of giving them. Even as a pre-teen, she personally took on the responsibility of taking care of her brothers, and sometimes of taking care of her mother. Nora Lee learned what responsibility was all about. She came to realize that for her and her family to survive, she would have to work hard and achieve, not sit back and be quiet. Her faith became central to her life, and guided her along the path of responsibility. She rejected the idea that all men were motivated by evil intentions. She knew that she needed to find a stable, responsible husband who believed in God and who looked at the world the same way she did.

The Great Depression hit Limestone County hard. About 43 percent of the farms in the county went out of business in the 1930s.[4] One of them was Clyde's. He decided to leave farming and go to where the jobs were. One of the few bright spots in the Texan economy of the Great Depression was oil and gas, and the area north of Amarillo was swimming in both. Clyde decided that this was where his future lay, and he decided to move his family to Borger, a small town north and east of Amarillo. Clyde did not own a motorized vehicle, so the family travelled to Borger by horse and wagon. The 460-mile (740-kilometer) trip took over a week.

Borger had sprung up around the nearby oil and gas fields, and it still very much had the look and feel of the Old West. Indeed, the town's founder was killed in a shootout by a long-time rival in 1934.[5] When Clyde and Nannie Mae arrived in Borger with their children, there was no home prepared for the family to live in. So Clyde found a shack that would do the job, and Nannie Mae fixed it up as best she could. Nora Lee spent her teenage years in that makeshift home, helping her mother out with her brothers, while her father worked in the oil and gas fields. The experience only reinforced her intention to do better in life than her parents had done.

Nora Lee at home in Borger, Texas, in January 1944 (courtesy Jenny Abeels).

Nora Lee graduated from the Borger High School in the spring of 1942 and decided to move to Amarillo that summer in search of economic opportunity. She shared a room with another girl to keep costs low, and she enrolled in the Amarillo Business College. She then got a job at the C.E. House Insurance Agency in Borger. She also joined the United Church of Christ in Amarillo, which became the anchor of stability in Nora Lee's life at that time. Despite the move to Amarillo, Nora Lee continued to feel a deep responsibility toward her family, and tried to look after their needs. Later on, after she had earned enough money, Nora Lee moved her mother and brothers from Borger to a real home in Amarillo, while Clyde was off working on a pipeline in Colorado.

Amarillo, and the surrounding area, was now undergoing a profound change. As Nora Lee was graduating from high school, the USAAF's Western Technical Training Command established the Amarillo Army Airfield nearby. The purpose of this base was to provide basic and specialized training for enlisted air crew and ground crew for the USAAF's B-17 Flying Fortress bombers. Classes began at the Amarillo Army Airfield in September 1942, and by 1943 thousands of young men from across the country were funneling into Amarillo. One of them was Jerry Sorensen, who was sent to Amarillo in mid–June following his wash-out from the Aviation Cadet program.

Jerry was in Amarillo for basic training as an enlisted airman. Basic training consisted of an eight-week program of physical training, military drill, and classes designed to adapt the newly inducted to military life and to prepare them for service in combat areas. For Jerry, basic training was easy. In the Aviation Cadet program, he had already learned everything he needed to know about military discipline, customs, etiquette, procedures, etc. He was already in excellent physical shape. He had already been on active duty for over eight months, and he knew the ropes of the USAAF. What was new for Jerry was basic training's emphasis on the skills required to survive on the ground in combat areas. Subjects like marksmanship, drill, bivouacking, chemical warfare, and camouflage had replaced the courses in things like meteorology, physics, mathematics, and code that he had learned when he was training to be a pilot.

Basic training at Amarillo also involved yet a new classification procedure to determine where Jerry would go for his specialized training. He could end up in any number of specialized positions, ranging from the combat role of an aerial gunner to the specialized skills of a mechanic, an intelligence specialist, a communications specialist, a military policeman, or any number of other positions. Since he was in the USAAF, most of these roles would involve service far away from the front lines. Given what had happened to him at Merced, Jerry could have adopted an indifferent or even bitter attitude and let the chips fall where they may. However, Jerry still wanted to fly, and he still wanted to fight. The only way he could do so now was as an aerial gunner, and becoming one involved yet a new rigorous classification process. Jerry set his sights on achieving that goal and made it clear that this was what he wanted to do.[6]

In the meantime, Jerry was now part of a broader socio-economic process that was transforming the city of Amarillo, and that would soon transform Jerry's life. The thousands of young men who were pouring into training in Amarillo brought both positive and negative changes to the city. On the positive side, the air base opened up a wealth of economic opportunities for the citizens of Amarillo. The construction and supply of the air base meant contracts for local businesses. The base brought new consumers to the area in the form of servicemen and sometimes their visiting families. All of this meant economic opportunities for local businesses and jobs for people in an area that was still recovering from the Great Depression. At the same time that new jobs were being created, the local young men were beginning to enter military service in large numbers. Labor shortages emerged that opened up economic opportunities for women like Nora Lee that had not existed before the war.

On the negative side, the Army Airfield created a new set of problems for the city of Amarillo. The thousands of young men who were stationed at the Amarillo Air Base came from many different backgrounds. Many were away from home and family for the first time in their lives and knew that they were only going to be there for a few weeks or months at best. Deep down inside, they also knew that there was a chance that their young lives would be cut short in a fiery death on a bomber in the skies above Europe or Asia. In what little free time they had from the base, many wanted to live for the day and throw caution to the wind. Even for the men who did not adopt this way of looking at the world, the temptation to do things off base that one wouldn't do at home was ever present. The off-base nightlife that developed in Amarillo brought excessive drinking, public disorderliness, and loose morals to what had been a quiet town. Prostitution became a problem in the area around the base. The prostitutes in turn complained about the "beer house girls" who gave sex away for free. The rate of venereal disease soared in Amarillo.[7]

The bars, dance halls and honkytonks that sprang up around Amarillo thanks to the air base were no place for a good Christian girl like Nora Lee. They also did not appeal to good Christian airmen like Jerry. That is why the United Church of Christ and other Christian churches in Amarillo organized socials for these like-minded young men and women to meet and enjoy wholesome company. It was at one of these socials organized by her church that Nora Lee Lewis met Jerry. The exact occasion of their meeting is lost to memory, but it may well have been a Fourth of July social. However, the consequences of that meeting would never be forgotten.

When Nora Lee first saw Jerry, she thought to herself that he was the most beautiful boy that she had ever seen. Jerry was the perfect gentleman. He was kind and respectful. He was a Christian who did not drink, did not smoke, did not gamble, and did not swear. He had a wonderful sense of humor. He was hardworking and responsible. His goals in life were to own a dairy farm, to marry a like-minded girl, and to raise a family. In short, Jerry was everything that Nora Lee was looking for in a man.

On his side, Jerry was taken by Nora Lee's beauty. She was a devout Christian woman who believed in principles. She was honest and sincere. She shared his sense of humor. She was also a woman of strength and responsibility. She believed in the importance of family and wanted a family of her own. She valued hard work, and she knew what the farming lifestyle was all about. She was everything that Jerry was looking for in a woman. Nora Lee and Jerry fell madly in love with each other at first sight. In the summer of 1943, they spent as much time together as Jerry's duties allowed.

This was not so difficult at Amarillo. The officers and the NCOs responsible for training Jerry knew his background. They were a lot less harsh on the aviation cadet washouts like Jerry than they were on the conscripts who were beginning to swell the ranks of the USAAF. After all, washouts like Jerry were volunteers, not conscripts, and they had already been in the service for many months. They had already been turned into military men long before they arrived at basic training. Relative to the recent inductees who now surrounded him, Jerry "had it easy" at Amarillo. His base passes for leaves were liberal enough that his romance with Nora Lee had time to bloom.

Bloom it did. Jerry and Nora Lee took advantage of every opportunity to see each other. They had time to talk and get to know each other. They talked about their families, and their backgrounds. They talked about their religions. They talked about everything. The more they talked, the more they realized that their first impressions of each other were correct. Although they came from different families and different traditions of Christianity, they shared the same values and the same outlook on life. They knew where their relationship was heading, but the USAAF brutally intervened before it could get there.[8]

Jerry's training at Amarillo came to an end, but he achieved his new goal for the war and was classified as a potential aerial gunner. This was great news. However, that good news was now tempered by the fact that it would now be awhile before Jerry and Nora Lee could see each other again. Jerry's next stop was the USAAF's gunnery school at the Las Vegas Army Airfield in Nevada.

Las Vegas was not a "fun" assignment. In fact, it was probably the most rigorous training program that Jerry experienced throughout his entire USAAF career. Although the beginnings of what the world knows today as Las Vegas can probably be traced to the existence of the air force base, today's casinos and nightlife were only in their infancy. At that time, Las Vegas was a sleepy town in the middle of a desert with a population of under 9,000 and not much to do. That was just as well for Jerry, since he was not interested in casinos and nightlife anyway. However, even the airmen who were interested in such things did not have much time to enjoy them. Jerry and the thousands of other airmen who passed through Las Vegas during the war were there for one purpose only: to learn how to be aerial gunners on B-17 Flying Fortress bombers. For Jerry, this meant that visits with Nora Lee were out of the question. Jerry and Nora Lee depended upon the United States Post Office to keep the relationship alive.

Jerry's gunnery school was an intense training experience, but it actually involved little time in the air. It was a six-week program, and the first five weeks were spent entirely on the ground in classes and on the shooting ranges. In the five weeks on the ground, Jerry had to memorize each and every detail of the machine guns that B-17s carried. He practiced taking the guns apart and putting them back together. He then learned how to do the same thing while blindfolded and wearing gloves, over and over again, until he could prove that he had it memorized. He had to learn every detail of the different types of ammunition that his guns would fire. He learned when it was appropriate to use armor piercing munitions, when it was appropriate to use semi-armor piercing munitions, when it was appropriate to use ball shot or tracer shot, when it was time to use incendiary or dummy shells. He learned how to aim and fire to compensate for the effects of wind, altitude, speed, and direction of attack. To simulate combat in the air while on the ground, he learned how to fire out of moving vehicles at moving targets. He learned to fire from standing platforms that tested his ability to fire in any direction (right, left, above, below, sideways), as he would have to do in the gun positions of the B-17. He learned about timing: when to fire and when not to. Firing too much could cause his gun to overheat and potentially misfire and kill him. Firing too little could allow an enemy aircraft the space it needed to bring down his bomber. He learned how to operate the bomber's turrets while shooting, which was done with the feet. He was taught to shoot with his right hand, how to shoot with his left hand, and how to shoot any other way possible.

Jerry was also tested for his ability to withstand the elements. The gunnery positions on B-17's were neither heated nor pressurized. Flying at high altitude in the skies above Northern Europe, the gunners would be subject to extreme cold and lack of oxygen. Jerry was tested in decompression chambers to determine his ability to withstand altitude. He learned how to wear sweaty, rubbery and smelly oxygen masks for long periods of time. Jerry was at Las Vegas in September and October, which were still warm months in the desert. In that environment, he trained with gloves and heavy flight suits to prove he could fire his gun while encumbered by such clothing. He was even tested on his ability to remain in this winter-type clothing in a cramped position for long periods of time, as he would be in a gunnery position on a B-17. Although doing so in the Las Vegas desert was unbearably hot, doing so in the skies of Northern Europe would be unbearably cold. His training was teaching him to bear the unbearable.

A vital portion of his training at Las Vegas was learning how to identify aircraft. In the upcoming combat in the air, Jerry would have a split second to decide whether or not to shoot at a nearby plane. He needed to know instinctively which airplane was a friend and which was a foe. Since neither the gunnery school nor Jerry knew if he would ultimately serve in Europe or Asia, he needed to learn all of the aircraft flown by the Germans, Japanese, Italians, British, Russians and, of course, Americans. He also had to learn Morse code to be able to pass messages between planes during periods of radio silence or communications equipment failures. That was easy for Jerry. He had already learned Morse code as an aviation cadet.

As was the case in the Aviation Cadet program, washouts could and did occur from gunnery school. Not everyone could master the manipulation of guns with gloves and flight suits. Not everyone could learn to identify twenty-seven different types of aircraft or master Morse code. Not everyone could cope with altitude, oxygen deprivation, or confinement to small, enclosed areas. However, Jerry could, and during his last week of training he was able to ride in an airplane once again, this time practicing what he had learned during the last five weeks by shooting at targets pulled by other aircraft. At the end of October, Jerry graduated from gunnery school. He received a diploma, a promotion to corporal, and a set of silver wings with a bullet at the center, indicating that he was now a qualified aerial gunner. He also received a two-week furlough to visit home.[9]

Jerry used his furlough to visit his parents and family in Tyhee. He had not been home to Idaho since he had left for the USAAF one year earlier. The whole family knew he was home and wanted to see him. His cousin Evelyn, one of Nephi's daughters, invited him to come up to Blackfoot to join her for a dance. Jerry agreed, and he brought along Wayne Murdock, an Army buddy who was also home on leave. They went to the Castell, a dancing establishment that facilitated youth contact in a wholesome atmosphere. Smoking and drinking were not allowed, and the attendees were strictly controlled. Evelyn still remembers the evening to this day. Jerry was the ideal surrogate "big brother date" to take to such an occasion.[10]

When Jerry's leave drew to a close, he reported to the Combat Reception Center of the 18th Replacement Wing at the Salt Lake City Air Base. He was only there for a few days before being sent to the Kearns Army Air Base near Salt Lake City, where he was administered yet another series of tests. This time the tests were used to determine his crew assignment and the specific role that he would serve on his future bomber. At the end of November, he was sent to the Combat Crew Training School at the Drew Army Airfield in Tampa, Florida. At Drew Field, he met the other members of his bomber crew for the first time. They would spend the next five months training together and preparing for combat.[11]

Meanwhile, Nora Lee got a job with Western Union. Although she was hired in Texas, the job held open the possibility of being transferred to other cities. Part of her training was in Salt Lake City. Although there is no documentary evidence to support this, it is probable that Nora Lee was in Salt Lake City for training when Jerry was home for his leave and when he was stationed at Kearns.[12] If so, the experience would have provided an excellent opportunity for Nora Lee to learn about the world in which Jerry was raised. She certainly knew that Jerry was going to be stationed in Tampa. It just so happened that Nora Lee's best friend at the time was Doris Fowler, whose boyfriend was Frank Lovelace, one of Jerry's army buddies from Amarillo. Frank was stationed near New Orleans, and Doris wanted to move there. However, since Frank and Doris were not yet married, appearances would not have been quite right if she had moved there on her own. Nora Lee's job at Western Union provided the excuse that everyone needed.

Following her training, Nora Lee managed to get assigned to the Western Union office in New Orleans, allowing her and Doris to move there together. They rented a room in the home of a family named "Pierre." Although New Orleans was still a very long way away from Tampa, the train and bus connections to Tampa were easier than from Amarillo. It gave Nora Lee and Jerry more of a chance to see each other, at least from time to time. For the farm girls from Texas, New Orleans was quite the experience. Nora Lee described the city as the "wickedest city in America," and she did not like the seedier things that she witnessed. At the same time she loved the Cajun food and found it fascinating to live there. After all, there were Cajun roots in her family.[13]

Jerry's training at Drew Field was all about bringing his bomber crew together as a team and preparing for combat. The instructors were nearly all combat veterans, with experiences to share and stories to tell. The aircraft that his crew trained in were B-17's that had flown in combat but had been retired to be replaced by newer models. Jerry and each of the other crewmembers received individualized training about their positions on the bomber. Although much of this was a repeat from what he had learned before, this time Jerry was hearing it from combat veterans who had real-life lessons to teach.

The Flying Fortresses were neither heated nor pressurized, yet they flew over the cold skies of Northern Europe at over 35,000 feet (10,000 meters). Wind would enter through gaps in the bomb bay, windows, and gun emplacements during flight, creating a frigid draft that grew worse toward the tail section of the aircraft. The seats, when they could be used, were little more than pieces of canvas strapped over metal rods. However, that did not matter a great deal in combat when all the guns were manned and only the pilot and co-pilot could actually sit. The crewmembers wore heavy, electronically heated suits to withstand the cold, and smelly, tight fitting, and generally uncomfortable oxygen masks to compensate for the lack of oxygen at the high altitudes. The noise of the engines was deafening, so crewmembers communicated through earphones and microphones connected to the Interphone that were worn with flak helmets and oxygen masks. To say that flying in a B-17 at altitude was uncomfortable is an understatement.[14]

At Drew Field the crew began to grow accustomed to the B-17, as they made practice flights at the high altitudes that they would experience in combat. More importantly, Jerry and the crew he was assigned to were training to fight as a team, with a heavy emphasis on crew discipline and coordination. They flew simulated bombing runs over the Gulf of Mexico, learning the mechanics of what each position on the plane would do and how they would coordinate with each other. The pilots practiced formation flying: joining a formation, flying in formation, and departing from a formation when landing. They also simulated flying under various emergency scenarios, such as how to stay in the air when one, two, or even three engines were taken out. The navigators practiced reckoning with and without instruments. The bombardiers practiced delivering their payloads by dropping "dud" bombs over the Gulf and by using cameras to simulate dropping bombs over cities. The gunners like Jerry practiced defending the planes by firing live ammunition at targets set up over the Gulf and by firing at drone aircraft that were towed by other planes. Most importantly, the crew did all of this together as a team, learning how to work together as a seamless whole.

Everyone on the aircrew practiced the basics of emergency preparedness, like the procedures for crash landing. They learned how to bail out of an aircraft, and the differences in what they would have to do if they were jumping at high altitude versus low altitude. At low altitude, the challenge was pulling the ripcord as soon as possible to break the fall, but not so soon as to entangle the parachute on the airplane or its motors. In jumping at high altitudes, the problem was learning to wait as long as possible before pulling the ripcord, as airmen falling to the earth in parachutes were easy targets for enemy fighters and anti-aircraft flak.[15]

The training at Drew Field was serious and purposeful. There was none of the pointless tasks or hazing that Jerry had known in his training the year before. Drew Field was about boosting morale, not lowering it. The Army Air Force knew that many of the young men who billeted there would soon have their young lives cut short in combat. The men who were stationed there knew that, too. So, when the men were not training or otherwise on duty, leave policy was liberal. The men could spend time off base and enjoy themselves.

Although Jerry was there in the winter and it was too cold to swim, Tampa was a pretty city with nice weather in the winter, especially when compared to Idaho. It had an active nightlife that appealed to many of Jerry's colleagues. The liberal leave policy did allow him to spend time with Nora Lee, whenever she could make the trek to Tampa to see him. Because of the more limited duration of his weekend passes, it was more difficult for Jerry to go to New Orleans. In 1943, Christmas and New Year's Day fell on Saturdays, and Jerry had leave for the holidays. There is no documentary evidence to support this, but it is highly likely that Jerry and Nora Lee spent those holidays together either in Tampa or in New Orleans. However, it is also possible that he spent the holidays with the LDS community in Tampa.

In any event, Nora Lee loved visiting Florida, which she described as "the land of whispering palms and romance." There was a park in St. Petersburg where the couple enjoyed walking. It was filled with palm trees, and there was a large oak tree in the middle. Nearby was a pier that jutted into the Gulf of Mexico. Pelicans frequented the water near the pier. The farm boy from Idaho and the farm girl from Texas were enamored with the setting, particularly in the middle of winter when their hometowns were buried in snow. It was under a palm tree near this pier that Jerry proposed to Nora Lee on a Sunday afternoon in January of 1944. She, of course, said yes.[16]

This was true love. The only real issue in the relationship that might have had an adverse impact on the future marriage was religion. Louella and Ephraim Sorensen probably would have preferred their son to marry a Mormon. However, the fact that Jerry loved Nora Lee was good enough for them to welcome Nora Lee to the family. Besides, Jerry was already twenty-three, and they thought that it was more than time for him to settle down. The fact that Nora Lee was a farmer's daughter, and that she knew the lifestyle of farming, was even better. Jerry and his family were convinced that he would eventually convert her to the LDS faith.

It was more difficult for Clyde and Nannie Mae Lewis to accept the marriage. Nora Lee's family belonged to the

Nora Lee immediately after her engagement to Jerry (courtesy William Jones Morton).

Nora Lee and Jerry's wedding portrait (courtesy DeLoy Larsen).

Church of Christ, a mainstream Protestant denomination. At the time, Mormonism did not have as many adherents as today, and the faith was not well regarded in the panhandle of Texas. Some Protestants at the time did not consider Mormons to be Christians at all, and false rumors about what Mormons believed and practiced were widespread. The fact that Jerry was a Mormon just did not sit right with Nora Lee's parents. They resigned themselves to her decision and continued to love her as their daughter, but they did not appear to accept Jerry. In fact, Nora Lee's parents never even met Jerry. As for Nora Lee, Jerry's religion did not bother her. She knew that she shared the same values that Jerry did. She also knew that she would eventually convert him to the Church of Christ.[17]

By early March, Jerry's training at Drew Field drew to a close. He and the men he had trained with had become a coherent, battle-ready team. Jerry's next stop was combat in the skies above Europe. Jerry underwent final physical and dental examinations to ensure that his medical records were complete and up to date. His immunizations were checked. He completed forms concerning whom to contact in the event that something would happen to him and whom to designate as the beneficiary of his government life insurance policy. He did a complete inventory of the personal belongings that he would bring with him to England. The crewmembers received two-week furloughs to say goodbye to their loved ones, and Jerry decided that he would use this opportunity to marry Nora Lee.

The wedding was hastily thrown together. He telephoned his parents and asked them to make the arrangements. He also telephoned his seventeen-year-old cousin Evelyn to ask if she would serve as Nora Lee's maid of honor. Evelyn was surprised to learn that Jerry even had a girlfriend, let alone that he was ready to be married, but she immediately agreed. At the time, Evelyn was dating a man named Marion J. Callister who lived in Groveland. Jerry barely knew him, but Marion was in the Army, too, and he just happened to be home on leave at the same time that Jerry would be there. Jerry asked Evelyn to ask him to serve as his best man. It would be an intimate wedding, attended only by a small group of Jerry's family and family friends. No one from Nora Lee's family attended the wedding but, of course, Tyhee, Idaho, was a long distance away from Borger, Texas.

The ceremony took place on Thursday, March 20, 1944, at 8:30 p.m. at Ephraim and Louella's home in Tyhee. Bishop Arden Hale of the local LDS ward presided over the ceremony. Nora Lee wore a navy blue two-piece suit with black and white accessories, and a rhinestone clip borrowed from Jerry's mother. Jerry wore his dress uniform, with the wings of an aerial gunner proudly displayed. It was double ring ceremony, but with an added touch. Jerry gave Nora Lee a bouquet of white chrysanthemums with a red rose in the middle. He told her that the white flowers symbolized hope for the future, while the red rose symbolized the blood being lost during the war to secure that future. Even during his wedding, Jerry was infused with patriotism and his commitment to the struggle for the future of a free world. It was, perhaps, also a foreshadowing of what was to come.[18]

For their honeymoon, Jerry and Nora Lee checked into the Hotel Bannock in Pocatello that evening, in a fancy room that cost $3.75 per night.[19] Two days later Jerry's parents arrived with a telegram that they had received from the USAAF: Jerry's furlough had been prematurely cancelled. He and the other members of the crew were ordered to report immediately to the Combat Crew Staging Center at Hunter Field in Savannah, Georgia. Jerry was heading to Europe. With sadness in his heart, but with the conviction of a man on a mission, Jerry boarded a bus on March 23 for the first stage of his trip to Georgia. Rather than return to Texas or New Orleans, Nora Lee decided that she would stay with the Sorensen family in Pocatello, at least for the time being. Those three days in March of 1944 were the only time that Nora Lee and Jerry would ever spend together as a married couple. When she kissed Jerry goodbye, Nora Lee did not know that she would never see her husband again.

· 4 ·

Jerry's Air War

The B-17 bomber was nicknamed the Flying Fortress for a reason. By the standards of the day, it was a colossal aircraft, with a wingspan of 103.9 feet (31.6 meters). It could take the war from London to Berlin and back with its range of over 2,000 miles (3,000 kilometers), and longer when extra fuel tanks were added. It could deliver over 8,000 pounds (3,600 kilograms) of bombs on its target, with terribly destructive and lethal results. To and from the target, it defended itself with thirteen .50-caliber Browning machine guns, two in the "chin," two in the "cheek," two in the "waist," two in a turret on the top, two in a ball turret on the bottom, two in the "tail," and one in the roof of the radio operator's position. With these guns pointing out in every direction, the B-17 even looked like a fortress as it flew in the air. Like a fortress on the ground, it gave the impression of being strong and impregnable. Its legend only grew as the war progressed. Countless aircrew recounted stories of B-17s sustaining horrific amounts of combat damage, and yet still somehow managing to stay in the air to return home. The men who flew the Flying Fortress believed in her. They believed her to be invincible, and therefore she was.

Yet the Flying Fortress was only a machine, and it was only as good as her crew of ten men. Each man had a distinct and well-defined role to play. The survival of the plane and crew depended upon these distinct roles fitting seamlessly together into a functioning whole. An outstanding tail gunner could not compensate for an underperforming waist gunner. One poorly trained or underperforming ball turret gunner could result in the loss of the entire bomber if an enemy fighter attacked from below. Even the best pilots were ineffective if their navigators could not get them to the target and if their bombardiers could not accurately deliver their payloads. All ten men needed to think and act as a team.

However, when a new crew met each other for the first time, they were complete strangers. The USAAF assigned men to specific crews based on a number of criteria. The first test, of course, was the training that they had received for the individual positions they occupied on the aircraft. For the officers, this was self-evident: pilots would serve as pilots, navigators as navigators, and bombardiers as bombardiers. However, the positions for the enlisted men were more fungible, and so tests of physical and mental aptitude were given to assign specific enlisted men to specific positions. These tests determined if one was best suited as a tail gunner, a ball turret gunner, a waist gunner, a radio operator or a flight engineer. Training for that specific position followed this classification. Then it was a question of putting together the crew itself. It was essential to avoid personality clashes, so psychological tests were used to help determine who should and should not serve together. On top of that, there were objective criteria that applied to all crews. No more than two crewmembers should be from the same state. At least one of them was supposed to be a universal (Type O) blood donor. As was the case with Jerry's crew, in practice these criteria could not always met, but they were the criteria that the USAAF aimed to meet.[1]

Jerry met his crew for the first time shortly after he arrived at Drew Field in Florida. His commanding officer and the pilot of the crew was Second Lieutenant Eugene Dingledine. Lt. Dingledine was from Hachington, Illinois, and he was not yet twenty-four years old when he was given command. Ultimate accountability for the crew, the plane, and their missions rested on his shoulders. It was his airplane, and his crew. Indeed, Dingledine was responsible for the crew at all times, not just when they were flying together. He was held accountable for each crewmember's training, performance, discipline, morale, and overall fighting spirit. He was held responsible for melding the crew so that they would function and fight together as a cohesive team. Although the crew was his primary responsibility, Dingledine was also accountable for the safekeeping of the plane itself, a piece of machinery that cost about a quarter of a million dollars, which was a fortune in 1944.

The co-pilot was Second Lieutenant George R. Smith from Alabama. Lt. Smith served as the crew's executive officer or, in other words, as Lt. Dingledine's right-hand man. His job was to assist Dingledine in any way that he was asked, and to be prepared to take on any and all of Dingledine's responsibilities at any time. He shared the flying responsibilities with Dingledine on long flights, or when Dingledine was otherwise absent from the pilot's seat. He monitored the progress of the flight and paid attention to the instrument signals. He also monitored the crew's performance, and stood ready to lead them at any time. In short, Lt. Smith's job was to be fully prepared to step into Dingledine's shoes if circumstances ever warranted.

The navigator was Lt. James MacConnell. His overarching responsibility was to ensure that the pilot could get the plane to its destination and home again. He was trained in all forms of sight and instrument navigation. He was responsible for calibrating the navigational instruments. He was responsible for knowing the weather forecasts, monitoring the development of the weather, and advising the pilot about course changes accordingly. He and Dingledine met before every flight to do the preflight planning and to plan alternative routes to be used if necessary. In addition to these roles, MacConnell could man one of two machine guns that were located near his position in the "cheek" part of the nose, one on the right and one on the left. Should the plane come under attack from enemy fighters, he would man whichever was appropriate. At the end of a flight, MacConnell and Dingledine would always meet to review what went right, what did not go right, and what they should take into account in the future.

The bombardier was Lt. Denuncio Street, who was 27 years old and from Baltimore, Maryland. The ultimate military success or failure of a mission rested on his shoulders because it was he who was responsible for ensuring that the B-17's lethal payload was delivered on target. In fact, from a military point of view, every other role on the aircraft was simply there to assist Street in doing his job. In dropping the bombs, he had to take into account a variety of factors like the speed, the wind, the weather, the altitude, the nature of the ordnance being dropped, and dozens of other things that would determine if the bombs would hit their target or not. When the plane reached its initial point of attack for its final approach to the target, absolute command of the aircraft temporarily passed from Dingledine to Street, who would be in command until the bombs were delivered. In addition to this responsibility, Street manned the "chin gun" when the plane came under attack from enemy fighters. This consisted of two machine guns at the very front of the airplane.

The remaining six members of the crew were enlisted men, whose ultimate job was to assist the officers in carrying out these missions. Vito A. Champa was twenty-one years old and from Columbus, Ohio. He was the flight engineer, and he had been trained specifically for this position. His job was to know more about the physical state of the airplane itself than anyone else on board, including the pilot. He monitored the performance of all of the mechanical systems on board, and he notified Dingledine if there was anything amiss or anything that Dingledine needed to be aware of. If there was a problem with any of the mechanical, navigational, bombing, gunnery systems, or anything else, he was the man who was supposed to know how to fix it. Effectively, Champa served as the bomber's ground crew in the air, fixing problems as they arose in flight. In an emergency situation, his role was pivotal. Champa was the man who was to keep Dingledine informed of how well the plane was and was not doing mechanically. When the bomber came under attack from enemy fighters, he also played an important defensive role. He manned the turret gun on the top of the aircraft, with its two machine guns.

John R. Glass was twenty-six years old and from New Cumberland, Pennsylvania. He was the Flying Fortress's radio operator, or "lifeline" with the home base. It was Glass who received instructions and updates to the mission while it was in flight and sent back progress reports as the mission progressed. The radio system of a B-17 was complex by the standards of the day, and Glass learned how to operate the radio systems at Drew Field. He was also the crew's first aid specialist and was responsible for the other emergency equipment on the bomber. In addition, Glass served as the flight photographer, taking pictures after the bombs were dropped to assess the results of the mission. When the bomber was threatened with enemy fighters, he manned a machine gun that was located in the radio room.

Otto Stange, Jr., was twenty-eight years old and from Queens, New York City. He was one of the two waist gunners who manned the two horizontal machine guns in the middle section of the aircraft. Stange was also qualified as a flight engineer. He therefore served as Vito Champa's assistant, helping Champa when needed. If Champa was killed or severely wounded, Stange had to be prepared to immediately step into the flight engineer's role. Lester Hutchinson was the other waist gunner. Hutchinson was from Hingham, Massachusetts, and was 23 years old. In addition to manning a waist gun, Hutchinson was the bomber's armorer, a munitions specialist who assisted Lt. Street with loading and fusing the bombs.

John R. Smith, a twenty-five-year-old from Cleveland, Ohio, was the ball turret gunner. He was also a trained radio operator who could fill in for Glass should the need arise. That was a rather unlikely possibility. For the entire flight, the ball turret gunner was normally suspended from the belly of the aircraft in a big, round Plexiglas bubble about three feet (a meter) wide. He was armed with two machine guns that, thanks to the turret, could be rotated to aim in any direction. The guns and the ammunition they would fire took up most of the space in the ball turret, so by necessity ball turret gunners were not tall men.

The ball turret was the least popular position on the bomber. Once in flight, the ball turret was lowered outside of the aircraft into a highly exposed position. In this isolated perch, Smith had no other means of contact with the other crewmembers outside of the interphone. The only thing separating him from the ground below was that piece of plastic, and he could see everything that was going on underneath the plane. On top of that, the ball turret was not easy to operate. The gunner would turn the turret with his feet, leaving his hands free to concentrate on the machine gun. Operating the ball turret was a bit like driving a car with one's feet and shooting the guns with one's hands at the same time. Evacuating from the ball turret in an emergency was not easy. In all too many bail-outs of bombers in distress, mechanical problems prevented the ball turret operator from escaping. The airmen believed that it was the most dangerous position on the aircraft. Statistically, that was not true. Both waist gunners and tail gunners had higher casualty rates than ball turret gunners. However, the airmen were never informed of the statistics, and it probably would not have mattered anyway even if they knew. The position looked and felt vulnerable and exposed to danger.[2]

There were two men named Smith in the crew, Lt. Smith the co-pilot and Sgt. John Smith the gunner. Although one might think that this would lead to confusion, it did not in practice because Lt. Smith was an officer, and Sgt. Smith was an enlisted man. The other officers in the crew called Lt. Smith by either his first name or last name, while the enlisted men addressed him strictly as "Lieutenant" or "sir." The enlisted men called John Smith by either his first or last name while the officers called him "Sergeant." An enlisted man would never call Lt. Smith "George" or "Smith," and the officers would never call Sgt. Smith "John." Therefore, military protocol ensured that the two Smiths would not be confused with each other. The fact that there were two Smiths in the crew must have struck some kind of chord with Jerry, as the founder of the LDS faith was Joseph Smith.

Finally, Jerry was assigned as the tail gunner, whose position was at the very back of the airplane. Like the ball turret gunner, the tail gunner was in an isolated and cramped position, and reaching the tail gun required squeezing around the rear wheel landing assembly. Once in position, his only connection with the other crewmembers was through the interphone. Since the Luftwaffe liked to attack B-17s from behind, he would usually be the first to see an enemy fighter attack coming, and therefore the first to react and to convey the necessary information about the threat to the other members of the team. Arguably, it was the most important defensive position on the bomber. It was also the most dangerous. Although the crewmen did not know it at the time, tail gunners suffered the highest casualty rates of all of the positions on the Flying Fortress.[3]

During the four months that the crew spent at Drew Field, Dingledine molded his men into a combat ready team. They spent hours flying together and rehearsing scenarios that they would encounter in combat. They learned to anticipate each other's thoughts, emotions, movements, and actions. Maurice Braswell, a former B-17 tail gunner, described the team-work experience of a Flying Fortress crew: "You develop camaraderie and trust within ten men. Therefore you develop a belief in them that they will do what they are supposed to do when you hit the hard place. You go through so much training that you develop instinct to do what you are supposed to do. You get past training and then you just do it. You just know that everyone will do what they are supposed to do when it counts. You have faith in them."[4]

When the crew finished their training at Drew Field, they were ready for combat. However, it was the USAAF, and only the USAAF, that would determine when they would go to Europe. Initially, it appeared that the crew would have a couple of weeks in between the end of their training and their deployment. Therefore all of the men were given a two-week furlough. This is when Jerry married Nora Lee. However, the USAAF's operational requirements changed, and it was decided that the crew would go to Europe sooner rather than later. The furloughs of Jerry and the rest of the men were cancelled and Jerry's honeymoon was abruptly cut short. He was reunited with his crew when he reported for duty at the Hunter Army Air-field near Savannah, Georgia.

Hunter Field was a Combat Crew Staging Center, the last base assignment in the United States that the crew would have before shipping to Europe. Dingledine's crew was assigned to a brand new B-17 and their assignment was to get that airplane safely to Europe. One morning in early April, Dingledine led Jerry and the other men to the new bomber for the first time, and each man went to his station and inspected it for combat readiness. They tested and calibrated their respective pieces of equipment and arms. Dingledine then took the crew up in the air for a test flight over the Atlantic. They tested the navigational, communications, and bombing equipment in flight. The guns were test fired over the ocean. Everything was in order. Dingledine landed, and while the plane was being refueled, the crewmembers were issued their overseas equipment. The crew then re-boarded the airplane and took off for Dow Field, near Bangor, Maine. They were now under the North Atlantic Transport Command, and on their way to Europe.[5]

The crew spent the night in Bangor, but it was purely a transit stop.

They were confined to base, and so they simply ate dinner and went to bed. The next morning, they took off and flew to Goose Bay, in Labrador, Canada. Again they were confined to base, and there was little to do in Goose Bay except eat and sleep. On the third morning, they flew to a base in Greenland. They landed in Greenland, where there was little sign of human habitation outside of the airbase. By now, the crew must have remarked upon the emptiness and bleakness of the frozen, barren terrain that they were flying over and that surrounded them. Again, there was nothing for the crew to do except eat and sleep. On the fourth morning, the crew left for Reykjavik, Iceland. It was the first real city that they had seen since Bangor. However, they were not there for tourism, and the crew was again confined to base. Besides, the Icelanders had a reputation among USAAF airmen for being as cold as the climate in which they lived, and some airmen suspected them of pro–Nazi sympathies. From Reykjavik, the crew flew to Prestwick, Scotland, where, upon arrival, they passed under the command of the European Theater of Operations.

At some point either during the journey to Scotland or shortly thereafter, Lt. Dingledine had the pleasure of promoting Jerry to the rank of sergeant. The promotion was routine. The USAAF knew that the Germans drew a distinction between the ordinary enlisted personnel like privates and the enlisted non-commissioned officers like sergeants. The Germans gave the latter slightly more respect and comfort than the former in their prisoner of war (POW) camps. Since the airmen's missions would all take place over enemy territory, the chances of an American airman becoming a POW were high. So, the Army Air Force adopted the practice of promoting flying enlisted personnel to the rank of sergeant before they entered combat in the European Theater of Operations.

At Prestwick, Dingledine's crew left behind the new B-17 that they had flown over from Georgia. By this point in the war, a superstition had grown among the airmen that it was bad luck to equip a new crew with a new plane in combat. The combat experience of an older plane was supposed to somehow make up for the inexperience of a new crew. However, the superstition had nothing to do with the separation. The reality was that the bomber would be sent where new bombers were needed, and the crew would be sent where new crews were needed. These were usually different locations. Now separated from the plane that brought them to Europe, Jerry and the rest of the crew spent the night at Prestwick and enjoyed a taste of hospitality from their British hosts. It was a welcome change from the perfunctory treatment that they had experienced on the bases on their journey overseas. The next morning, they boarded a bus for the long ride to the 11th Combat Crew Replacement Center at Bovingdon, north of London.[6]

It was now that the war started to become a reality for Jerry and the crew. Many of the instructors at Bovingdon were British aviators who had considerable combat experience. Some had been shot down over enemy territory and had escaped back to England. Their job was to mentally prepare the crew for combat. The crew underwent a few days of lectures from the veterans about combat experiences. More particularly, they learned about ditching procedures, how to hide parachutes, and how to escape from the occupied continent if they were shot down. The crew also began to feel as if they were in a war zone. England was under blackout at night, and there was plenty of evidence of the Luftwaffe's bombing campaign against England earlier in the war. Although the Luftwaffe was finding it harder and harder to strike at England at this stage in the war, it is possible that the crew witnessed the Luftwaffe's final manned air raid on nearby London on April 18, at the end of the "Baby Blitz." From the beginning of June 1944 until the end of the war, the Luftwaffe would only be able to strike England with its unmanned V-1 and V-2 rockets.[7]

On April 19, Jerry and the rest of the Dingledine crew were sent by bus to their new assignment: the 339th Squadron of the 96th Bomb Group at Army Air Force Station No. 138 at Snetterton Heath. Snetterton is six miles southwest of a small town called Attleborough in East Anglia. The 96th Bomb Group was a proud unit with high morale. They called themselves the Snetterton Falcons. The unit had already flown over 110 combat missions by the time the Dingledine crew and Jerry had arrived, and it would end up flying 321 combat missions over the course of the war. Since the 96th Bomb Group was located relatively close to the Army Air Force's 3rd Division Headquarters at Elveden Hall, it often participated in major operations that carried commanding generals. On August 17, 1943, then colonel, and soon to be general, Curtis LeMay led his famous "North Africa Shuttle Mission" to bomb Regensburg in a bomber of the 96th. The Snetterton Falcons also led the 3rd Division on the infamous Black Thursday raid of Schweinfurt on October 14, 1943. That mission was so named because the USAAF suffered its highest losses on a single mission of the war on that day.[8]

The motto of the Snetterton Falcons was "*E Sempre l'Ora*" or "It is Always the Hour." They were an elite unit, ready to risk their lives at a moment's notice. They were proud of their combat record, and they had the attention of the USAAF's senior generals. The Snetterton Falcons also had a unique honorary member, a donkey named "Lady Moe." The crew of *The Miracle Tribe* had bought Lady Moe back from the North Africa Shuttle Mission, having purchased her from a family in Algeria. The crew improvised an oxygen mask for her for the trip, and when they arrived at Snetterton, her head was sticking out of the waist gunner's position for all to see. Lady Moe had full freedom to wander about the base. She was known to walk inside buildings if the door was open, including the barracks where the men slept.

When Jerry and the other members of his crew arrived at Snetterton, they were assigned to their barracks with the 339th Squadron, the officers in one location, the enlisted men in another. It turned out that Jerry had some coincidental connections with this unit. The 96th Bomb Group itself was activated in July of 1942 at Salt Lake City, Utah, where Jerry first reported for duty and the home of the LDS Church. From November 1942 to January 1943, it had been based near Jerry's hometown of Pocatello, Idaho. From January 1943 until it shipped to Europe in April of 1943, it had been based in Peyote, Texas, Nora Lee's home state. Although these connections with Jerry's life were purely coincidental, he must have felt some natural affinity with the unit. It also turned out that Jerry knew three of the other enlisted men in his barracks: Everette Howe, Harry Shirey, and Claud Meadows. The three of them had trained with Jerry at gunnery school in Las Vegas, and they had been assigned to the 96th Bomb Group and the 339th Squadron shortly before Jerry had arrived.[9]

Jerry and the other members of Dingledine's crew began to talk with the other men in the barracks about what the Snetterton Falcons had been through. The month of April 1944 had been the deadliest in the Snetterton Falcons' proud history. They had lost a total of twenty-six bombers, the equivalent of nearly two squadrons. Although they did not know this at the time, May 1944 would be even worse, resulting in a loss of thirty bombers. Over the course of the war, the Snetterton Falcons lost more bombers to enemy action, and probably suffered higher casualties, than any other bomb group in the U.S. 8th Air Force.

In principle, in May of 1944 a B-17 crew that completed 25 missions would be considered to have completed its tour of duty. The crewmembers would be withdrawn from combat and returned to America for reassignment to train future bomber crews or other non-combat duties. In practice, not many bomber crews made it to that magic number, particularly in the early stages of the war. Although estimates vary, in 1942 the average bomber crew would be expected to complete only 8 to 12 missions, and in 1943 it was estimated that only 26.6 percent of all crews completed 25 missions. By the autumn of 1944 as the Luftwaffe weakened, the chances of survival improved, but they were still not great. The overall casualty rate of the U.S. 8th Air Force in Europe during the war approached 50 percent.[10]

Jerry knew that he was about to be thrown into a cauldron of fire, and that his chances of coming out of it were not so high. On April 20, Jerry wrote the following letter to his cousin Harold:

> Dear Harold,
> Hello ole chap. How is every little thing? I suppose the folks or your parents have told you that I am an old married man already. It hardly seems believable. Here I am clear over here in England so soon afterwards. The army finally saw fit to give me a rating, and I may get Staff soon. If I can only get out of this thing as easy as I got into it, I'll be happy. As our radio operator on our crew says, "They have us in a hell of a tight spot now." They can have the ratings, the money, and everything else if I can only get back again. After we finish our combat missions, we can go back to the States. Supposed to get a furlough and then be reclassified. Drop me a line when you get time. I haven't heard from home yet. Hope I get some mail from someone soon.
> As Ever,
> Gerald[11]

Fear and the feeling of isolation from home was a common psychological phenomenon among aircrews during their first six or seven combat missions. Jerry's apprehensions were certainly shared by the other crewmembers. However, there was also a sense of pride of belonging to an elite group of warriors bringing the war to Germany long before the Allied invasion of the continent. The men of Dingledine's crew were proud to fly a Flying Fortress. The Snetterton Falcons had more than their share of stories to tell about their bombers returning home crippled when they probably should have been lost. The stories gave the crew courage.

Shortly after their arrival, Dingledine and his crew were assigned to their bomber. It was a B-17 G, with serial number 42–31152. It had been built at one of the three B-17 assembly lines on the West Coast and delivered to the USAAF on September 25, 1943, at the Cheyenne Modification Center in Wyoming. It was one of the first batch of the "G" series of the B-17, which had just begun delivery to the USAAF on September 4. It entered service with the Snetterton Falcons on October 14, 1943, the same day that the Snetterton Falcons were suffering their Black Thursday. The bomber was probably assigned as a replacement for a bomber that was severely damaged or

Crew of the *Wolverine*: Top row, left to right: Vito Champa, Eugene Dingledine, Denuncio Street, George Smith, James MacConnell. Bottom row: Jerry, John Glass, Otto Stange, Lester Hutchinson, John Smith (courtesy DeLoy Larsen).

lost in that raid. The pilot of the first crew that flew 42–31152 in combat nicknamed it the *Wolverine*. When Dingledine and his crew were assigned to the *Wolverine*, it had already been in service for six months, and it had already been damaged in combat and repaired. It was an experienced plane, a good omen for the inexperienced crew. The pride of Jerry and the other crewmembers in the *Wolverine* is evident in their official photo taken with the airplane.[12]

During the next three days, the Snetterton Falcons bombed Hamm, Friedrickshaven, and Dijon while Dingledine and his crew completed their final training for combat. Part of this training consisted of talking to the experienced men of the Snetterton Falcons who briefed them on their own experiences and what the conditions they would be flying in were like. Experienced pilots, navigators and bombardiers briefed Dingledine and his officers. Experienced aerial gunners briefed Jerry and the other enlisted men about what aerial combat and anti-aircraft fire were like in practice. The experienced gunners shared with them tips on how to survive, such as how to position oneself in the tail gun to take advantage of the little protection that was available and minimize exposure to machine guns and flak. The crew then flew some final practice flights together, with the stories that they heard forefront in their minds. If the men had not paid attention to any of the other aspects of their training to date, they certainly paid attention now. The meaning behind all of the training had become very, very real for them.

The enlisted men were given one last round of promotions to help them should they become prisoners of war. Jerry was promoted to staff sergeant, as was Hutchinson, Stange, and John Smith. Champa, the flight engineer, and Glass, the radio operator, were now technical sergeants. The crewmembers also underwent one last set of physical examinations. The point of these examinations was to ensure that all dental records were up to date, as well as the medical history of any broken bones or other physical abnormalities the crewmen may have had. This information would be needed to identify their remains in the event that they were killed in combat. The crew was fully aware that this was the point of the medical and dental examinations. They knew about the losses that the Snetterton Falcons had suffered in April. It was all deadly serious now. They had trained for what was to come, but no amount of training could ever replace the actual experience of combat. Their first mission would be the final test of whether their skill, physical stamina, and psychological courage were ready for the challenges ahead.

When the Flying Fortresses flew into battle, they did so as part of a "wing." A typical wing consisted of eighteen bombers, although wings of thirty-six were also used starting in 1944. For the pilots, formation flying itself was quite a test. Keeping the bombers close together created a constant risk of mid-air collisions, particularly when things got confusing as a wing came under enemy fire or encountered bad weather. On the positive side, however, eighteen bombers flying in formation presented a formidable obstacle to enemy fighter aircraft. Since each Flying Fortress was equipped with thirteen machine guns, an enemy fighter approaching a formation faced a wall of fire of 234 .50-caliber machine guns that covered the approach to the formation in every direction. For the Flying Fortresses, there truly was safety in numbers. As long as long as the bombers remained in formation, the men felt relatively safe. However, if a bomber fell out of formation, it became an easier target for enemy fighter aircraft, and a more inviting target for anti-aircraft artillery flak. The aerial gunners felt like they had a chance to defend themselves against the enemy fighter aircraft. However, that feeling of empowerment disappeared against anti-aircraft artillery when a bomber approached its final target.

As a Flying Fortress approached its initial point of attack, command passed from the pilot to the bombardier. The pilots simply held the aircraft at a steady altitude as the bombardiers waited for the target to come into the cross-hairs of their Norden bombsight. At that moment, the bombardier would release the lethal payload and announce, "Bombs away." Control of the aircraft would revert to the pilots, who would turn their aircraft around and bring them home in formation following the predetermined route. The length of time between the initial point of attack and the signal "Bombs away" was a harrowing experience, and it could last as long as twelve minutes. As the pilots kept the bombers at a level altitude and steady speed, anti-aircraft artillery had plenty of time to calculate where the bombers were going to be and to target them. Normal flak from the anti-aircraft artillery would send deadly shrapnel ricocheting through the bomber. Explosive flak could detonate next to the plane and break off a wing, the nose, or the tail. Flak could also hit the fuel tanks or the payload, turning the bomber into a giant fireball in the sky. The flak probably took its greatest psychological toll on the aerial gunners. The pilots, navigator, and bombardier all had tasks to occupy their minds during the final bomb run and did not have much time to think about the danger they were in. The aerial gunners had nothing to do except wait. Enemy fighter aircraft would never enter the flak, and the B-17 gunners could do nothing to defend themselves against anti-aircraft artillery on the ground. For the ball turret gunner, flak was particularly frightening since he had an unobstructed view of the tracers rising from the ground toward him.[13]

The weather over Northern Europe posed another psychological challenge for the crew. The Flying Fortresses were not pressurized, so the crew fought in freezing cold temperatures wearing heavy flights suits, gloves, and oxygen masks that were uncomfortable and that inhibited their mobility. The weather also wreaked havoc with the combat missions themselves. Between 60 and 80 percent of the 96th Bomb Group's planned combat missions in the winter, and 50 to 60 percent in the summer, were cancelled due to poor weather. All too often, a bomber would approach its target under heavy anti-aircraft fire, only to watch as the target disappeared in a blank space of clouds at the last moment when the bombardier was supposed to drop bombs. Airmen were willing to risk their lives to accomplish their missions. However, failed missions only served to lower morale, particularly when they occurred under enemy fire.

To get around this problem, the USAAF and the Royal Air Force (RAF) began experimenting with electronic guidance systems, or "weather weapons," that would enable their bombers to operate and bomb effectively in cloudy weather. The USAAF's initial guidance system was called the H2X or MICKEY device, and it was introduced in the spring of 1944. When weather conditions warranted it, the MICKEY device was installed on one of the bombers in a wing whose job was to lead the other bombers to the target. These aircraft were known as "Pathfinders." To make room for the MICKEY, Pathfinders were stripped of most of their armament, and were therefore vulnerable. German fighters soon learned to identify the Pathfinders and make them a priority target.

The first combat test for Jerry and the other members of the Dingledine crew finally came on Wednesday, April 26, 1944. Their target was Brunswick (Braunschweig) in Germany. Brunswick was a significant industrial center, with machine and munitions factories, a harbor, canneries, a railway center, and a Volkswagen factory nearby. It had already been the target of dozens of air raids, and it was surrounded by significant anti-aircraft artillery. The *Wolverine* and seventeen other Snetterton Falcons left for Brunswick that day in poor weather led by a Pathfinder. Unfortunately, the Pathfinder's MICKEY failed. The bombs were dropped off-target, resulting in little or no damage to the intended target. The mission was a failure. However, there was one silver lining to the story. Since the bombers were off-target, the formation encountered no significant opposition. No enemy fighters challenged them, and they encountered only light anti-aircraft flak. All eighteen bombers returned to Snetterton unharmed.[14]

For the veterans of the Snetterton Falcons, it was a disappointing day, but not a disheartening one. It is true that they had not accomplished their mission, but they had also lost no one. It was simply a "milk run," and the veteran crews had notched up one more mission on their count that would determine when they could go home. However, the Dingledine crew was on its first mission, and had nothing to compare the experience of that mission with. What was routine and easy to a veteran could be perceived as difficult and dangerous to an inexperienced crew.

Sgt. John Smith had spent that first mission suspended from the bottom of the aircraft, isolated from the other crewmembers in the Plexiglas ball turret. He watched the entire mission unfold from that particularly exposed vantage point. Sgt. Smith could clearly see just how deep over enemy territory they had travelled. He could clearly see whatever anti-aircraft fire that they had faced that day. Maybe it was the thought that he was deep over enemy territory. Maybe it was the stories ringing through his head that he heard from the veteran crewmembers before he left. Maybe it was his imagination exaggerating the minimal danger that he had faced that day into something that it was not. Maybe it was simply the thought of being alone, isolated, and dangling over enemy territory. Whatever it was, something snapped inside of him. When the *Wolverine* returned to Snetterton, Sgt. Smith asked Lt. Dingledine to remove him from the crew. Despite the consequences that he knew would befall him, Sgt. Smith refused to operate the ball turret again in combat.

This turn of events was a real blow to the Dingledine crew. Critical to the crew's training was the trust that they had developed in each other to perform their assigned task to their utmost when the call of duty came. Sgt. Smith was now refusing the call of duty. Although it was better that Sgt. Smith made the decision that he did when the *Wolverine* was on the ground rather than when it was in the air, the fact remained that the trust was now broken. Moreover, the combat effectiveness of the bomber depended upon all ten crew positions being filled. The *Wolverine* could not fly without a ball turret gunner. Dingledine requested a replacement ball turret gunner from the 96th Bomb Group's Operations Officer. It would be less than an ideal solution, since the new man would not have trained with the crew, but it would have gotten the *Wolverine* back into the air. However, the request was denied. Because of the losses that the Snetterton Falcons were now experiencing, there simply were no replacement gunners available. The Dingledine crew was grounded.

On the next day, the Snetterton Falcons bombed V-1 installations in Bois d'Enfers, France. On April 29, they bombed Berlin itself. On April 30, they bombed a German airfield at Clermont Ferrand, France. The Dingledine crew sat out all three missions. This was very hard for Lt. Dingledine, Jerry, and the other members of the crew to take. The Snetterton Falcons were a battle-hardened unit, one that was used to taking damage to its airplanes and suffering casualties. The Snetterton Falcons did not like to take casualties, of course, but they were prepared to risk their lives to win the war. They were an elite unit and their morale was high.

One can only imagine the attitude that the other members of the 339th Squadron adopted toward Dingledine's crew during those three days. Dingledine and his men were "NFGs" (New F**king Guys) among battle-hardened veterans. They had participated in only one mission, and it was an easy mission at that. Now these NFGs were sitting on the ground doing nothing while the veterans of the squadron were bombing Berlin itself! Dingledine's crew must have been the subject of innuendo, ridicule, and ostracization. The situation was particularly unbearable for Jerry. His friends Howe, Shirey, and Meadows were out there flying and risking their lives on missions while he sat on the ground. He knew that his crew was letting the squadron down. However, there was nothing Jerry could do. Sgt. Smith refused to fly and as long as he did so, the *Wolverine* could not fly without him.

Finally, the operations officer suggested a compromise to Dingledine. The problem was that Sgt. Smith refused to operate the ball turret position. He did not refuse to fly per se. The operations officer suggested that Dingledine take Smith back on board in a different position on the bomber and use someone else in the ball turret. Sgt. Smith agreed to the idea, as long as he did not have to go back into the ball turret. Dingledine probably did not like the idea. Sgt. Smith had trained for the ball turret, and his crew had trained to operate with Sgt. Smith in the ball turret. However, Dingledine also had a responsibility to get his crew back into the air, and the reputation of him and his crew was suffering. Dingledine asked Jerry if he would take the ball turret so that he could put Sgt. Smith at the tail gun. Inside his heart, Jerry did not like the idea. He had not trained much on the ball turret and had only an elementary understanding of how it operated. Moreover, nobody wanted that job in the crammed Plexiglas bubble dangling from the bottom of the airplane. However, Jerry kept his reservations to himself. When Dingledine asked him to switch with Sgt. Smith, Jerry said, "Yes, sir." It was the only thing that Jerry could do that would get the crew back in the air.

It was Monday morning, May 1, 1944, and the Dingledine crew was immediately placed on flight status. The squadron was tasked with a bombing raid against Metz in France that same afternoon, and the Dingledine crew would be part of it. At this point in the war, the USAAF's bombing campaign was turning to the task of disrupting Germany's ability to reinforce its forces on the coast to resist the pending Allied invasion of Normandy. Metz was an important railway-marshaling yard, and the squadron's mission was to hit those railway yards. Jerry and the other crewmembers dressed for the mission and deposited their personal property. They went to their briefing where they learned about the mission and the dangers they would face. They were issued their escape kits with maps, money, and other items that they would need if shot down over Belgium or France. The briefing was classified and they were now prohibited from discussing it with anyone, including the ground crew that was getting the *Wolverine* ready for the mission. They took a jeep out to the *Wolverine,* and each crewmember talked to the relevant ground crew member about the condition of his position. The ground crew responsible for the ball turret told Jerry that they had some problems in adjusting the solenoid firing mechanism, and they couldn't get it to load its ammunition properly. Since Dingledine's orders were to start the engines at 1:40 p.m., they did not have time to finish the adjustments. Jerry would have to make the adjustments in the air.

The *Wolverine* took off as scheduled, and Jerry was now in a small race against time. To fix the problem with his machine guns, Jerry had to remove the guns' covers, rearrange the cables, adjust the solenoids, and put everything back in place. In the three-meter-wide cramped space of the ball turret, this would even be a challenge on the ground. Once the *Wolverine* reached cruising altitude, he would have to do it while wearing gloves, using oxygen, and dealing with air turbulence all at the same time. Since he had not really trained on the ball turret, he was not comfortable with the idea of trying to fix the solenoids while wearing all of that equipment. So, as soon as the plane took off, Jerry rushed to the ball turret to work on the problem. He worked frantically, and finished the job just as it was getting cold and the air was getting thin. He went inside to put on his gloves and oxygen equipment. He then returned to the ball turret. By now, they were over the English Channel. Jerry test fired his guns, and they worked. He was ready for combat by the time the *Wolverine* reached the Continent.

About forty-five minutes from the target, bad luck struck the *Wolverine*. An oil line on one of the engines broke, forcing Dingledine to "feather" (or shut off) the engine. Although B-17's could fly on three engines without a problem, it meant that the *Wolverine* would fly slower than the other bombers in the formation. It was inevitable that the *Wolverine* would leave the formation and become an inviting target for enemy fighters and flak. Dingledine asked the flight commander for permission to return to base. The flight commander refused the request and ordered Dingledine to press on. The fact that the crew consisted of NFGs who had been grounded for three days for reasons related to the courage of one of the crewmembers was probably a factor in the flight commander's decision. As they progressed to the target, the inevitable occurred, and the *Wolverine* began to fall behind the other bombers in the formation.

Over Luxembourg, enemy anti-aircraft artillery attacked the *Wolverine* and hit another engine, feathering it out, too. They were not far from the target, and Dingledine pressed ahead with the attack. It was too late for Dingledine to do anything else. However, the *Wolverine* was still laden with bombs. The remaining two functioning engines could not support the weight of those bombs, and the bomber began to lose altitude even before reaching the target. As the now isolated *Wolverine* approached the railway

yards at Metz and reached the initial point of attack, command passed to
Lt. Street, who delivered the payload on target. From Jerry's position in the
ball turret, he could see that they had made a direct hit. Command then
reverted to Dingledine, whose job was to try to get the *Wolverine* home.
This was going to be a challenge. Flying Fortresses were mighty aircraft.
Although they could fly on two engines, they were not intended to. The
Wolverine continued to lose speed and altitude despite the fact that it no
longer carried the weight of the bombs. It appeared that the anti-aircraft
flak had done even more damage to the bomber than Dingledine or Champa
had originally thought.

By the time it reached the middle of Belgium, the *Wolverine* had already
dropped to 7,000 feet (2,100 meters), compared to the altitude it should
have been at of 15,000 feet (4,500 meters). Dingledine conferred with the
flight engineer Champa. The two remaining engines were losing power,
and Champa did not think that they had enough engine power to make it
back to Snetterton. Dingledine decided to at least try to make it to the
English Channel, where they could ditch and an Allied ship could pick
them up. Dingledine ordered the crew to throw all unnecessary equipment
overboard in the hope of lightening the aircraft enough to keep it in the
air. It did not work. By the time the *Wolverine* had dropped to 6,000 feet
(1,800 meters), it was still thirty minutes from the Channel. The remaining
two engines began to smoke from overwork, and it became clear to Champa
that one of those engines would soon quit working, too. Champa informed
Dingledine that the *Wolverine* could not stay in the air for much longer.
Dingledine ordered the crew to prepare to bail out.

Jerry and the rest of the enlisted crew left their positions and moved
to the main door in the middle of the aircraft. Speaking to the crew over
the interphone, Dingledine pointed out a small woods below the aircraft
that the crewmen could see through a window. He told the crew to orient
themselves to the woods, and to assemble there once they were on the
ground. He then asked Jerry to serve as the jumpmaster for the enlisted
men. Sgt. Smith jumped first, followed by Sgts. Stange, Hutchinson, Glass,
and Champa. While the enlisted men were jumping through the main door,
Lts. Smith, MacConnell and Street bailed out through the nose. Jerry notified Dingledine that he was the only one left, and Dingledine told him to
jump.

Jerry paused for a moment at the door, and briefly thought about what
lay before him. If he could get to the ground safely and hide until nightfall,
he had the chance to make contact with the Belgian underground and

escape back to freedom. If not, he would spend the rest of the war in a German POW camp. Jerry took a deep breath, and then leaped into the vast empty space below. Meanwhile, Dingledine pointed the airplane in the direction of what he believed to be empty farmers' fields, and he bailed out. Dingledine was no longer in control of the *Wolverine*.

For the first few moments of his fall, air rushed about Jerry as he tumbled every which way. But as the plane grew farther and farther away, he lost his forward momentum and felt more quiet and calm. He waited to pull the ripcord in order to minimize the chances that the Germans would see him. However, he probably waited too long, as he was falling faster than he realized. When he finally pulled the ripcord, he felt an abrupt jerk, followed by "a feeling of extreme quietness, a feeling of almost complete oblivion from all earthly existence." He relaxed, but the moment did not last long. Jerry realized that the next few moments could mean life or death, freedom or captivity. He looked around to orient himself. In the sky around him, he saw three parachutes from other members of the crew. Below him, he saw that he was falling fast toward either a telephone or electrical line. Hitting it could mean electrocution or entrapment in the wire. He looked up at his chute and let a little air out to try to avoid the line, but this accelerated the rate of his fall.

Suddenly, something very fast moving and terribly hard slammed against his body. It was planet Earth. Jerry found himself lying in a grain field. As he adjusted to the shock of the hard landing, he looked around. He could see that he was close to a farmhouse, a road, and the power line that he was trying to avoid. He did not know it at the time, but he was just outside of the village of Silly in Belgium, not far from its train station.[15]

The now pilotless *Wolverine* slowly descended to the earth. Twenty-year-old Madelaine Petit lived with her parents in the village of Lanquesaint, about ten kilometers away. She liked to listen to the B-17's as they rumbled far over head each day, bringing the war to Germany. It was the sound of liberation on its way. However, this time something was different. As the empty and pilotless *Wolverine* passed over her home, it made an infernal noise like she had never heard before. She rushed outside to see what was happening and was terrified to realize just how close above her head the Flying Fortress was as it glided toward the ground with two smoking engines. The *Wolverine* narrowly cleared the roof of the last house in the village. It then slammed on its belly into a farmer's field next to the home of Madelaine's brother Henri. Lanquesaint had barely escaped a horrific tragedy. If the *Wolverine* were only three or four meters lower in altitude, it would have hit the last house in the village, killing its occupants and their neighbors. If it had taken a slightly different direction of travel to the right, it would have slammed into Henri's home, killing Madelaine's brother and his family. If it had fallen at a slightly faster rate of descent, it would have struck the middle of the village and killed or wounded dozens of civilians. Instead, the *Wolverine* fell harmlessly into a farmer's field, just outside the village. The citizens of Lanquesaint knew that God was watching out for them that day.[16]

Jerry knew nothing about the events in Lanquesaint. He was facing a more immediate problem. As he stood up, a sharp pain quickly emanated from his left ankle and shot through his body. He fell back to the ground and took off his electric flight to examine his foot. No bones appeared to be broken, so he knew it wouldn't be so bad. However, his ankle was sprained and it did hurt a lot as put on his GI boots. As he was pulling the boot over his injured ankle, a farmer came up to him holding a pocketknife. The farmer was speaking French, and Jerry could not understand a word that he was saying. However, he sensed that the farmer was trying to help him. The farmer cut Jerry's chute off and took it away to hide it from the Germans. He made some motions that Jerry understood to mean that he should go hide in a nearby ravine on the other side of the road. Jerry stood up to move toward the ravine. Pain from his ankle shot through his body. As he hobbled across the road, a bicycle passed. The woman on the bicycle also pointed to the ravine and made body motions that Jerry knew were meant to tell him that he should hurry up. His ankle really hurt, but he did his best. He fell to the ground and crawled into the ravine, where he laid down in pain and waited until it was dark.

After reaching the ravine and catching his breath, Jerry's first thought was to pray. He thanked God for his survival, and he put his fate in God's hands. He asked God for guidance to lead him safely to the Belgian Resistance. He prayed for strength and courage to see him through the ordeal that he knew was ahead. Having put his faith in God, Jerry then put his faith in his country. He pulled out his escape kit to see what Uncle Sam would tell him to do in this situation. There was a map and he did his best to orient himself based on what Dingledine had said about their location before they bailed out. He looked for the woods that Dingledine had pointed to from the air. However, there were so many woods in the area that he was no longer sure which was the right one. In fact, he had no idea where he was. What he did know was that his ankle was swelling, and that he was in pain.

As darkness fell, he found a stick to use as a cane, and he began to hobble off through the fields looking for an area that would be relatively safe from German patrols. Sometimes dogs would start to bark as he limped by a farmhouse. When that happened, Jerry laid still until they were quiet in order not to give away his presence to the Germans. After a couple of hours of this limping under pain through the fields, he found a place to hide in some woods that he thought would be safe for the night. It was midnight, and Jerry did his best to try to get some sleep. Jerry's air war was finished. His underground war was about to begin.[17]

• 5 •

The Underground

A lot of people were looking for Jerry when he awoke the next morning. The Germans had seen the crew parachute to the ground as the *Wolverine* crashed near Lanquesaint. They recognized that it was a B-17, and they knew that there would be ten crewmembers on board. By the morning of May 2, they had already captured MacConnell, Champa, Glass, and Stange. There were six other Americans out there somewhere, and the Germans were determined to find them. So, too, was the Comet Line (*La Ligne Comète*).[1]

The Comet Line was a Belgian Resistance organization that was dedicated to finding, sheltering, and returning to the Allies airmen who were shot down over occupied Europe. When an Allied fighter or bomber was shot down, the American and British militaries lost more than just a piece of machinery. They lost a cohesive combat crew that was expensive to train. Pilots, in particular, were valuable assets that the Allies could not afford to lose. By returning downed airmen to the United Kingdom, the Comet Line played an invaluable role in the Allied war effort. However, returning airmen to England was something that was much easier said than done. The Nazis occupied almost all of continental Europe, and there were no transportation links of any type between occupied Europe and the United Kingdom. However, Spain was neutral during the war, and the British maintained a diplomatic presence there. That fact planted an idea in the mind of a twenty-five-year-old Belgian woman named Andrée de Jongh, who went by the nickname of Dédée.

When the British evacuated Dunkerque in 1940, a small number of British soldiers were left behind. Some of these successfully evaded capture and were secretly sheltered in the homes of Belgian families. In August of 1941, Dédée left Brussels with one of these soldiers, Private James Cromar of the First Gordon Highlanders, along with two other Belgians. Using trains and forged identity papers, they travelled south to Valenciennes in the north of France, southeast to Hamelet (near Amiens), south to Bayonne, and from Bayonne to Saint Jean de Luz, near the border of France with Spain.

Standing in between them and Spain were the Pyrenees Mountains, a formidable obstacle policed on one side by the Germans and on the other side by Generalissimo Francisco Franco's Spanish security forces, who were sympathetic to the Germans. To avoid detection, Dédée and her charges needed to cross the mountains at night on narrow, winding, and steep mountain trails. Even today, these trails can be tricky in the daylight hours. At night, they are outright dangerous, as one wrong step can result in a plunge of hundreds of feet off of the side of the mountains. To surmount this obstacle, Dédée found a Basque guide named Tomas to help them, and he led them across using smuggling routes that the Basques had used for centuries. Thanks to Tomas, the group made it safely across the Pyrenees, and they went to Bilbao, where there was a British Consulate. Dédée took Private Cromar to the consulate, where they met Vice Consul Arthur Dean.

Dean could not believe his eyes. Sitting in front of him was a young Belgian woman who claimed to have made a long and dangerous journey with a fugitive British soldier all the way from Belgium, across occupied France, and through the Pyrenees mountains to see him in this office. He could not imagine how Dédée, a slim and delicate young woman, could have made such a perilous voyage, and particularly how she made the arduous trek on foot at night across the Pyrenees. Dean was further shocked when Dédée asked him for the British government's financial support to help her make the route that she took a permanent escape route for other servicemen. Dean did not believe that she was serious, and he even considered the possibility that Dédée was a German spy. However, Dédée eventually convinced Dean that she was for real, and he communicated Dédée's request to the Foreign Office in London.

The British bombing campaign of continental Europe was in its early stages, but it was already clear that the air war would only grow larger. The British government recognized that it would lose more and more airmen over occupied territory as the war progressed. Therefore, it needed the service that Dédée was offering them. After three weeks of negotiations between the Consulate in Bilbao and the Foreign Office in London, Dédée got what she wanted. The Foreign Office agreed to provide the financial and material support that Dédée needed to buy transportation tickets, pay guides, forge documents, and cover the other costs associated with such an operation. With this assistance, Dédée could now make the Comet Line a reality, and she returned to Brussels to do so.

Throughout the course of the war, thousands of Belgian, French, and Spanish civilians helped the Comet Line in this task. Some were spotters who searched the skies during bombing missions and tried to find the airmen who parachuted to the ground from crippled aircraft. Some were individuals and families who provided safe houses to shelter the airmen. Some were guides who led the airmen to the safe houses and ultimately on the trek to Spain. Others supported the guides and safe houses by forging documents, arranging transportation, and securing food and clothing for the airmen. All of this was very dangerous, and the penalties that the Germans laid down for helping downed airmen included death.

Betrayal was a constant threat. On several occasions during the war, the Nazi secret police, the Gestapo, arrested the leadership of the Comet Line, temporarily decapitating it. Each time that the Gestapo did so, other brave volunteers stepped forward to take over the reins of the organization and risk their lives for the cause. Over time, the Comet Line evolved into a system of organization that helped it to survive the betrayals and arrests that it would periodically suffer. The central organization was in Brussels, but underneath were three separate sectors for Belgium, the border region of Belgium and France, and France itself. Underneath each sector were various "sections" headed by individuals who would recruit the guides, the safe houses, and the other volunteers. In principle, beneath the level of the section heads and principal guides, any one person in the organization would know only two or three others who were involved in the organization. In this way, if the Gestapo arrested, interrogated, and tortured an ordinary volunteer, at worst that person could only give up the names of two or three other people in the organization. Yet, betrayals did occur, and sometimes the Nazis successfully infiltrated the organization.

The consequences were catastrophic for those who were compromised. The Nazis executed over 200 Comet Line volunteers during the war, including Dédée's father. Hundreds more were sent to concentration camps, including Dédée herself, who was arrested in January of 1943. The following is the text of one of the many notices of an execution that the German military authorities published:

> The Belgian citizens, Eric de Menten de Horne, Jean Ingels, Emile Delbruyère, Albert Marchal, Henri Rasquin, Ghislain Neybergh, Gaston Bidoul, also the Frenchmen Edouard Verpraet and Anoine Renaud, were condemned to death by a war tribunal for their activities on behalf of the enemy. The judgment has been executed by firing squad. Some of the condemned were acting as members of an organization set up with this intent. The others had no connection with the organization but had prevented occupying forces from arresting enemy airmen who had been shot down, by providing them with civilian clothing, sheltering them and helping them by

other means to escape. In this notice it is necessary to draw attention once again to the fact that the military tribunals will enforce without pity the most severe penalties the law provides for any future cases of aiding the armed forces of the enemy. Consequently, anyone who gives help in any sort of way to enemy airmen, anyone who fails to report members of enemy armed forces to the nearest German headquarters, must realize the consequences of his action and may not count on any indulgence on the part of the tribunals.[2]

Why did members of the Comet Line take such risks? Mme. Anne Brusselmans, one of the Comet Line's section chiefs, wrote this in her diary during the war:

It's no use pretending otherwise, I do feel sometimes like nothing on earth. This continuous strain is getting me down. Yet I must keep on. I know that by now the Allies are counting on us. Again and again I remind myself that each man we send back is a man of experience, and that the mere fact they do go back is good for the morale of those who, day after day, night after night, go out into the skies to face and meet death. And what a death! Burned alive or machined-gunned as they come down by parachute. Yes, we must keep on.[3]

Thanks to the sacrifices of these brave civilian volunteers, the Comet Line saved about 800 American and British airmen from the Nazis.

Jerry and the other crewmembers of the *Wolverine* did not know the name of the Comet Line or how it worked. However, they did know that something like it existed. An important part of their final training in England was learning what to do if they found themselves shot down over enemy territory. British airmen who had undergone the ordeal and had successfully returned to England had briefed Dingledine's crew in England. The crew was given tips on how to avoid capture and how to make contact with the Resistance. It was now time for Jerry to put that training to use.

Jerry's ankle was badly sprained and had swollen even larger during the night. He knew that he could not move far and fast, and he knew that both the Germans and the Resistance were looking for him. Using a stick as a crutch, he hobbled off as discreetly as possible to find a friendly Belgian civilian to help him. To avoid the Germans, Jerry stayed off of the main road, and he limped along a parallel path at a distance that permitted him to monitor the main road for any signs of the Germans. The path was a little sunken, which would allow him to dive for cover if necessary. At some point during the morning, he spotted a Belgian woman who appeared to be "safe" walking along the road, and he made contact. She was a spotter for the Comet Line, and she was looking for Jerry. She had probably been tipped off about Jerry's presence in the area by either the farmer or the bicyclist he had encountered the day before. Her name is lost to history, and Jerry described her only as an "English lady." However, she was undoubtedly a Belgian who spoke English with an English accent. This unknown woman led him to the home of Gisbert Edouard Germain Van Delft, who owned a chateau-farm in Saint-Marcoult, an isolated location that was not far from where he landed.[4]

Van Delft was a patriotic Belgian who was active in the Belgian Resistance. He was more than happy to help Jerry. However, because he was so active in the Resistance, there were a lot of secret activities taking place in and around his home. If Jerry had stayed at the Van Delft home for long, he might have seen things that would have compromised the Resistance had he had been captured. Since the Germans were actively looking for Jerry, the risk that he would be captured was too high. Therefore, Jerry would have to be moved sooner rather than later. The next day, Wednesday, May 3, Julien Schotte arrived with his bicycle to take Jerry to another location. With his swollen and injured ankle, Jerry could not pedal a bicycle on his own. So, he sat on the back of Schotte's bicycle, and Schotte pedaled him to the village of Thoricourt, which was about five kilometers away. At Thoricourt, Jerry and Schotte were met by a Monsieur Durez, who took Jerry by car to the home of Charles and Sylvie Lepoivre.[5]

The Lepoivres and their three children, Marcel, Lucie and Carmen, lived on a thirty-five hectare farm called *l'Espinette* near the village of Gondregnies. In 1942, their parish priest, Father Voordeckers, began sheltering Allied airmen. However, a collaborator tipped off the Gestapo about Father Voordecker's activities. The Gestapo sent an English-speaking German Nazi to Father Voordeckers' rectory posing as a downed airman. Father Voordeckers took the bait, and the Gestapo promptly arrested him. Father Voordeckers was sent to a concentration camp, where he later perished. The patriotism and bravery of their parish priest inspired Charles and Sylvie Lepoivre to follow in his footsteps. They volunteered to assist the Comet Line, knowing all too well the risks that were involved.

The Comet Line turned the Lepoivre farm into an important first stop for downed Allied airmen recovered in the area. At the Lepoivre home airmen were issued civilian clothes and false identity papers while the Comet Line planned the next steps in their journey. Lepoivre's eldest daughter, Lucie, often accompanied the airmen on their journey to the next safe house, posing as their girlfriends. If the Germans saw a young man walking down the road alone, particularly in an area with a lot of downed airmen, they would have stopped the young man to determine his identity. However, if they saw the same young man arm-in-arm with a young woman, this would reduce their suspicions, since they would assume that the man was Belgian. The practice of using young women to pose as the girlfriends of the airmen in civilian clothes was a common deception employed by the Comet Line. Dédée herself had pioneered the practice, and she found it be very valuable. Moreover, since the American and British airmen spoke no French or Dutch, the "girlfriend" could speak for the "couple" if they were ever stopped by the authorities or otherwise needed to communicate with people they did not know.

Lepoivre's farm occupied an ideal location for this task. It was situated in a relatively isolated spot in a peaceful countryside, and many citizens in the area were sympathetic to the Resistance. However, no safe house was ever truly safe. Almost every community had a few collaborators who were only too willing to betray the Resistance. Every community also had a much larger number of innocent civilians who were simply indifferent to the Resistance, and just wanted to be left alone. The primary objective of these indifferent civilians was to stay out of the war as best they could and not stir up trouble. If one of these indifferent civilians saw something unusual at the Lepoivre's farm, they would remain silent. However, if the Nazis would ever question them about what they had seen or heard, they would tell the truth in order to avoid getting themselves into any trouble with the authorities. The danger of being betrayed under these circumstances was probably greatest in smaller communities in the provinces where everyone knew everyone else. It was somewhat easier to shelter airmen in one of the nineteen communities of Brussels. In Brussels, there was a larger pool of potential safe houses to draw from, more opportunities to acquire food and clothing without attracting notice, and certainly more anonymity in the population of a large city. Therefore, the Comet Line in the area of Silly tried to move the airmen to Brussels as fast as they could.[6]

When Jerry arrived at the Lepoivre farm, three of the four officers from the *Wolverine* were already there, Lts. Dingledine, Smith, and Street. They informed Jerry that Lt. MacConnell had been taken prisoner along with Sgts. Champa, Glass, and Stange. However, they were happy to report that Sgt. Hutchinson was safely in the hands of the Comet Line at another location. No one was sure what had happened to Sgt. Smith. It turned out that Sgt. Smith, too, was in the hands of the Resistance, albeit a different Resistance organization than the Comet Line. He had parachuted into a courtyard in the middle of a square farmhouse. The startled farmer at first laid low, not knowing if the person who had fallen into the middle of his home was a German or an Allied airman. However, after watching Sgt. Smith's behavior for a while, the farmer realized that he was not German. The farmer took Sgt. Smith in, and turned him over to Astride d'Adam, who was a volunteer for a different Resistance organization.[7]

Of the four crewmembers in the Lepoivre home, Lt. Dingledine was the most important one to move. He was the pilot and his rapid return to England would have the most military value to the Allies. So, Dingledine was sent toward Brussels on the next day. However, Jerry had a badly injured ankle, and he would have to recover for a few days before he could travel. The Comet Line decided to keep Jerry, Lt. Smith, and Lt. Street at the Lepoivre home for six days. During that time, Jerry must have made quite a positive impression on the Lepoivre family. When it was time for Jerry to leave, Charles Lepoivre pulled him off to the side to have a private word with him. Lepoivre told Jerry that could always count on him if he were ever on the run and needed a place to hide. Little did anyone know at the time that Jerry would take Lepoivre up on that offer three months later. For now, however, Jerry would be heading to Brussels with the others.[8]

On Monday, May 8, Lucie Lepoivre took Jerry and Lts. Smith and Street to the home of Cyrile Suys in Tollembeek, where they spent the night. Lt. Dingledine had not yet been moved to Brussels and was staying at the same house when Jerry, Smith and Street arrived there. The following morning, Victor Schutters came to collect Jerry and Lt. Dingledine and move them to Brussels, while Lts. Smith and Street stayed in Tollembeek to be moved later.

Schutters was one of the unsung heroes of the Comet Line who took enormous risks for the airmen. He worked for the Belgian National Railroad (SNCB), where he was a foreman in the maintenance department. During the occupation, the Germans ran the SNCB, which was vital to the German war effort. Schutters ranked high enough in the SNCB that his responsibilities were nationwide. Schutters did his job for the SNCB well enough that the Germans left him alone and allowed him get on with his work. Because of the nature of his work and his proven track record of competence, the Germans authorized him to drive any car or truck that belonged to the SNCB, and he had permission to go anywhere in Belgium, except the coast. He also had papers exempting him from having his car searched. Only collaborators normally enjoyed such privileges. However, Schutters was anything but a collaborator. He used his privileges to transport airmen like Jerry from the provinces to Brussels using SNCB vehicles under the

At the Lepoivre family farm *L'Espinette*, left to right, top row: Denuncio Street, Sylvie Lepoivre, and George Smith. Bottom row: Jerry, and Marcel and Charles Lepoivre (courtesy Jenny Abeels).

very nose of the Germans. It was the ideal cover for such a job. The members of the Comet Line who knew Schutters appreciated the irony of the fact that he was using his position to subvert the German war effort with their own resources. However, if the Germans had ever discovered what Schutters was up to, there is no doubt that he would have suffered a slow and painful death at the hands of the Gestapo.[9]

Schutters brought Jerry to the South Train Station in Brussels and handed him over to Mademoiselle Odette Gryspeirt. Odette was twenty-one years old. She was the child of a Belgian father and a British mother. She grew up in Bel-

Odette Gryspeirt (courtesy Jenny Abeels).

Lester Hutchinson, Marguerite Schreyen, and Jerry (courtesy Jenny Abeels).

gium, and had graduated from the Belgian school system. However, her mother had ensured that her English was perfect and that she spoke it with a proper British accent. Odette identified with both of her parents' cultures, and she felt a natural affinity with the British airmen flying above her head every day on their way to bomb Germany. She was determined to help both of her homelands win the war. Like Dédée, Odette was headstrong, and a woman who believed in acting upon her beliefs. Mme. Anne Brusselmans recruited Odette to join her section of the Comet Line in January of 1944. Mme. Brusselmans initially assigned Odette to the tasks of collecting food, clothing, and money to support her section. Odette's motivation was so strong and her performance was so outstanding that Mme. Brusselmans promoted Odette to the status of a guide in February, despite her young age.[10]

Odette brought Jerry to the home of Victor Schreyen. Schreyen was a senior guide for the Comet Line and he played a key organizational role in Mme. Brusselmans' section. He sometimes offered his own home as a safe house as well. Schreyen in turn brought Jerry to the home of Marie De Stobbelier, who lived in Koekelberg, one of the nineteen communities that constitute Brussels. Jerry stayed with Mme. De Stobbelier for four days before Odette moved him to the home of Mlle. Bertha Fillée's in the Etterbeek community of Brussels. While he was at Mlle. Fillée's home, Jerry was reunited with Sgt. Hutchinson, who was also staying there. It was the first time that Jerry and Hutchinson had seen each other since they were shot down. Two days later, another guide, Mme. Madeleine Mounier, took Jerry and Hutchinson to the home of Jean-Pierre Brichard in the Ixelles community of Brussels. Jerry and Hutchinson stayed there for one week, until May 23.[11]

The Comet Line was now facing an acute crisis of finding safe houses for the airmen. It was clear that the Allies would soon invade Europe in either France or Belgium and open the long-awaited Western Front in the war. What was not known was exactly when or where they would invade the continent. Given the extreme risks involved in moving airmen from Belgium to Spain, the Comet Line decided to stop the movement. Orders came down to the Brusselmans Section in May to shelter the airmen in the safe houses where they were, and to wait for the Allied armies to reach them. However, the invasion had not yet come by the end of May, while more and more airmen were continuing to be shot down.

Finding safe houses for this growing pool of downed airmen became a harder and harder task. Not only did the Comet Line need to identify individuals who would take the potentially lethal risk of sheltering an airman, but the homes also had to be suitable for the task. The safe houses could not be located near German military facilities, or railway junctions, or other areas where the Germans were constantly on the watch. Homes with children were dangerous because of the risk that children might talk at school. Petty personality issues also came into play. Not all husbands were ready to bring gallant young airmen under the same roofs as their wives, while some unmarried women thought of the possibility as a golden opportunity. For Mme. Brusselmans, finding suitable safe houses was a significant challenge, a challenge that was made more difficult by occasional betrayals that would remove existing safe houses from the available pool.[12]

Compounding this problem, the Gestapo became more active in its pursuit of the Comet Line at the end of May. To stay one step ahead of them, Mme. Brusselmans ordered her guides to move the airmen around the existing temporary safe houses more frequently while they searched for new safe houses that could provide more permanent solutions to the problem. On May 23, Mme. Meunier moved Jerry and Hutchinson to the home of Jacques De Coen in the Auderghem community of Brussels. The next day, Victor Schreyen picked them up and took them to his home. On the 25th, he brought them back to Bertha Fillée's home in Etterbeek. On the 26th, Odette took them to the home of Gilbert Tedesco in Auderghem. Four days later, Odette moved Jerry back to Bertha Fillée, while she took Hutchinson to Waterloo.

The situation then became extremely dangerous. On June 1, the Gestapo arrested Victor Schreyen, as well as his pregnant wife and his sister Suzette. Given his position in the Comet Line, Schreyen knew too much, and his arrest put the entire Brusselmans Section at risk. All of the airmen under the care of the Brusselmans Section needed to be moved immediately. Fortunately, the Comet Line had already recruited a new family who would serve as a suitable safe house for Jerry. Only Mme. Brusselmans, Odette, and a third person named Willy knew about this new family. Whatever happened to Victor Schreyen under torture, Jerry would be safe with this new family, at least in the short term. On June 2, Odette bought Jerry to the home of Arthur and Clémy Abeels, who lived at *avenue de la Constitution* 19 in Ganshoren, another one of the nineteen communities of Brussels. It was a move that would irreversibly change the life of Jerry and the Abeels family.[13]

Although he did not know it at the time, Jerry was now in the middle of the Belgian Resistance, of which the Comet Line was only one small part.

In fact, there was no national movement or organization called the "Belgian Resistance." Rather, the Belgian Resistance consisted of multiple organizations that were fragmented along functional, ideological, and linguistic lines, much like the country itself. There were varying degrees of coordination among some of these organizations, and varying degrees of cooperation between them and the Allied authorities and the Belgian government-in-exile in London. However, there was no effective Belgian equivalent of the French National Resistance Council (CNR). The Belgian Resistance fought the war as separate groups of isolated bands of volunteers, and sometimes as rival gangs.[14] Sometimes there were overlaps in membership and activities among these groups; sometimes there was not. The only common denominator was their collective goal of ridding Belgium of the occupiers.[15]

At times, the fragmentation in the Belgian Resistance represented a functional division of labor. Some Resistance groups, like the Comet Line, were specialized in sheltering downed airmen and helping them to escape capture. They were known as "evasion lines." Although the Comet Line was the largest and most well-organized of the evasion lines, it was not alone in this venture. In Belgium, there was also an organization named "EVA" that eventually merged with the Comet Line. A Belgian named Albert Guérisse also set up one of these networks in France that he called "Pat O'Leary." Other lines were active in the Netherlands, France and Denmark.

Some Resistance organizations specialized in the clandestine press. Since the German authorities controlled the official press, the clandestine press played an important role in reporting what was really happening in the rest of the world. The clandestine press was also instrumental in restoring the morale of the Belgian population and urging them to resist. Around 600 such resistance publications appeared at various times during the war. Most of these were small with only one to four pages, and a circulation of a couple of hundred copies. However, there were some notable exceptions. *La Libre Belgique* was published by a group calling itself "Peter Pan," which had links to the Independence Front. At its peak, this clandestine newspaper had a circulation of over 60,000, and was distributed across the country. This was a remarkable feat considering the need for secrecy, the shortages of paper and ink, and the fact that the penalty for publishing such a work was death. Over the course of the war, some 2,000 Belgian writers, printers, and distributors paid the price for engaging in this activity.

Other Resistance organizations focused on espionage and intelligence-gathering for the Allied Forces. Belgians with military backgrounds and strong pro–British feelings tended to be behind the creation of these networks. They were normally established with the active assistance of the British Secret Intelligence Service (SIS), with which they continued to have close links. By providing information about German troop formations, air force capabilities, military installations, critical infrastructure, and political developments within Belgium, they provided invaluable support to the Allied war effort in general and its bombing campaigns in particular. One example was the group "Luc," which was later renamed "Marc." Georges Leclercq, a World War I veteran, founded the organization. His son Georges Lucien Leclercq, who went by the nickname Luc, was in the Belgian army at the time of the German invasion in 1940. Luc was killed in the opening stages of the war and is buried in the community cemetery of Ganshoren. Leclercq named his espionage organization in honor of his fallen son, and it had a network of agents across the country that did direct physical spying on the Germans. Another example is the group *Zéro*, which set up radio signal transmission stations to help guide Allied aircraft. There were over forty-three such intelligence networks during the war, involving over 18,000 Belgians.

There were also Resistance organizations that specialized in sabotage. One of the most successful of these was the *Groupement Général de Sabotage*, more commonly known as Group G. Scientists and engineers from the Free University of Brussels founded Group G, and because of their background, they were ideally suited for the task. They had the expertise to identify the most critical junctures in the industrial, communication, and transportation networks and to apply just enough force at those junctures to bring these networks down. In a spectacular operation in January 1944, Group G took out almost the entire Belgian electricity grid for nearly a week, costing the factories fifteen million to twenty-five million lost man-hours of labor needed for the German war effort. The members of Group G knew what they were doing, and because of that, Group G enjoyed considerable support from the British Special Operations Executive (SOE).

Some Resistance organizations spanned all three activities but were separated from each other on linguistic or political lines. One example is the *Witte Brigade* (or White Brigade), which took its name from the fact that the paramilitary units of the fascist collaborators were called the Black Brigades. It was founded in Antwerp and was mostly active in Flanders, the Flemish part of the country. The White Brigade began with a clandestine newspaper called *Steeds Verenigd* (or Still United). From there, it moved into evasion-like activities by protecting Jewish families from the authorities, and then into acts of sabotage. Similar organizations originated in

Brussels and Wallonia, the francophone part of the country such as the *Mouvement National Belge* (Belgian National Movement). Just to be clear, the linguistic division of Belgium was not as strong in the 1940s as it is today. Both of these organizations operated across the linguistic division of Belgium. The White Brigade was known as *Fidelio* to its francophone members, and the Belgian National Movement was known as the *Belgische Nationale Beweging* to its Flemish members. However, their origins were in different parts of the country, and their membership and activities tended to be concentrated in the areas where they originated.

There were also Resistance organizations that strove to be truly national in character. One of the initially best-organized and most successful groups was the Communist Armed Partisans (*Partisans Armées/De Gewapende Partizanen*). The Partisans sprung into action after the German invasion of the Soviet Union in June of 1941. They successfully ran a clandestine press, engaged in acts of sabotage, targeted collaborationist Belgians for execution, and trained to engage the Nazis in combat so that they would be ready for the moment when the Allied invasion of the continent would arrive. This latter fact was discomforting to both the Belgian government-in-exile and the Allied governments. The last thing the authorities in London wanted was a large, well-organized, and well-armed Communist paramilitary force to contend with in Belgium after the liberation.

However, in late 1942, the Partisans made a critical mistake when they began targeting ordinary German soldiers for assassination, which provoked the Nazis into executing innocent Belgian civilians in retaliation. Although the Belgian public would accept (and perhaps even largely support) attacks against collaborators, most Belgians thought that attacking ordinary German soldiers, most of whom were conscripts and not Nazis, was going too far. Most Belgians certainly believed that such actions were not worth the cost in the innocent civilian lives that the Nazis would take in retaliation. So, public opinion began to turn against the Partisans. Moreover, the targeting of German soldiers redoubled the efforts of the Nazis to eradicate the Partisans.

By July of 1943, the Germans had succeeded in infiltrating both the party and the Partisans. They arrested almost the entire Communist leadership, crippling the Partisans' political organization. For the rest of the war, groups of Communist Partisans remained active in the clandestine press, sabotage activities, and the execution of collaborators, particularly in Wallonia and especially the area around Charleroi. However, as a nationwide political organization, the Partisans never recovered from this blow, and they became less and less of a worry to the authorities in London as time went on.

This change of fortunes for the Partisans enabled the Independence Front (*Front d'Indépendance/Onafhankelijkheidsfront*) to emerge as a major actor in the Belgian Resistance. Originally, the Communist Party was behind the foundation of the Independence Front. However, the Communists had intended the Independence Front to be a more broad-based anti-fascist movement that would reach across Belgium's political divides. In fact, many of the leaders of the Independence Front were non–Communists, and one of its founders was André Bolland, a Catholic priest. However, because of the presence of Communists in its leadership, the authorities in London were initially skeptical of the organization and kept it at a distance. This changed with the collapse of the cohesiveness of the Partisans, and the subsequent dominance of the Independence Front by its non–Communist members. The government-in-exile finally officially recognized the Independence Front in November of 1943, and a representative of the front joined the Belgian government after the liberation.

The Independence Front was involved in a wide variety of activities. It published about 167 different titles in the clandestine press, including tracts in German that were designed to demoralize the occupiers. It established a Jewish Defense Committee to shelter Jews in hiding and that was credited with saving the lives of 2,000 children. In 1942, the Germans introduced labor conscription, which forced young Belgian men who had finished school to go to Germany for service in the factories while German men were fighting the war. If a Belgian refused to do so, he was known as a *réfractaire* and would be subject to forced deportation or criminal penalties. The Independence Front was very active in combating the labor conscription. It encouraged Belgian men to become *réfractaires* if conscripted, and it helped to shelter them when they did so. Finally, as the war progressed, the Independence Front moved into limited acts of sabotage and limited assassinations of collaborators through its "Patriotic Militias" (*Milices Patriotiques*).

The Independence Front was behind one of the greatest propaganda victories of the Belgian resistance, the fake *Le Soir*. Before the war, *Le Soir* was a regular Belgian newspaper and it had the largest circulation of all of the francophone newspapers. For that reason, the German authorities took it over during the occupation and continued to publish the newspaper as a mouthpiece for their propaganda. Under German supervision, *Le Soir* remained the largest francophone newspaper in the country, and it was the primary source of official information for French-speaking Belgians. However, it provided only pro–German information.

A group of writers and printers who belonged to the Independence Front decided to use *Le Soir* against the Germans. They put together one edition of the newspaper that looked exactly like the real *Le Soir,* except that its content was filled with satirical, anti–German content, including an announcement that the Axis Powers had decided to unconditionally surrender to the Allies. The content revealed the fake *Le Soir* to be an obvious farce, but on the surface it had the look and feel of the real thing. They delivered it to the newsstands at 5 a.m. on November 9, 1943, just before the normal delivery of the real *Le Soir.* Because it looked like the real thing, the newsstands sold it as *Le Soir,* without giving it any thought. Thousands of copies were sold before the Nazis caught on and immediately suspended sales. It was a spectacular work of subversion, but it came at a heavy cost. The embarrassment of the Nazis was so great, and the effect of that act on Belgian public opinion was so significant, that the Nazis made it a special point to hunt down everyone who had been involved in the operation. Seventeen of the twenty-two people behind the project were arrested and executed.

However, the largest and most "official" of the Belgian Resistance organizations would come to be known as the Secret Army (*Armée Secrète/ Geheim Leger*). In 1941, a group of Royalist military officers led by Charles Claser founded a resistance organization that they called the Belgian Legion (*Légion Belge/Belgisch Legioen*). Claser intended the Belgian Legion to be a real army, and he organized it as an army with ranks, records, written orders, geographic areas of responsibility, etc. Originally, Claser and the other founders envisioned the Belgian Legion engaging in combat against the Germans and providing the country's law and order after the liberation, at which point it would become the new Belgian army.[16]

Initially, the Belgian government-in-exile was suspicious of the Belgian Legion, since it exercised no control over the organization. The Belgian Legion's stated goal was to become the Belgian army, and the government-in-exile feared that the Belgian Legion might in time constitute a potential threat to its own authority. However, given the numbers of Belgian ex-military personnel in its ranks, the British Special Operations Executive (SOE) embraced the Belgian Legion for its military expertise and its potential to commit professional acts of sabotage. So, with the assistance of the SOE, Claser managed to escape to London in August of 1942 to negotiate a reconciliation between his organization and the government-in-exile. The meeting worked, and Claser succeeded in allaying the suspicions of the government-in-exile.

By the end of 1942, the government-in-exile had recognized the Belgian Legion as its armed force on the ground in Belgium. In turn, the Belgian Legion changed its name to the Army of Belgium (*l'Armée de Belgique/ Leger van België*). It agreed to recognize the authority of the government-in-exile and to take orders from the Belgian Prime Minister and Minister of Defense. The government-in-exile changed the name of the Belgian Army to the Secret Army a few months later to emphasize the fact that the Secret Army would disappear at the liberation when the new Belgian government would create a new Belgian Army. At the time of the liberation, the Secret Army claimed to have a membership of over 50,000, making it by far the largest of the Belgian Resistance organizations. However, it is also clear that a large percentage of these 50,000 joined only in the final weeks of the war.

By 1944, the Secret Army had divided Belgium into five zones designated by the Roman numerals I through V. Each zone was subdivided into several sections. Each section in turn was divided into "refuges" which were the operational units of the Secret Army where forces would be mobilized and missions planned. The refuges were designated by code names, usually referring to animals. Through these code names, the government-in-exile and the SOE could transmit secret messages and instructions directly to the members of the Secret Army via BBC Radio. They did this by using coded messages that appeared in the script of the regular broadcasts of the BBC's nightly *Radio Belgique* program. For example, a radio actor might say the line "*Mettez le tarin en cage*" (or "Put the siskin [bird] in the cage") as a part of his script in an ordinary broadcast. The members of the Secret Army in Belgium who tuned into the program each night would know that this was actually an instruction to mobilize the *Refuge Tarin* for a mission. Hearing that coded message, the members of that refuge would then assemble in a pre-designated location and wait for further instructions. When the order for the mission arrived, the commandant of the each refuge designated teams of men to carry out the missions. The missions would include espionage, receiving parachute drops, acts of sabotage, and eventually combat. The teams were not necessarily formal standing units of the organization within the Secret Army. Depending on the commandant, the teams could consist of either *ad hoc* groups of men assembled for specific missions, or *de facto* standing units.

Once the formal relationship between the government-in-exile and the Secret Army was established, the government-in-exile issued a number of directives, which constituted the Secret Army's orders from the political leadership. The most important of these was a directive issued on March 31, 1943, and then revised on May 27 that established the strategic goals of the Secret Army. Hubert Pierlot, the Belgian Prime Minister-in-Exile, signed the directive. It ordered the Secret Army to divide its operations into three phases. The first phase was for the period before the British and American forces invaded Northern Europe. In this phase, the Secret Army was to collect information, engage in acts of sabotage as directed by SOE, and to begin collecting arms and other material parachuted into Belgium. The second phase would begin when the Allied invasion was imminent. In this phase, all of the refuges would be mobilized. Acts of sabotage would intensify and aim to disrupt German communications and transportation links to the front. The SOE's parachute drops of arms and other material would increase, and the men would prepare for combat. The third phase would only begin as the Allied armies were approaching Belgium. In this phase, the Secret Army was to engage the Nazis directly in combat in order to hinder their retreat and to maximize the number of Germans who could be taken prisoner or killed.

The government-in-exile prescribed a uniform for the Secret Army. The most important element of this uniform was an armband with a lion's head in an inverted triangle, which was the symbol of the Secret Army. The armbands were manufactured in London and parachuted in to the refuges during the second phase of operations. The government-in-exile maintained that this insignia identified the members of the Secret Army as soldiers of the Kingdom of Belgium, and that those who wore it were entitled to the protection of the Geneva conventions governing prisoners of war. The Nazis thought differently.

Some 4,000 members of the Secret Army lost their lives in various actions against the Nazis. The Nazis never treated any of the members of the Secret Army as soldiers, and never accorded any of them the status of prisoner of war. When the Nazis captured a soldier of the Secret Army, they treated him as less than a common criminal. At best, a captured Secret Army soldier could expect a summary execution. More often, he would face a slow death by torture. All of the soldiers of the Secret Army knew that if they were ever in danger of being captured by the Nazis, it was better to fight to the death than to surrender.

• 6 •

King, Law and Liberty

Thirty years earlier, on the eve of the First World War, the ordinary citizen of the Kingdom of Belgium had a lot be proud of. Economically, Belgium was an advanced, wealthy, and industrialized country. It was the first country in continental Europe to undergo the Industrial Revolution. In terms of GDP per capita, it was the richest country in continental Europe in most of the years leading up to 1914, with only the United Kingdom ranking higher.[1] Belgium also owned the Congo, a colony in the heart of Africa that was ten times its size and rich in natural resources. Although Belgium's colonial experience is not remembered with pride today, in 1914 it was a completely different story. The Congo not only provided resources for the Belgian economy, but it also made Belgium one of the smallest members of an elite colonial club that included the greatest powers of the day.

Politically, Belgium was (and is) linguistically divided between Dutch speakers in Flanders in the north and French speakers in Wallonia in the south. It was (and is) politically divided along ideological and religious lines. Consequently, Belgian political parties represented nearly all points on the political spectrum, and the competition among these parties was vigorous. However, the Belgian constitution was a model of European liberal parliamentary democracy that ensured that these parties settled their disputes at the ballot box. Belgians were proud of their vibrant democracy with its constitutional monarch who stayed out of politics. King Albert I embodied the unity of the nation across its linguistic and political divides, and he was popular among the people.

Belgians were also proud of their country's neutrality. Austria, France, the Netherlands, Prussia, Russia and the United Kingdom had all recognized and guaranteed Belgium's neutrality in the Treaty of London of 1839. Neutrality served Belgium well throughout the nineteenth century, keeping it safe from the periodic conflicts that engulfed the great powers, such as the Franco-Prussian War of 1870–1871. Since it became independent, Belgium had never been invaded and its citizens had not experienced the sufferings of war. Therefore, the Belgian government made neutrality the cornerstone of its foreign policy.

Belgium's military planning and doctrine were built solely upon defending its neutrality. Its armed forces were spread around the country, not garrisoned on any one particular border. With its west anchored on the North Sea, it built defensive fortifications on all of its remaining borders, north (Antwerp), east (Liège), and south (Namur). The disposition of its forces and fortresses symbolically demonstrated that Belgium sided neither for nor against any other country. Belgium threatened no other nation, and it regarded no other nation as a threat. Despite the country's internal divisions, Belgium was peaceful, prosperous and free. It was much like Switzerland is today.

The First World War brought an abrupt and violent end to this happy existence. As the storms of war gathered in the summer of 1914, France and Germany had reasons to go to war with each other. Neither had a reason to go to war with Belgium. Belgium should have been an innocent bystander in their conflict, as it had been in 1870. Besides, both France and Germany (as Prussia's successor) were guarantors of Belgium's neutrality. However, the cold military logic of Germany's war strategy dragged Belgium into a war that it neither wanted nor deserved.[2]

At the beginning of August 1914, Germany faced the prospect of a two front war, fighting France in the west and Russia in the east at one and the same time. To achieve victory in such a war, Germany's military strategy was to defeat France in the west first, and then to turn its full military weight against Russia in the east. However, significant barriers stood in the way of the German army's path to Paris. The Franco-German border was only about 150 miles (240 kilometers) long. The south of this border ran along the Vosges Mountains, a natural obstacle protecting France from Germany. In the area to the north, the French had built a system of fortresses, such as the one at Verdun, that tens of thousands of French troops could quickly garrison once mobilized. Plowing through those natural and manmade barriers would take time that the Germans would not have. In the event of a two front war, Germany would need to defeat France quickly and decisively. Field Marshal Count Alfred von Schlieffen, Chief of the Imperial German General Staff from 1890 to 1905, developed the plan for how to do so.

Von Schlieffen argued that the German Army should bypass the Vosges Mountains and the French forces amassed on the border by invading Belgium in the north first. Germany would rapidly overcome neutral Belgium's much smaller and weaker army, and then turn south to invade France across the Franco-Belgian border, which was undefended by the French. If the timing went as planned, the German Army would be able to capture Paris before the French Army could reorient itself from its positions in the east and move to the north and west to oppose them. The war against France would be over in six weeks. Militarily, it was a brilliant plan. Morally, it was reprehensible since it meant that Germany would attack Belgium, a neutral country with whom Germany had no quarrel and whose neutrality Germany itself had guaranteed.

Partially for this reason, but mostly for reasons of military expediency, Germany at first attempted to realize the von Schlieffen plan through diplomacy when war was declared between Germany and France. On August 2, 1914, Germany's ambassador to Belgium delivered a communication to the Belgian government demanding that Belgium allow Germany's armed forces to pass through the country unmolested on their way to France. In exchange, Germany promised not to harm the lives and property of Belgian citizens and to respect the independence of the Belgian government. Accepting this demand might have spared Belgium from the ravages of the war. However, it would have also represented a renunciation of Belgium's neutrality and a *de facto* military alliance with Germany in its war against France. Therefore, the Belgian government formally rejected the German demand the next day, stating that Belgium was prepared to defend its neutrality. It is reputed that King Albert sent a communication to Kaiser Wilhelm in which he said, "I rule a nation, not a road."[3]

With its diplomatic initiative rebuffed, Germany invaded Belgium on Tuesday, August 4, as the cold military logic of the von Schlieffen plan required. However, this decision had an unintended consequence for Germany. Under the Treaty of London, the United Kingdom was pledged to guarantee Belgium's neutrality. The United Kingdom reminded Germany of that fact on August 3 when it learned that Germany had demanded to pass through Belgium. The British government announced that it was prepared to go to war to defend Belgium's neutrality. This threat did not deter the German government from going forward with the invasion. Subsequently, the United Kingdom declared war on Germany at 11:00 p.m. on August 4. The German chancellor, Theobald von Bethmann Hollweg, was surprised that the United Kingdom had actually declared war because of the Treaty of London, which he dismissed as a "mere scrap of paper."[4] However, the Treaty of London certainly was not a scrap of paper for the British government. It was a commitment under international law and a point of honor. For the British people "Remember Belgium" became the rallying cry of the war.

For the von Schlieffen plan to work, the German army would have to move fast through Belgium, and standing squarely in front of the German line of attack was the Belgian city of Liège. The von Schlieffen plan called for the German army to pass through Liège within two days, and initially the odds looked good for the Germans. Only 40,000 Belgian soldiers surrounded Liège and they faced over 120,000 attacking Germans. However, those 40,000 Belgian soldiers were dug into positions surrounding the city that included twelve fortresses of recent construction and that embodied the state of the art in the defensive military technology of the day. Although they were outnumbered three to one, the Belgians defending those fortresses were not going to give up without a fight. The initial German assault on Liège began on August 5 and was repulsed. Repeated German assaults over the next few days were likewise repulsed, at a heavy price in German blood. One contemporary report states that the Germans suffered 5,000 dead in the first three days of the battle of Liège.[5] The Germans in turn tried out a new military strategy to dishearten the Belgians. That is, Liège earned the dubious distinction of becoming the first city in history to suffer an aerial bombardment when a German zeppelin dropped bombs on the city, killing nine civilians.[6]

By August 10, all but one of the twelve fortresses surrounding Liège were still in Belgian hands. So stubborn was the Belgian defense of Liège that Kaiser Wilhelm wrote a strongly worded note to King Albert threatening to take the fortresses by brutal force if they did not surrender and threatening the defenders with consequences. King Albert replied with a one-word response, "Try!"[7] The bravery of King Albert inspired the Belgian Army to resist the Germans even more. It was not until the Germans brought in heavy naval siege artillery, and particularly the famous "Big Bertha" howitzer, that the fortresses were demolished into submission one by one. The last of the fortresses did not fall until August 16, eleven days after the siege had begun, and nine days after the German war plan had required it to.

Although the Battle of Liège was a tactical military defeat for the Belgians, it was a moral and perhaps even a strategic victory of sorts. The Belgians had bought valuable time for the French to reposition their forces to oppose the German advance that was now coming from an unexpected direction. They also bought additional time for the British to deploy expeditionary forces to France. Even more importantly, tiny Belgium demonstrated that it could resist the military weight of the mighty Germans, killing thousands of the invading forces in the process. In a nutshell, Liège was a victory because Belgium resisted, and through its resistance, Belgium validated the morality of its cause. "Remember Belgium" now meant something concrete. As the historian Barbara Tuchman wrote, "What Belgium gave the Allies was neither two days nor two weeks but a cause and an example."[8]

One of those Belgians who so stubbornly defended Liège was Corporal Arthur Henri Abeels. Arthur was born in Brussels on October 31, 1893. He was the son of Isidore Abeels and Constance Krijkamp, and they lived at *rue de Chemiste* (Scheikundigestraat) 1 in Anderlecht. Isidore was a furniture maker, and Constance was from the Netherlands (or at least her parents were). The couple ensured that Arthur grew up bilingual, speaking both French and Dutch at home. Like most Belgian young men of his generation, Arthur was conscripted into the Belgian army for fifteen months of duty. His service began on September 13, 1913, and he was assigned to the 4th Company of the 1st Battalion of the 11th Line Infantry Regiment (*11ème Régiment de Ligne*). He was promoted to corporal on December 11, 1913, and on July 30, 1914, he was recommended for promotion to the rank of sergeant. However, the looming German invasion of Belgium put that promotion on hold.[9]

On August 1, Arthur's regiment was rushed by train from its base in Hasselt to Herstal as a precautionary measure against the rising military tensions. General Gérard Leman, who commanded the forces in and around Liège, assigned the regiment to the 11th Mixed Brigade of the 3rd Army Division. On the 2nd and 3rd of August, Arthur's company was put to work building up some defensive works near Milmort. When the Germans invaded Belgium on the 4th, Arthur's company took up an interval position at Micheroux, between Fort Fléron and Fort Evegnée. This was on the east side of Liège, square in the path of the German thrust into Belgium. Initially, the company was positioned at the edge of the woods on the east side of the village of Micheroux in order to protect forward artillery observers. However, that evening the company was ordered to withdraw to a better defensive position 200 yards west of the chapel in the village.

Shortly after midnight, the German 34th Brigade attempted to break through the Belgian lines through the positions of the 11th Line Infantry Regiment. It was a confusing fight in the middle of the night. Col. Charles Dusart, the commanding officer of Arthur's regiment, was killed in action at the head of his troops, becoming the first high-ranking Belgian officer to die in the war. Arthur's company came under attack at about 4 a.m., and it held its ground in a fight that lasted about 50 minutes. The 11th Line Infantry Regiment had temporarily stopped the German advance, dealing the German Army one of its first military blows in Belgium.

At 10 a.m., Arthur's company received the order to withdraw to Queue-du-Bois to protect the artillery, a distance of under 2.4 miles (4 kilometers). They dug in and waited for the next attack, which came at 1:00 a.m. the next morning. It was a fierce battle that lasted three hours. The company again held its ground and stopped the Germans who were attacking them. However, this valiant stand came at a heavy price as Arthur's company suffered 25 casualties (dead, wounded or missing) in that action. One of those casualties was Arthur himself, who was hit by a rifle bullet in his left calf.

Medics took Arthur to the civilian Hospital *de Bavière* in Liège, where he underwent surgery. As he lay in his bed recovering from surgery, Arthur could hear the sounds of Big Bertha pulverizing the fortresses surrounding the city. In his heart, he knew that his comrades-in-arms could not hold out for long. When the Germans entered Liège, they searched the hospitals looking for Belgian soldiers. They found Arthur and made him a prisoner of war. Before his leg had fully recovered from his surgery, the Germans removed him from the hospital. They packed him into a cattle car with other wounded prisoners and sent him to a POW camp in Parchim, Germany. Because of that premature move, Arthur's leg never did properly heal, and his health never fully recovered.

Over the next few years, Arthur was transferred to POW camps at Mannheim and Gustrow, and his leg needed additional surgery twice. Eventually, he contracted acute anemia and his health debilitated. In July 1918, he was transferred to the *Hôtel de la Couronne* in Unterseen, Switzerland. Although Switzerland was neutral, the Red Cross had brokered an agreement between the German and Allied forces under which seriously ill POWs like Arthur could be sent there for recovery, provided that the Allies paid for it, of course. The war ended on November 11, 1918, and in December Arthur was repatriated to Belgium. For the rest of his life, Arthur suffered leg pains and walked with a limp. It was a daily reminder of what the Germans had done to him and his country.[10]

In one sense, Arthur was fortunate. He spoke French, Dutch, English, and German, skills that were rare in 1914. So, when his health permitted, the Germans used him as an interpreter in the camps where he was interred, and he was spared the labor duty that most prisoners of war endured. As an interpreter, he was able to see and experience things that most POWs did not. He assisted in the questioning of newly arrived prisoners who brought with them stories of the horrors that the Germans had unleashed on the battlefield. He learned about the killing fields of the trenches, and the terrible death toll that machine guns and artillery were now bringing to the conflict. He learned about a horrible new and inhumane weapon that the Germans introduced on the battlefield to overcome trench warfare, the flamethrower. He was shocked to learn of the Germans' intro-duction of the most evil of all weapons on the battlefield, poison gas. Both poison gas and the flamethrower made their debut in Belgium.

Newly arrived POWs also told Arthur about the suffering of the Bel-gian civilian population. The Germans had destroyed the city of Leuven and its great university library, despite the fact that it was occupied only by civilians and played no role in the war. He learned that Germany was stripping his country of its wealth and resources. He knew that his fellow countrymen were literally starving, as the Germans shipped food from Bel-gium to Germany. Arthur expected starvation and privation in a POW camp. He was appalled that the innocent civilians of his country were now, in effect, living in one giant POW camp.

Arthur's position as an interpreter put him in regular contact with the Germans who ran the camp. He saw how they treated the Belgian prisoners, and the differences in how they treated different nationalities. The German attitude was that "might makes right," and they looked upon people from other cultures with disdain. Their arrogance sickened him inside. As a POW, Arthur developed a hatred for the Germans and for what they had done to his country. Arthur was already patriotic when the war broke out. When he was released at the end of the war, his patriotism ran even deeper.

The final stirring refrain of the Belgian bilingual national anthem is "*Le roi, la loi, la liberté/de voorst, de vrijheid, en de wet.*" In English, each translates as "King, law, and liberty." For Arthur, these were not simply words. They were values that defined his outlook on life, particularly after the war. He had witnessed a large, powerful, and aggressive neighbor with whom Belgium had no quarrel trample on international law and rob his own country of its peace, prosperity, and freedom. He learned about the atrocities that the Germans committed both on and off the battlefield. He witnessed first-hand the economic consequences of the occupation as he returned home to a country that was starving and economically devastated. He discovered that Germany had tried to divide Belgians against each other politically, and absorb his country into the service of its empire. Arthur believed that the roots of all of this lay in a fundamental contempt for the rule of law, a disregard for the freedom of ordinary citizens, and a contempt for other nationalities that characterized the autocratic regime of Kaiser Wilhelm.

While his experiences during the war created Arthur's hatred for the

Germans, they deepened his pride in his king. King Albert was the Commander in Chief of the Belgian Armed Forces. He had inspired Arthur and his comrades in their heroic defense of Liège, and in the Belgian army's orderly, fighting withdrawal across the country to the Belgian coast. Throughout the war, King Albert remained at the head of his troops and doggedly defended one small corner of Belgium wedged against the coast that the Germans never conquered. King Albert never surrendered, and when he returned triumphantly to Brussels at the end of the war, he was greeted as a hero. Albert had defended the rule of law and the liberty of the Belgian people against an autocratic empire that had tried to crush both. To Arthur, King Albert was a saint.

When Arthur returned to civilian life, he was employed as a salesman for the clothing store Clébau. He spent his entire career with Clébau, gradually working his way up in the company to become an accountant who could support a family in comfort. Arthur was acutely interested in world affairs, and his linguistic abilities allowed him to follow the news through foreign newspapers and radio broadcasts as well as the Belgian media. He took up stamp collecting as a hobby, undoubtedly because of his interest in the world at large. He became active in the local veterans' association and other patriotic activities.

In 1923, Arthur married Clémentine Alice Maria Noël, and they moved into their home in Ganshoren. Clémy was nine years younger than Arthur, and she was a devoted wife. She was proud of Arthur and his service in the military and regarded him as a war hero. Like Arthur, Clémy was proud of her country and her king. The couple was deeply patriotic in ways that, frankly, most Belgians are not today. Like the overwhelming majority of Belgians at the time, they were Catholic.

During the German occupation of the First World War, Clémy was a young teenager. She was too young to play an active role in resisting the occupation, but she did have one moment of taking a personal stand against the Germans. Her family lived in a row house in Ixelles, one of the nineteen communities of Brussels. The entrance to the house in the front facing the street had a small stairway leading up into the house, but there was also a stairway at the rear of the house leading down to a basement. The stairway in the rear was not visible or evident from the front of the house. At one point during the war, the Germans enacted a decree requiring Belgians to turn over everything they owned that was made of copper. The items were to be melted down for war material. Obviously, compliance with this decree was less than what the Germans had hoped for, so they began searching the homes of Belgian civilians looking for copper items that could be melted down.

One day, the Germans arrived at the Noël family home looking for copper. The Noëls owned a large copper clock that was a family heirloom, and Clémy was not about to let the Germans have it. As the Germans came up the stairs in the front of the house to begin their search, Clémy grabbed the clock and went out the back door. She ran down the stairs in the back of the house and found a hiding place in the basement. The Germans searched the house, but they never realized that there were stairs leading to a basement in the back. Clémy was not found, and the Germans left the house empty-handed. Until the end of her life, Clémy's daughter owned that clock.

Arthur and Clémy's first child was a boy named Roger Marie Théodore Abeels, who was born on August 15, 1924. Roger was highly intelligent and an excellent student. Following primary school in Ganshoren, he attended the *Atheneum Léon Lépage* in Brussels, and then transferred to the *Royal Atheneum* in Koekelberg. This edu-
cational track would have normally led to a university education, had the war not intervened. He was active in the Catholic Youth Association. He was an avid and accomplished fencer, and was a prominent member of the fencing club *La Rapière*. He practiced gymnastics, and he liked to bicycle. Everyone who knew Roger described him as a serious young man who embraced knowledge, physical fitness, and personal responsibility. He was not particularly interested in popularity at school if popularity meant betraying his principles. Roger's dream was to attend the Royal Military Academy and to become an air force pilot. Roger was clearly inspired by his father, and he was the apple of his father's eye.

Arthur and Clémy's second child was a daughter named Janine Con-

Roger's portrait on August 15, 1942 (courtesy Jenny Abeels).

stance Abeels, who was born on May 8, 1930. Janine attended the local primary school in Ganshoren, and then the Emile André Secondary School. Janine wanted to study nursing because she wanted to do something with her life that would help people. Unlike her brother, Janine was just an average student, and she had particular difficulties in mathematics. However, Roger always helped her with her math homework, and it became one of the special times of day that they spent together. Janine's favorite toy was a stuffed teddy bear that she simply named "Teddy." Her best friend was Marie Louise Poncer, who went by the nickname "Pompon." Janine and Pompon met in primary school and went to the same secondary school. Pompon's parents owned a candy store, and they had a large backyard where the children could play. For both reasons, Janine loved visiting Pompon's home. Unlike her brother, Janine was not all that interested in joining organized clubs. However, she did belong to the Guides, which in Belgium was analogous to the Girl Scouts.

Clémy brought life to the Abeels family. Clémy was young in spirit, optimistic, and fun. She taught her children games and sports, like how to play Ping-Pong and how to roller skate. When the kids sat down to play a board game, Clémy would always jump in and join them. She had a wonderful sense of humor and would joke around with her children. In fact, she was so young in spirit and playful with the kids that sometimes people would mistake her for Arthur's eldest daughter rather than his wife. She was sociable with the neighbors, with whom she played Whist on Saturdays. (Whist is a card came that is similar to Bridge and was popular in Belgium before the war.)

Arthur, on the other hand, was more serious, and he viewed his role in the family through the lens of responsibility. He thought that his job was to be a good provider for the family at all times, and the family disciplinarian when necessary. He believed that it was his duty to raise his children as patriots. Arthur talked often about the war and made sure that Roger and Janine knew what Germany had done to their country. In fact, he forbade Roger and Janine from calling the Germans "Germans." Instead they were to use the words *Les Boches* to describe them, a derogatory term for Germans that francophones use. It was an unspoken rule that the children were never to say anything good about Germany in general. Arthur brought up his children to revere King Albert as the defender of the rule of law and the freedom of the Belgians. When King Albert died in 1934, Arthur insisted that his children show the same devotion to their new king, Leopold III, that they had shown to King Albert. The children took this to heart. The children's patriotic upbringing was reinforced by the fact that Arthur had become the president of the Ganshoren Veterans Association (*Association des Anciens Combattants de Ganshoren*) by the eve of the Second World War. The children attended all of the various patriotic ceremonies in which Arthur represented the veterans.

On September 1, 1939, Nazi Germany invaded Poland. Two days later the United Kingdom and France declared war on Germany. As was the case twenty-five years before, the Belgian government clung to its neutrality in the hope that this would spare the country from the conflict among the great powers of Europe. As was the case twenty-five years before, in order to preserve the appearance of its neutrality, the Belgian government refused to coordinate its military strategy with the French or the British. As was the case twenty-five years before, Germany faced the prospect of a two-front war. As was the case twenty-five years before, the cold logic of German military strategy dictated that Germany would invade France by passing through Belgium, as the von Schlieffen plan dictated. On May 10, 1940, the Nazis unleashed their blitzkrieg on neutral Belgium. This time they did not even bother to pretend to ask for permission to pass through the country.[11]

In 1914, the Germans had expected little opposition from the Belgians, but found the opposite. This time, the Germans not only anticipated opposition, they also came prepared to emasculate it. The Belgians fought hard to defend their country against the invaders, and the commander of the German 18th Division remarked on the "extraordinary courage" of the Belgians.[12] In a letter that he wrote to Benito Mussolini, Hitler himself mentioned the bravery of the Belgian soldiers and described their tenacity as amazing.[13] However, the extraordinary courage and tenacity of the Belgians was no match for the extraordinary tactics and weapons that the Germans employed in the blitzkrieg. By May 17, the Belgian government had fled to France and the Germans had captured Brussels. By May 20, the Germans had reached the English Channel, cutting off the Belgian Army and the British Expeditionary force from France. The two armies were pushed back to the coast. By May 24, the British had withdrawn towards Ieper, the scene of so much bloody fighting in the First World War, while the Belgians made a two-day stand at the Lys River. By May 27, the British had withdrawn towards Dunkirk in France. The Belgian Army was to their north, holding a line that stretched from Menen to Bruges. The Luftwaffe mercilessly pounded the Belgian roads and railways leading from the coast to the Army, destroying the ability of the Belgian army to resupply itself.

The Belgian government urged King Leopold to attack south and attempt to break through the German lines. The government's hope was that Leopold would be able to reconnect with the British and then French armies to the south and carry on the battle from France. However, King Leopold and his senior military advisors believed that the situation was hopeless. The army was running out of ammunition, supplies, and men. There were no natural barriers like rivers or canals lying between the Belgians and the Germans to cover a move to the south. The Luftwaffe had absolute air supremacy and the Belgian Army was hopelessly exposed to that airpower if it tried to move from its positions. In seventeen days of combat, over 6,000 Belgian soldiers had died, and over 30,000 more were wounded or captured. Leopold requested an armistice on the night of May 27. Over the objections of his government, Leopold unconditionally surrendered the Belgian army to the Germans at 4:00 a.m. on Tuesday, May 28.

The British offered Leopold himself the opportunity to escape on one of their naval ships that was docked at Middelkerke. Belgian Prime Minister Henri Pierlot pleaded with him to do so in order to underscore the legitimacy of the now government-in-exile of the country. Leopold refused. Believing that the war was lost for the Allies and stating that he did not want to desert his army, Leopold chose to remain in Belgium. He would spend the next four years under house arrest in his palace at Laeken.

The German invasion of Belgium did not surprise Arthur and Clémy. They knew what the Germans were all about from their experiences in the First World War. They certainly were under no illusions about the intentions of Adolf Hitler. When the invasion finally did come, Arthur dreamed that brave little Belgium would stand up to the German empire once again. He truly wanted to fight with the Belgian Army again, and he tried to volunteer. However, Arthur was now forty-six years old, plus he had a bad leg and two children. The Belgian army politely declined his offer to enlist. In those three weeks of May 1940, Arthur followed the progress of the war closely, and what he saw, heard, and read bewildered him. He was surprised that his king had ignored the advice of his government and did not at least try to link up with the British and the French armies in the south. If that was not possible, he did not understand why Leopold did not leave Belgium and join the government-in-exile, as Queen Wilhelmina of the Netherlands and Grand Duchess Charlotte of Luxembourg had done. Unlike those neighbors, Belgium would now have to suffer the indignity of seeing their king as a prisoner of the Nazis.

On the other hand, Arthur also realized that German invasion of 1940 was overpowering in a way that it was not in 1914. The blitzkrieg was so rapid and so effective, and so many more Belgians had been killed, captured and wounded in those eighteen days of conflict than in the opening stage of the First World War. King Leopold said that the Belgian Army could not continue to fight, and the king knew more about the military situation than Arthur did. Who was Arthur to question the decision of the king? Arthur was a patriot first, and he remained loyal to his king. However, he resolved to work for the freedom of his country under Nazi occupation, and he distilled this determination in his children.

In 1941, Arthur joined the Independence Front. Politically, Arthur was a liberal, on the center right of the Belgian political spectrum, and he was therefore uncomfortable with the communist links of the Independence Front. However, the Independence Front was one of the few Belgian Resistance organizations at that early stage in the war that had attempted to bridge the political and linguistic divisions of the country. That is why Arthur chose to join it. His linguistic skills were his primary contribution to the Independence Front.

Arthur listened to the BBC radio broadcasts each night and translated them into French. These translations were then published in the clandestine press as a counterbalance to the news available through the official newspapers that were controlled by German propaganda. Arthur also wrote pamphlets and other tracts in French to keep up the patriotic morale of the population. He especially liked to write pieces that encouraged young Belgian men to refuse the mandatory labor conscription for Germany and that explained how the Independence Front could help them do so. He also used his German language skills for the Independence Front, writing flyers in German to try to make ordinary German soldiers sympathetic to the plight of the Belgian people and to demoralize their commitment to the German war effort. Those were the activities that he told his children about. However, there was probably another side to Arthur's activities in the Independence Front as well.

Arthur hated Germany for what it had done to his country twice in his lifetime. However, he held no personal animosity against the individual German soldier in the Wehrmacht, the regular German Army. He recognized that the overwhelming majority of the ordinary German soldiers were not Nazis. They were conscripts, as he had been in 1914, and those German soldiers were simply doing their duty to their country. He did loathe those Germans who were the true believers in the Nazis' evil ideology, and who served in the forces of the Waffen SS (armed wing of the Nazi party) and the Gestapo. However, they, too, at least were Germans, so he could kind of understand that they were serving their country, albeit in an evil way. What Arthur could not tolerate were the Belgians who actively collaborated with the occupiers. On the French side of the country, the collaborationists belonged to the *Rexist* movement. On the Flemish side, they belonged to the *Vlaams Nationaal Verbond* (VNV). How Belgians like the *Rexists* and VNV could betray their own people was incomprehensible to Arthur.

In the case of the true collaborators, it was also unforgiveable. Arthur owned a gun, and sometimes at night his children would see him leave the house with it. He never, ever, talked about what he did on those evenings, even after the war. However, a day or two after one of the evenings when he had left the house with his gun, conversation at the dinner table would turn to news that Arthur had heard about the Resistance recently executing or attacking a collaborator. The stories were told with a sense that justice had been served.

However, not all collaborators were necessarily evil, even in Arthur's eyes. The Abeels lived in a three-story home, with an additional bedroom in the landing of the stairs between the ground floor and the floor in the middle. The Abeels family occupied the ground floor and the bedroom in between. A couple named Cellens lived on the floor above them. The Cellens were from St. Truiden in Belgium, and had rented the space in the home before the war. After the occupation began, Arthur learned that they were members of the VNV, and collaborators. Mr. Cellens worked for the government of occupied Belgium, and his wife was a teacher. However, the Cellens were not true believers in the Nazi cause. They were opportunists.

One day Arthur and Mr. Cellens got to talking about the war in the stairway of the house. Cellens expressed a dislike for all of the violence that the war had brought, and for some of the things he was witnessing under the occupation. Cellens admitted to Arthur that he was working for the Germans, and therefore helping them. However, he said that he was doing so only for his own self-interest rather than for the ideology. As Cellens said to Arthur, "My religion is my wallet." So, the Abeels and the Cellens families had an implicit agreement to leave each other alone. Ironically, on the top floor of the house lived Madame Delvigne, who belonged to the White Brigade. Unknown to them, the Cellens collaborators were living sandwiched in between two families who were active in the Resistance.

For Roger Abeels, the occupation of Belgium meant a change in his career plans. Although he still wanted to be a military officer and a pilot, that plan was now impossible in Belgium. He developed a new plan to achieve this goal. That is, he would escape to England and become a pilot for the Royal Air Force, as some other young Belgian men whom he had heard about had done. However, Roger was still in secondary school, and he knew that he had to complete his schooling before he could become a pilot. So, Roger dedicated his remaining time at the *atheneum* to preparing for a career as a British air force pilot. He studied hard, particularly in mathematics, which is an essential subject for an aviator. Perhaps most importantly for someone who wanted to join the Royal Air Force, he worked hard on improving his English at home under the tutelage of his father.

Roger also joined the Belgian Resistance. In 1941, Roger was only sixteen years old, too young to engage in acts of violence. However, like his father, he did join the Independence Front, and did non-violent tasks like delivering copies of *La Libre Belgique,* the largest of the clandestine newspapers. As Roger became older, his fencing teacher, Olivier De Keyser, recruited him for a different Resistance organization. De Keyser had served in the Belgian military in the First World War. In 1941, he joined the Belgian Legion, which would later become the Secret Army. He had a son who was about Roger's age, and he promised Roger that the three of them would escape together to England when the two boys were old enough. In the meantime, De Keyser told Roger that he could fight the Germans by helping what would become the Secret Army. Roger only too gladly volunteered. Around the time that Roger turned eighteen, De Keyser and his son did escape to England, but they left Roger behind. It was a bitter disappointment for Roger, but he did not let it discourage him from his dream. By then, he was a full-fledged member of the Secret Army, and he began engaging in acts of sabotage. He remained determined to find a way to get to England.

However, Roger's greatest challenge when he turned eighteen was the same as for all young men of occupied Belgium: avoiding labor service in Germany. In 1942, the German authorities enacted a decree that required all Belgian young men who turned eighteen and who were no longer enrolled in school to report for labor service in Germany. Initially, this was not a problem since Roger was still in school when he turned eighteen. However, it became a problem when he graduated. Through the Independence Front, Roger secured a document from a local automobile garage that said that he was working there, although he really was not. The garage was considered vital for the German war effort, and its employees were therefore exempt from the labor draft. This worked for Roger until the garage came under investigation and he could no longer use the paper. Between March and June of 1944, the Belgian authorities who were responsible for enforcing the labor draft turned up twice at the Abeels home to find Roger and to order him to report for labor service. Both times, Arthur and Clémy claimed that they did not know where he was when, in fact, he was hiding in the house. Both times, the authorities left behind the notice requiring him to report for duty. If this were to happen a third time and Roger did not respond to the summons, he would be classified as a *réfractaire* and would be subject to criminal penalties, or worse, to the hands of the Gestapo. By June, this fact was very much on the minds of the Abeels family.

Roger's sister Janine had only just turned ten when the blitzkrieg overpowered Belgium. At first, she did not really understand what was going on around her, but the reality of the war and occupation sunk in with time. The first thing she noticed was that the family home got crowded. Clémy's sister Cécile was a nurse who had married an Englishman named Daniel Cracklow. Cécile had moved to England where Daniel worked in a museum. Purely by chance, Cécile and Daniel were visiting Belgium when the blitzkrieg came. Daniel left immediately for England, and Cécile was supposed to follow right away. However, she did not leave in time, and found herself stranded in occupied Belgium. Cécile moved in with the Abeels for a few months. She later went to work at a hospital and got her own apartment.

The next thing Janine noticed was that many of the things that her family used to buy and consume were no longer available. That situation only grew worse as the war progressed, and it began to affect the traditional holidays like Christmas. Her parents and older brother made sure that Janine knew that it was because of the Germans. When Janine turned eleven, she celebrated her first communion, which is an important rite of passage for Belgian children, even to this day. Roger gave her a necklace with a crucifix on it made of plaster, and apologized for not being able to do better because of the war. However, he promised that when the war was over he would replace it with one made of gold.

As they grew older, the broader political context of oppression by the Nazis became more obvious to the young Janine and her friends. Janine and Pompon went to school with three Jewish girls whose father owned a shoe store in Jette, another one of the nineteen communities of Brussels. Janine, Pompon and the Jewish girls were friends at school and they played together at recess. In June of 1941, her friends were suddenly required to start wearing the yellow Star of David. Janine and Pompon could not understand what that was supposed to mean. Then, one day the Jewish girls simply stopped coming to school. After a few days, Janine and Pompon went to the shoe store of the girls' father to find out what happened to them. They found that the store was closed and empty. Janine and Pompon did not know what had happened to her Jewish friends. However, Janine had a feeling that, whatever it was, it was very, very bad. As she grew a bit older, Janine finally understood what had happened to her friends. The realization filled her with a deep revulsion toward the Nazis. She could not understand how someone could do something so mean to her innocent friends.

Resistance was part of the Abeels family tradition, and Resistance took many forms in occupied Belgium. One day, the family went to see the opera *The Merry Widow* at the *Théâtre Royal de la Monnaie* in downtown Brussels. The opera was performed in French, and there was one point in the libretto where the prince was to sing, *Je ne te dirais jamais que j t'aime*. Rather than sing the scripted verse, the singer playing the prince sang "*Je ne te dirais jamais que* I love you." The crowd burst into a standing ovation. It was only three words, and not overtly seditious. But the words were spoken in English, and that fact was not lost on the audience.

The anniversary of the armistice that ended the First World War, November 11, was one of the most important national holidays in Belgium in the interwar period. Each year a ceremony was held on that day at the Congress Column in Brussels, a ceremony that the Abeels family attended. The Congress Column was a monument to Belgium's independence, and five unknown Belgian soldiers from the First World War were buried at the foot of the column on November 11, 1922. There was (and is) a tram that runs down the street in front of the Congress Column, and a tram stop just in front of it. Not realizing its significance, the Germans ignored the monument in 1940, and this proved to be a mistake for them. Although no formal ceremony was scheduled, of course, Belgians flocked to the monument on November 11 in an impromptu outpouring of Belgian nationalism under the occupation. The Abeels were among the people who visited the Congress Column that day. The next year, the Germans had realized their mistake, and they were determined that this would not happen again. They sealed off the area around the Congress Column and banned the tram from stopping in front of it. Arthur decided to take the family there that day anyway. As the tram passed the Congress Column without stopping, the Belgian driver of the tram slowed the vehicle. Everyone on the tram stood to attention, faced the monument, and bowed. Such small acts of defiance may seem trivial today, but they were very important for the spirit of the Belgians living under the occupation.

At the same time, the Abeels tried to do their best to maintain as normal a childhood as they could for their children in the midst of the occupation. One day in 1941, Arthur brought home a live rabbit. It was a "Flemish Giant," a breed that is native to Belgium. Arthur's intention was for this rabbit to become dinner. However, Jenny and Roger fell in love with it immediately, and it ended up becoming a family pet. In a display of ironic humor, they named it Benito Mussolini or Bénis for short. Bénis became a true part of the family. Normally, he lived outside in a small brick house with windows where the family also kept some chickens for eggs. Bénis was the king of the chicken coup. At night, he would wait for all of the chickens to go up the little plank into the henhouse before he would follow them. In the morning, Roger would go to the chicken coop and open the door and say, "*Allez* Bénis, we go to gymnastics." The rabbit would come out of the coop and come into the house. He would follow Roger upstairs to the attic, where Roger had set up a small area to work out. Bénis would watch Roger doing his gymnastics, and then follow him back downstairs again so they could enjoy their breakfast together.

Roger's fencing club met on Wednesdays and Fridays at the *Café Léon* at *Place Simonis*. Because of their coach, several members of the club were active in the Resistance, and all were patriotic.[14] The fencing club was a venue to at least symbolically project the fighting spirit of the young men who belonged to it. On May 24, one of the members of the club who was named Willy approached Roger to ask if his family would be willing to hide an Allied airman. Roger was willing, but he needed permission from his parents. He went home and asked his parents about the idea. Arthur and Clémy enthusiastically said yes. So, on May 29, Odette arrived to interview the family.

The Abeels home was less than ideal. Not only were there collaborators living in the same house, but the Abeels also had a young girl who might talk at school. However, Arthur's patriotism and his devotion to duty were well known in Ganshoren, as was his reputation as a man who could be trusted to do what was right. Besides, Janine was now fourteen years old and could probably be trusted. The fact that there were collaborators in the house might also prove to be an advantage since the Nazis would assume that nothing untold would occur there. Provided that Arthur and the family were careful, and Odette had every reason to believe that they would be, everything would probably be all right. Besides, the Comet Line was running out of choices for housing airmen. Odette left saying that she would be back the next Thursday.

On Thursday, June 1, Odette arrived at the Abeels home with an American airman named Bernard Lourance McManaman. "Mac," as he preferred to be called, was born on March 21, 1924, in Lapeer, Michigan, the third of five children. Mac's parents were Catholic, but their marriage was loveless and his father was abusive. For a Catholic living in the 1930s, Mac's mother took the unheard of step of divorcing her husband for the sake of her children. She moved to Flint, Michigan, and supported her family of five as a single mother working as a beautician. Despite the hardship, it was the right move for the family. They struggled to survive, but Mac's mother gave the children a happy home and a loving environment. She had a wonderful sense of humor, which rubbed off on the children. She was also a talented artist on the side. Her children adored her. Mac graduated from Northern High School in Flint. In 1942, he enlisted in the U.S. Army Air Forces.[15]

Mac was assigned to the 712th Bomber Squadron of the 448th Bomber Group based at Seething, England. The 712th Squadron flew B-24 "Liberator" bombers, and Mac was part of Second Lieutenant Everett P. Musselman's crew. He served as the crew's flight engineer and held the rank of technical sergeant. He was also responsible for manning the top turret gun. On March 9, 1944, the Musselman crew was flying an older B-24 named *Baby Shoes*. Their target that day was Nienberg in Germany. *Baby Shoes* successfully bombed its target, but it was brought down on its return trip by anti-aircraft fire near Arendonk in Belgium. Mac parachuted to safety. The Comet Line picked him up and sheltered in a number of homes, including that of the Countess Limbourg-Stirum.[16]

When Odette arrived with Mac in the afternoon, Pompon was visiting Janine. Clémy told the girls that it was time for Pompon to go home, and she promptly left without realizing what was going on. Clémy then brought Janine into the dining room where she saw Mac for the first time. Janine greeted him with a kiss on the cheek, which was (and is) normal in Belgian homes. Mac was young, and Janine was struck by his soft hair and blue eyes. He was the first liberator that Janine had seen, and she was impressed.[17]

However, the civilities of the introductions did not last long because Odette had a problem. Earlier that day, the Gestapo had arrested Victor Schreyen, his pregnant wife, his sister Suzette, and a half dozen other members of the Brusselmans Section of the Comet Line. Schreyen was one of the leaders of the Brusselmans Section. He knew too much and his arrest put the section in significant danger.

Odette and her family lived at *Place Surlet de Chokier 2*, not far from the *Botanique* in Brussels. Her father owned an electronics store, and the family lived above the store. Odette had left an envelope with her father containing the names and photographs of over forty Allied airmen that the section was sheltering, as well as the families that they were staying with. If Schreyen's arrest had compromised Odette, the probability was high that her father's store would come under surveillance by the Gestapo looking for Odette. It was also likely that the Nazis would search the store and find the envelope after they arrested Odette. Odette needed to get that envelope out of the store. However, if the store were already under surveillance, she would be arrested if she tried to recover the envelope herself. In anticipation of such an emergency, Odette had made an arrangement with her father. If an unknown Belgian arrived at the store and said the proper code words, her father was to turn over the envelope to that person. It would also be a sign to Odette's father that the store might be under surveillance and that Odette would not be coming home for a few days.

Odette explained her problem to Clémy, and Janine promptly volunteered to go fetch the envelope. Arthur probably would have objected to subjecting his fourteen-year-old daughter to such a risk. However, Arthur was not home, and Clémy agreed to the plan. Odette gave Janine the code words for receiving the documents, which were, "Do you have an electric heater?" Janine jumped on her bike, and pedaled off toward the Botanique.

If it were ever necessary for someone other than Odette to come looking for that envelope, Odette's father was expecting it to be an adult. So, when a fourteen-year-old girl walked into the store and asked, "Do you have an electric heater?" he did not know what to do. At first, he simply dismissed the question and pretended that he didn't know what the young girl was really after. After all, it was the beginning of June and no one was looking for an electric heater in that month. Janine asked a second time, and Odette's father again dismissed the question saying it was too warm for an electric heater. Janine grew more insistent and said, "I want an electric heater. Do you have an electric heater?" Odette's father again said that he did not, but this only made Janine angry. Janine looked at him directly in the eye and exclaimed in an annoyed and loud voice, "Mademoiselle Gryspeirt wants an electric heater!" Odette's astonished father handed Jenny the envelope, and waved her out of the store.

If the Gestapo had been looking for Odette and if Janine had been overheard, that incident would have been the end of the line for many a brave soul. However, the store was empty of customers and no one overheard the conversation. It also turned out that Victor Schreyens had not cracked under torture from the Gestapo. Odette had not been compromised. A very proud Janine pedaled her way back to Ganshoren and delivered the envelope to Odette. Janine had done her patriotic duty for her country, and she, too, was now part of the Resistance.[18]

That evening, Arthur returned home and met Mac for the first time. He invited Aunt Cécile over for dinner since she also spoke English, and that would help make Mac feel more at home. Clémy prepared mushrooms for dinner, and Mac told all kinds of stories about his experiences. However, he refused to say how old he was. It was clear that Mac was a "talker," but that he also had a great sense of humor. When it came time to turn in for the evening, Mac slept in Roger's room on a sofa borrowed from Mme. Delvigne.

The next day was Friday, June 2. All day long, Odette and the other members of the Brusselmans Section worried about the men under their care. No one was yet sure what Schreyen's arrest would mean for the Brusselmans section, and Odette knew that it was possible that the Gestapo would find out about Bertha Fillée, with whom Jerry was staying. She had to move Jerry. That evening, Arthur was out of the home, and Roger was with his fencing club. So, Clémy, Mac, and Janine had dinner together alone. Mac turned the event into a little party and taught Clémy and Janine an American dance. Roger returned home a little later.

Around 10:30 p.m., the doorbell rang. Given the Gestapo's penchant to arrest people at home at night, a nighttime ring at the door was always a frightening experience in occupied Belgium. Janine hid while Clémy went with trepidation to answer the door. Roger sat with Mac in the living room. If they had already been betrayed, it was too late to hide. Fortunately, it was Odette at the door. She had Jerry with her as well as some clothes for Mac. Odette explained the situation to Clémy, and she asked Clémy to take Jerry in for a few days until the situation had calmed down. Without hesitation, Clémy agreed. She brought Odette and Jerry into the living room, and introduced Jerry to Roger and Mac. After speaking to Roger and Mac for a few moments, Odette left the house, promising that she would return to pick up Jerry in a few days.

While Roger and Mac were getting to know Jerry, Janine emerged from her hiding place and walked into the living room. Jerry immediately impressed her as a fine young man with brown curly hair, gray-blue eyes, and a heart of gold. Jerry turned to Roger and asked him what his sister's name was. Roger said "Janine." Either Jerry did not hear the name properly or he decided to Americanize it. He turned to Janine and said, "Hello Jenny.

I am Jerry," and they shook hands. From that moment forward Janine was known as Jenny. Mac and Roger immediately began calling her Jenny, too. The newly christened Jenny loved it, claiming that she never liked her given name in the first place. She insisted that everyone call her Jenny, including her family, friends, and the world as a whole. For the rest of her life, she was known as Jenny Abeels.[19]

After talking for a little while longer, it was time to go to bed. The three young men retired to Roger's room for the evening. Jenny went to her bed in her parents' room and Clémy went to bed shortly thereafter. Arthur was not yet home. Jenny had trouble falling asleep that night. She was elated by the idea that two dashing, young American liberators were now living in her home.

• 7 •

The Summer of 1944

On the morning of Saturday, June 3, the Abeels family awoke with two fugitive American airmen living in their home. The situation was dangerous for Arthur and Clémy. It was exciting for Roger and Jenny. It would irreversibly alter all of their lives within the next three months. However, in the short-term the situation created a number of challenges for the family that would need to be overcome.[1]

The first challenge was that Arthur did not even know that Jerry was now living in his home. When Jerry arrived on the previous evening, Arthur was out of the home and probably busy with Resistance activities for the Independence Front. He got home after his family had gone to bed that evening. Arthur had to go to work early the next morning, and he left the house before anyone else was awake. When he returned home from work in the early afternoon, Clémy finally had the chance to tell him about the events of the night before and to inform him that Jerry was now living in their home. Arthur took the news very well. He was happy to learn about the newcomer, and he was amused that he did not already know that there was another man living under his roof.

Arthur went to Roger's room to meet Jerry and the new young man living in his home impressed Arthur. He could tell that Jerry was a polite, decent, and serious young man. He knew that Jerry would get along fine with the family. However, Arthur was concerned about Jerry's health. Jerry's ankle had never fully healed from his parachute fall a month before, and Jerry suffered occasional pain. Given his own leg injury, Arthur could relate to what Jerry was experiencing. On top of that, Mac said that his right shoulder was bothering him. So, Arthur fetched the family doctor to have a look at Jerry and Mac. The doctor was also a family friend who could be trusted with the knowledge that Jerry and Mac were there. The doctor gave Jerry and Mac some prescriptions under the names of Roger and Arthur and he wished them good luck when he left.

Arthur and Clémy admonished Jenny to never, ever say anything to any of her friends about the two American airmen staying in their home. That rule applied to Jenny's conversations with Pompon as well. Jenny promised, and the first big test of that promise came on Sunday when she had a Guides meeting. Jenny wanted to stay home with the Americans rather than go to the Guides meeting. However, her parents made her go so that nothing would appear out of the ordinary. It took everything she had to say nothing to her friends in the Guides about what was happening at home, but she managed to keep the secret. As soon as the meeting was over, Jenny rushed home to continue to get acquainted with the young men. The family spent the rest of Sunday getting to know each other, and Jerry and Mac wrote some nice words in Jenny's scrapbook. On Monday, Arthur had to go to work, but everyone else was at home. Roger was already finished with his schooling, and Janine's school was closed because of damage that the building had recently suffered in an Allied bombardment. Another full day was spent with Jerry and Mac getting to know Roger, Jenny and Clémy. Jerry and Mac were rapidly becoming part of the Abeels family.

On Tuesday, June 6, 1944, the world changed. Although Arthur was at work, everyone else was again at home. The family radio was tuned to the BBC, which in and of itself was a punishable offense in occupied Belgium. Clémy heard something on the radio that she thought was great news, but she did not speak English so she was not sure. She asked Roger to come in to the room and confirm what she thought she had heard. The news was true: The Allies had landed at Normandy! Roger told Jerry, Mac, and Jenny. The four of them broke into a fit of happy hysteria that ended up in a small pillow fight. Even Clémy was swept up in the gaiety of the moment, as she grabbed a pillow and joined right in. It was the happiest moment that the Abeels family had experienced in years. The liberation of Belgium was now only a question of time. As Jenny wrote in her diary, "Our joy is indescribable. After four long years, we will again be free. We will be able to speak. We will be able to listen to the radio. We will be able to do what freemen do, without being afraid of being taken away by those horrible soldiers, having the home destroyed and the family killed. We shall be FREE!"

Arthur came immediately home from work that day. He had already heard the news at work and wanted to celebrate with his family. They all talked about how happy they were, and the four men debated how long it would take for the Allied armies to reach them. However, the doorbell soon rang. It was Odette, and she had arrived to take Jerry to another home as she promised she would four days earlier. Arthur and Clémy could see the disappointment on their children's faces. They also sensed that Jerry was happy in their home and did not want to go somewhere else. Arthur and Clémy told Odette that they would be happy if Jerry remained at their home, and they had a small discussion about it. Odette turned to Jerry and asked him if he wanted to stay or go. With a childish glee, Jerry clapped his hands together and shouted, "stay." Odette smiled and left without him.

As the joy of the news of the Allied landing in Normandy subsided over the next few days, new challenges began to emerge for the Abeels family. It was obvious to everyone, Belgian and German alike, that Belgium would be liberated in a matter of weeks, or months at most. The Comet Line had already decided in May that it was less dangerous to leave the airmen where they were sheltered in Belgium and wait for the Allied armies to come to them, rather than to try to move the airmen to Spain. Barring any security emergency, it was obvious that Jerry and Mac were going to be staying with the Abeels family for some time to come. This fact meant that simple things about everyday life that were already difficult under the occupation became potentially dangerous trials of skill and ingenuity for Arthur and Clémy.

Food was a particular challenge. The Nazis tried to divert as much food as possible from occupied Belgium to Germany in order to feed the German war machine and the German people. They imposed food rationing on Belgium. Each Belgian household was issued ration coupons that allowed them to purchase just enough food for the number of people in the household. The rations were sufficient to purchase an amount of food that was barely adequate for survival, and that was far less than what Belgian families usually consumed in peacetime. There was no possibility of receiving extra food rations. Arthur and Clémy now had to find a way to feed two young American men in their twenties in addition to their own children. How could they do this on their limited rations?

One way was to turn to the black market. Arthur knew some farmers who lived in the area around Aalst. Every now and then, he and Jenny took the train to Aalst to buy food from these farmers. This was both expensive and dangerous. It was illegal for the farmers to sell food directly to civilians, so the farmers charged high prices for the risk that they took in selling. Purchasing food directly from farmers was also a punishable offense. To deter people from doing this, the Nazis would occasionally inspect people coming into Brussels on trains from the countryside to look for food. If they found someone carrying food into the city, at the very least the food would be seized. However, if the Nazi doing the searching was so inclined, a Belgian civilian caught bringing food into Brussels could be arrested, tried, fined, or even sent to prison. The situation was even worse in the eastern part of Belgium that bordered Germany. Certain Belgian farmlands in that area were annexed to Germany, effectively dividing Belgian communities like Thimister-Clermont between Belgian and German territory. Bringing food from the newly annexed German territories into the areas that remained Belgian was made a capital offense. Some Belgian civilians in that area were executed for nothing more than trying to bring food home that they had purchased from nearby farmers they had known for their entire lives.[2]

There were other sources of food beyond the black market. Like most Belgians, the Abeels grew some vegetables in their small back yard, which helped a little bit. They had a chicken coop that provided eggs. The Comet Line and their friends in other Resistance organizations sometimes gave the Abeels food to help them feed the airmen, particularly if that food had been "liberated" from the Germans. Edible plants growing in the parks and forests around Brussels also entered the food chain. However, the main burden of making the food work fell on Clémy's shoulders, who never tired of trying to figure out how to make a little bit stretch a long way. Butter, sugar, coffee, tea, and often bread simply were not available. So, Clémy did her best to find substitutes from other edible plants. Beef, pork, and chicken were in short supply, and were considered treats when they were available. However, for some strange reason, herrings were often available. Clémy developed an amazing number of ways to serve herrings. The same was true for mushrooms, for which Clémy invented several new recipes. Clémy did not mind this role. She viewed feeding this new extended family, which now included four grown men, as her patriotic responsibility. She made it work, and the men never complained about the food.

Clothing likewise posed a challenge. When Jerry arrived at the house, he was dressed as a poor farmer, something that stood out in the city of Brussels. Mac had only one set of clothes when he arrived, until Odette brought him another. Although Arthur worked for a clothing store, clothes, too, were rationed and Arthur was carefully watched and controlled at work. Taking or even buying extra clothes at the shop was not normally an option, although he could occasionally get away with buying extra clothes that could not be sold by claiming they were for Roger. Second-hand stores were an alternative, and they became important sources of clothing for everyone in occupied Belgium. However, for that reason, the Nazis and their collaborators would watch these stores for unusual buying behavior. Clothing had to be purchased piece-by-piece and discretely, so as not to arouse suspicion. On more than one occasion, collaborationists working for second-hand clothes stores betrayed members of the Comet Line. Extended family members and trusted friends of the family would also provide second-hand clothing for Jerry and Mac.

Then there were the things that we take for granted in everyday life but were anything but granted in occupied Belgium. Cleaning products immediately disappeared from the stores after the German occupation. Lightbulbs were seldom replaced because there were few or no new ones to be found. Cosmetics and shampoo vanished. This was particularly hard on Belgian women, who viewed such items as an essential part of their feminine identity. Even soap was hard to come by and was hoarded when it was available. Toilet paper and other sanitary products were likewise scarce or not available. When the American and British armies finally did reach Belgium, one of the things that they noticed was how dirty and unhygienic many of the civilians appeared to be. What the American soldiers did not realize was that the Belgian civilians were not that way by choice. The circumstances of the occupation forced them to live that way.

School supplies posed a special problem. Jenny was in secondary school in June of 1944, and she needed things for school like paper and pens. However, there were none to be found. The Abeels saved every scrap of paper that they had for writing. Every blank space on these scraps of paper that could be used for writing was used for that purpose. School textbooks and other books disappeared. Jenny, Pompon, and their friends had to share the meager stocks that were available from before the war. Although Jerry and Roger did not smoke, Arthur and Mac did so from time to time. Arthur generously shared his cigarette ration with Mac. Wine, beer, and other special drinks that Arthur had possessed when the war broke out were used for only the most special occasions.

All of this cost money, particularly when Arthur had to turn to the black market to find what the family needed. Although the Abeels lived a comfortable life compared to many of their compatriots, they were by no means wealthy. Housing the two Americans put a considerable strain on the family budget. While staying in the Abeels home, Jerry insisted that he could work in whatever way was practical to help support the family. Of course, no way was practical. If Jerry were caught doing anything outside of the home, the consequences would have been devastating. However, Jerry did do everything he could to help out around the house. Mac would sometimes follow Jerry's example.

The collaborators living upstairs posed another challenge. The Abeels lived on the ground floor of the house and the Cellens couple lived on the floor above them. In between was a room off of a landing, which was Roger's bedroom. Arthur had no choice but to sleep Jerry and Mac in that room. The risk that the Cellens would run into the two Americans was high. However, there were different degrees of collaboration, and as mentioned in the previous chapter, the Cellens were "soft" collaborators. They basically stuck to themselves and did not ask questions. They left the home early in the morning and came back in the evening at regular, predictable hours. They left the house on weekends. Although they collaborated with the Nazis, the Cellens did not care for the random acts of violence perpetrated by the Nazis that they saw. They were opportunists who preferred to look the other way rather than cause trouble. However, these qualifiers did not negate the fact that they belonged to the VNV, and that they could have denounced the Abeels at any time if they had chosen to do so.

Willy Nipper, the collaborator living across and down the street at No. 48, was a bigger challenge. He was a "hard" collaborator, who pretended to help young Belgian men escape to England but instead turned them over to the Nazis for labor service in Germany. If he had ever even suspected that Allied airmen were living down the street, there is no doubt that he would have denounced the Abeels immediately.[3] If gossip among the neighbors had arisen that there were two Americans living in the street, the consequences would have been catastrophic. Therefore, outside of their close personal friends, the Abeels said nothing to anyone about the Americans who lived with them.

Beyond one's closest friends, no one ever really knew who to trust in occupied Belgium. Was the person who owned the second-hand clothing store a closet collaborator who would say something about a large purchase of clothing? Would the photographer who developed the family's photos denounce them if he saw something suspect in a film roll? Would a pharmacist report an unusual prescription that was needed for one of the Americans? Would the wrong neighbor see something unusual coming into or out of the house? What if a collaborator overheard two of the Abeels' real friends talking about the nice Americans staying in the home? All of the children in the neighborhood played together. What if Jenny would say something on the playground to the daughter of the wrong couple?

Arthur took precautions to minimize these risks. Jerry and Mac were ordered to be strictly out of sight when the Cellens couple came in and out of the house at their normal hours. Jenny was admonished time and time again to never under any circumstances say anything to her friends or anybody else about the airmen in her home. The front door was kept locked at all times, and to ensure that no one would forget, Roger rigged together an electrical device that emitted a signal when the front door was unlocked. In the event that the Gestapo would come knocking, Arthur cut a deal with one of their neighbors. The Abeels' back door led to a small courtyard with a fence. On the other side of the fence was another small courtyard belonging to the home of the Wueron family. The Wueron family agreed to keep their back door unlocked at all times. In that way, if the Gestapo arrived at the Abeels' front door, Jerry, Mac and Roger could run across the courtyard, jump the fence and go into their neighbor's home. This precaution did not eliminate the danger. When looking for someone, the Gestapo would often block off an entire neighborhood and search each and every house. If the Gestapo did this, it would have rendered the escape route via the Wueron family useless. However, despite this obvious shortcoming, it was a better plan for escape than no plan at all.

Periodic arrests of volunteers for the Comet Line posed another challenge. Regardless of one's patriotism or devotion to the cause, interrogation under torture could cause anyone to say anything. If someone detained and tortured by the Gestapo had given any indication that the Abeels were harboring American airmen in their home, the result would have been disastrous. One such arrest that could have compromised the Abeels occurred on June 9, and Odette had to move Jerry and Mac out of the house for a couple of days. She took them to Anderlecht where they stayed with a Mr. Locus. When it became clear that the danger had subsided, she moved them back to the Abeels home.

Perhaps the greatest challenge that Jerry, Mac, and the Abeels family faced was the sheer boredom of life underground. Jerry and Mac were, in effect, under house arrest in the Abeels home. They certainly could not go out on the streets of Brussels and walk around the city. The Nazis and their collaborators were authorized to stop people without cause and ask to see their identity papers. The Nazis particularly liked to do this to young men who were of age for military or labor service. Even if Jerry and Mac had possessed decent forgeries of the required documents, it would have been impossible for Jerry from Idaho and Mac from Michigan to pass themselves off as real Belgians. Moreover, even if they were not stopped directly by a Nazi, they could be observed and reported by collaborators, like the ones who lived across the street. The risk of being caught outside of the home was too great, and so Jerry and Mac were confined to the home. Although they did gymnastics in the attic with Roger, they could not participate in any sports or engage in any physical exercise outside of the home. They could not go sightseeing or shopping. They could not go to restaurants or cafés. They could not explore their surroundings. They could not make friends outside of the family. They could not make a lot of noise. They simply could not do any of the things that normal men in their early twenties would do. Instead, they could only sit and wait for the Allied armies to come and liberate them.

Jerry and Mac were quite different individuals, and they handled the waiting differently. Jerry was the more serious of the two. He was twenty-four years old, and he had left behind a wife in America whom he loved dearly. Jerry was also a devout Mormon who did not smoke, drink, swear, or engage in any other vices. He passed the idle time in the Abeels home thinking about his newlywed wife, and he talked about his wife and family every day. He dreamed about how Nora Lee and he were going to own a farm and raise a family. He thought about the war and what the world would look like after it was all over. He was only all too happy to talk about these things. Jerry used his time in the Abeels home to make plans for the future. He did not really feel the need to go outside. In fact, the only trouble that Jerry ever caused the Abeels family concerned a photograph of Nora Lee.

When Jerry bailed out of the *Wolverine,* he was carrying a photograph of Nora Lee and him together. The photograph was taken on the day of their engagement, on the pier in Saint Petersburg shortly after he had proposed to her. Jerry was in uniform, while Nora Lee was dressed in white. At the Lepoivre home in May, the Comet Line had taken Jerry's uniform, dog tags, and other personal items. They gave him a set of civilian clothes so that he could be more easily moved in the open. They also gave him forged papers that indicated that he was unable to speak for medical reasons. If a Nazi had stopped Jerry and his guide for an identity check, his guide had the possibility of talking their way out of the situation since the documents said that Jerry could not speak. However, if the Nazis had searched Jerry and found that photograph, the ruse would have been all over with. The photograph clearly identified Jerry as an American airman in a place that was clearly not Belgium. Therefore, the Comet Line confiscated the photograph at the same time that they took Jerry's uniform and other belongings.

Jerry desperately wanted that photograph back. It was his one and only link to Nora Lee, and Jerry pleaded incessantly with Arthur to get that photograph back for him. Having had enough of this, Arthur spoke to Odette, who spoke to Madame Brusselmans, who spoke to the appropriate people in the Comet Line to see if a solution could be found. A compromise was reached. Someone took the photo and clipped Jerry and the background out of it. This left only a woman dressed in white. It was now a photo of a woman who could have been anyone, in a location that could have been anywhere. Thus sanitized, the photograph was returned to Jerry. To say that he was elated is an understatement. Jerry told the Abeels that the day that the photograph was returned to him was one of the happiest days of his life. In a way, he had been reunited with Nora Lee. It seemed like every time he looked at the photo, he thanked Arthur for bringing it back to him.

Jerry was so grateful to the Abeels family for everything that they were doing for him that he sat down to write a letter to his family back home. He knew that the letter could not be sent or delivered until after the liberation, but he felt compelled to write it while he was in the Abeels home anyway. At the top of the letter, Jerry drew a small Belgian flag. The letter said:

> Brussels, Belgium
> June 26, 1944
>
> Dearest Wife and Family,
>
> Just a few words to let you know that at this time I am very well and happy, under the circumstances. I and another American have been living for the past three weeks with a grand family here in Brussels. They are very good to us, they try at all times to make us feel as much at home as possible. I have met many other truly wonderful people here in Belgium. I shall not forget the things that they have done for me.
>
> I suppose by this time you have received a notice that I was "missing in action." I hope that you have not worried too much about it and that you will soon get the news that I am safe and on my way home.
>
> I think of you always and dream of the day when we can be together again. We have much to be grateful for in America.
>
> With all my love,
> Your husband, son and brother
> Gerald

Mac was a different type of character. He was a "talker." The day that Jerry arrived in the home, Mac told the Abeels that he was twenty-four years old, the same age as Jerry. However, it quickly came out that he was only twenty years old. Mac was always full of stories. His imagination had created fanciful tales of his exploits while evading the Germans, despite the fact that these adventures would have been impossible while he was under the care of the Comet Line. Mac was also a "ladies man" and he liked to tell stories about his girlfriend in America. However, even these stories

Jerry and Nora Lee's engagement photograph taken in St. Petersburg, Florida. Jerry carried a copy on the *Wolverine*, and while fighting with the Resistance (but with his image removed for his own protection) (courtesy Jenny Abeels).

Left to right: Mac, Jenny, Clémy, and Jerry (courtesy Jenny Abeels).

Mac (left) and Jerry enjoy the sunshine on their shower day (courtesy Jenny Abeels).

did not always make sense. The name of this girlfriend would change from time to time, and he would sometimes use a different girlfriend's name the second time he told the same story. Mac never realized the inconsistencies in his stories, and no one else saw the need to embarrass him by pointing them out.

On the positive side, Mac was always full of jokes. He had an infectious sense of humor, one that he had inherited from his mother. When Mac was home in America and when he was stationed in England, he clearly liked to go out at night and have a good time. He was fun to be around. For Mac, his confinement in the Abeels home seemed like a prison, and he did not understand why he was not allowed to leave the house. At times, Mac acted like a child. He was always asking to go outside, and he never really seemed to understand the dangers.

At one point, Mac's frustration grew so great that in a fit of anger at the dinner table he said to the Abeels family that he thought that he would be better off as a POW than to stay in their home because at least then he could spend some time outside. Those words cut through the heart of the Abeels family like a dagger. Jerry immediately asked Mac to step into the next room, and he administered a severe rebuke, pointing out the sacrifices and the risks that the Abeels family had taken for them. Mac returned to the room and apologized. However, Mac never really seemed to get it. No matter how often Arthur, Roger, and Jerry explained the dangers and the risks, Mac could not seem to accept that the danger was so grave. He never really understood just how far the Abeels had risked their lives for him, and the danger that his discovery would have created for himself, for the Abeels, and for everyone else in the Comet Line with whom he had come in contact.

Arthur did his best to help relieve Jerry and Mac's boredom and their occasional homesickness. Both Jerry and Mac mentioned that one small thing that they missed about home was being able to take a decent shower.

Mac (left) and Jerry with Bénis, the family rabbit (courtesy DeLoy Larsen).

Belgians, at least at that time, took baths rather than showers, and there was no shower in the Abeels home. On one sunny day in June, Arthur allowed the men to recreate that small taste of home. Jerry and Mac took a garden hose and connected it to the kitchen faucet. They strung the hose outside into the back yard and made a makeshift showerhead. Turning on the water, Jerry and Mac enjoyed their first shower since England in the rare bright sunshine of a Belgian summer day. Roger joined in too, and the three young men spent the afternoon pretending that they were in America.

Being a patriot himself, Arthur knew that Jerry and Mac needed to do something special for the Fourth of July. He organized a special dinner for them, and tried to make it as American as they could. Making an American dinner was, of course, impossible under the circumstances, but Clémy did manage to serve beef, which was a rare treat during the occupation, and which was the closest she could come to something "American." Arthur decorated the table with homemade American and Belgian flags. Jerry and Mac taught Roger and Jenny the words to the American national anthem, and they sang it together. The Abeels family also sang *La Brabançonne*, the national anthem of Belgium. They tried to teach Jerry and Mac the words in French, but the Americans could not quite master it.

Arthur then put a Belgian twist on this American patriotic holiday. When a simple patriotic act is called for at a Belgian dinner, it was and is the practice that a master of ceremonies raises his glass and proposes a toast to the King. Arthur therefore poured everyone a glass of European Martini and proposed a toast to the United States of America. Unlike an American martini, what Arthur was offering was a wine-type drink that is a bit sweet and that has a low alcohol content. Even so, as a devout Mormon, Jerry was not allowed to drink any alcohol at all and so he politely declined to join in the toast. To Arthur this was incomprehensible. How could an American serviceman not participate in this simple and common patriotic act in honor of his own country? Arthur insisted quite firmly, and pointed out that it was only a Martini, something that even children like Jenny were allowed to taste. In fact, Arthur insisted so firmly that Jerry finally broke down and gave in. Jerry joined in the toast, and for the first and only time in his life, he tasted alcohol. However, the experience was not pleasant for him. After only a few sips, Jerry turned beet red and grew dizzy. He felt out of control of himself for the first time in his life, and he left the table and headed to bed. For Mac, Roger, and Jenny, this was a moment that they would tease Jerry about for the rest of the summer. For Jerry, the experience reinforced his commitment to a lifetime of abstinence.

One sunny Sunday in early July while Arthur was away from the house, Clémy decided to give in to Mac's incessant demands to be allowed to go outside. The Abeels lived near the National Basilica at Koekelberg, and surrounding this church was a large park. Sundays were quiet days when almost everything was closed, and it was typical for families to spend their Sundays by going on a walk. Clémy reasoned that if they looked like a normal family taking a walk in the park after church on a Sunday, the Nazis would not pay any attention to them. Just to be sure, however, Roger and Jenny scouted out the park to ensure that there were no Germans or uniformed collaborators to be seen. Having established that the coast was relatively clear, Clémy, Roger, Jenny, Jerry, and Mac went for a stroll in the park. They took some photos while Jerry and Mac enjoyed a walk outside of the home on that sunny afternoon. They were careful to not stay out for long, and they were home again within a couple of hours. When Arthur got home and found out what had happened, he was furious. The risks were so great, and a walk in the sunshine was not worth the risk. After all, he lectured them, what would have happened if someone had overheard them speaking English? It was the one and only time that Jerry and Mac would leave the Abeels home for fun. It was also the closest thing to sightseeing that Jerry would ever do in Belgium.

During their long hours of confinement, Jerry and Mac decided to learn French. They had lots of time to study and practice, and their progress was quite remarkable. This was particularly true for Jerry, who could carry on conversations and write basic letters in French by the end of July. However, both Jerry and Mac spoke the French that they knew with very thick American accents. One day in July, this led Mac into trouble.

For some reason that he could never really explain to Arthur, Mac walked out of his room at exactly the same time that the Cellens couple were coming down the stairs at the normal time that they left the house each day. They looked at each other, and Mac said, with his strong American accent, *Bonjour! Je parle français très bien.* (Good morning! I speak very well French.) He then came downstairs to the breakfast table where Arthur, Clémy, Roger, Jenny and Jerry were seated. Clearly proud of himself for the way he handled the situation, Mac told everyone what had just happened.

Initially, the others were stunned into silent disbelief by the stupidity of this act. Disbelief was soon replaced by horror, and horror was quickly followed by anger. How, they demanded, could Mac seriously believe that he had fooled the Cellens into thinking that he was Belgian? How could they possibly explain the presence in the house of a new twenty-year-old who the Cellens had never seen before, particularly a twenty-year-old with an American accent? Mac did not understand everybody's concern. He had spoken to the Cellens in French after all! Except for Mac, everyone else in the household spent the rest of the day gripped with fear about what would happen next. Would the Cellens betray them or were they actually the soft type of collaborators that they claimed to be? Would they ask questions? How could they explain why Mac was in the house if the Cellens asked? That evening, the Cellens came home at their normal time, and quietly went to their rooms. No one said anything to anybody. The next morning, the Cellens left the house in silence with some suitcases. The Abeels family never saw them again. They must have kept their mouths shut, because the Gestapo never came looking for Jerry and Mac.

Most of the time, Jerry, Mac, and the Abeels family passed the time by talking. Clémy was the only person in the household who did not speak at least some English. However, that did not prove to be an obstacle to communication since Arthur or Roger were normally around to interpret. Clémy's youthfulness impressed Jerry and Mac. During his first day in the Abeels home, Jerry thought that Clémy was Roger and Jenny's older sister, not their mother. Her cheerfulness and optimistic outlook toward life remained a constant feature of the home, despite the circumstances of the occupation.

The Abeels were full of questions for the Americans. Jerry and Mac were from a faraway land where things were very different than in Belgium, and the Abeels were keen to learn all about it. Jerry and Mac told the Abeels about television, which the average Belgian family at the time knew nothing about.[4] The thought that a box could transmit images from far away in the way that a radio could transmit sound intrigued them. Like all Europeans, the Abeels thought of America as a land of cowboys and Indians. Jerry was from Idaho, which was in the Wild West. That made him a real cowboy as far as the Abeels were concerned. He had stories about his grandparents' trek to Utah across the Great Plains in a wagon train. He grew up riding horses and tending sheep and cows. He could talk with authority about how hard life was in the West and what it took to eke out a living on the frontier. He talked about the natural beauty of the area where he was from, and about Yellowstone National Park, which was not far from where he grew up. Like all Belgians interested in America at the time, the idea of the Indians fascinated the Abeels. Jerry personally knew Indians when he was growing up, and he could talk about their life and culture. Jerry personified the image that the Abeels had of what America was all about.

There was never a shortage of things to talk about that summer, and there were always things to compare and contrast between Belgium and the United States. They talked about differences in school systems and compared each other's experiences in school. They talked about sports. The Abeels learned about American football and baseball while Jerry and Mac learned about soccer. They talked about differences in clothes, like the fact that the tails on men's shirts were longer in Belgium than in America. Food shortages prevented Clémy from introducing Jerry and Mac to many traditional Belgian dishes. However, the Abeels could at least tell them about traditional dishes like *waterzooi* and mussels while Jerry and Mac talked about hamburgers and hotdogs. They talked about differences in habits, like the Belgian penchant for kissing friends on the cheek, which Americans would never do.

Religion likewise provided hours of conversation. The Abeels and Mac were Catholic, so they obviously understood each other's religious beliefs rather well. However, Jerry was LDS, and proud of it. Neither the Abeels nor Mac knew anything about this quite distinct form of Christianity. They had a lot questions about Jerry's faith. Jerry was devout, and he cherished the values that he held. He welcomed the opportunities to talk about his faith when given the chance to do so. After all, he knew that God had led him to the Abeels home. However, Jerry never tried to force his religious views upon anyone, nor did he try to convert anyone through anything more than example. That was a fact that was appreciated by both the Abeels family and Mac. However, it was clearly the values that Jerry learned in his Mormon upbringing that made him so polite and easy to live with. Jerry knew what a family was supposed to be all about, and he lived that way with the Abeels.

Although Mac and the Abeels were Catholics, there were differences between them concerning their shared faith. Mac was from a midwestern American Catholic family with Irish roots. He went to church with his mother on Sundays, and he attended catechism classes. Mac even carried a Catholic, prayer book with him on the *Baby Shoes*. The Abeels were Catholic too. They believed in their faith, but they were not particularly devout nor did they particularly care for ritual practice. They attended mass from time to time, but they were not regular attendees. They did not say grace before meals. Perhaps it was because of their experiences during the wars, but Arthur and Clémy could be quite cynical about the Catholic church at times. They thought of the church as a human institution and of its leaders as human, with all of the weaknesses that human nature embodied. Mac had some difficulty accepting these points of view. Mac wanted to go to mass on Sundays. However, to do so was just too dangerous, and it simply was not an option for Arthur to allow him to do so. Mac did insist that the family say grace before meals. The desire to do so was something that Jerry and Mac shared in common, and so the Abeels went along with it. However, the Abeels never really understood the point. Fortunately, none of these discussions about religion ever turned ugly. Things were said and taken in a spirit of mutual respect. No one ever tried to convince anyone that their religious views were the best.

Jerry was particularly interested in Arthur's experiences during the First World War. He wanted to hear his stories of the siege of Liège, and about his time in the German POW camp. He was curious about life under occupation, both in the First World War and in the years of the Second World War before he entered the Abeels home. He was fascinated by Arthur's work for the Independence Front and the activities of the Belgian Resistance. Although he had nothing personally against the Germans, Jerry shared Arthur's intense hatred of the ideology of Nazism. Jerry was as disturbed as Arthur by the fact that collaborators were in their midst who would betray their own country. Jerry respected Arthur deeply, and could relate to his patriotism.

Over the summer of 1944, the bonds of friendship that had developed became bonds of kinship. Arthur and Clémy came to regard Jerry and Mac as adopted sons, and Jerry and Mac came to regard Arthur and Clémy as second parents. By July, Jerry and Mac were calling Clémy and Arthur "mom" and "pop." The bonds between the two American young men and Roger and Jenny were even stronger.

Roger turned twenty in August. All that he had ever wanted to do was to become an officer and a pilot. Now living in his home were two airmen with combat experience. Roger wanted to be just like them. The bonds between Jerry and Roger were particularly strong. Jerry was four years older than Roger and Mac. Like Roger, Jerry was serious, intelligent, mature, and convinced of the righteousness of the war they were all a part of. Jerry acted and behaved like a gentleman. Jerry had even piloted airplanes during his days as an aviation cadet. Roger looked up to Jerry, and Jerry taught Roger how to act like a soldier. Jerry and Roger became best friends and regarded themselves as brothers. Although they were quite different in terms of their upbringing, nationality, and religion, Jerry and Roger were identical in the values that they shared and in their outlook toward life.

Jerry and Roger's relationship with Mac was also close, but somewhat different in nature. Like Jerry, Mac was an airman with combat experience. In fact, Mac had actually flown more combat missions than Jerry. However, his personality type was different. Mac was full of jokes and a lot of fun to be around. He was naughty enough to make people laugh and to sometimes cause embarrassment. He was nice enough to be likeable at the same time. He brought laughter to life under the occupation. However, Mac sometimes would go too far and, when it was necessary to do so, Jerry did not hesitate to remind Mac that Mac was an American soldier, a representative of his country, and a guest in the Abeels home.

Both Jerry and Mac knew that they would have never been friends if they had known each other in America. However, they developed a mutual respect for each other and they came to understand those values that they did have in common. To put it simply, Jerry came to regard Mac as his rogue younger brother, and Mac looked up to Jerry as a serious older brother, with all of the ups and downs that such a relationship entailed.

The bonds of friendship that were established among these three men were immediate, natural, and deep. All three considered themselves to be brothers, and began calling themselves the three musketeers. As the summer progressed, "all for one and one for all" developed a new meaning for them. Roger had already been involved in the Independence Front for years, and he was now a full-fledged member of the Secret Army. At night, Jerry and Mac would sometimes see Roger leave the house on secret missions, and Roger would return with stories to tell. Jerry and Mac were enthralled by Roger's double life in the Secret Army and impressed by his patriotism. By the middle of July, the two Americans had resolved to join Roger in the Resistance to fight for the liberation of Belgium. To underscore the fact that this was his own decision, Jerry wrote the following letter on July 11 and gave it to Arthur for safekeeping in the event that something happened to him:

> To whom it may concern:
> I Gerald Sorensen, Army Serial Number I9095816, United States Army
> Air Force, voluntarily offer my services for action in a common cause, in
> case of the invasion of Belgium, by the United States Forces or their Allies. I
> will take arms and fight under the orders of the leaders of the underground
> movement. In case of my death, it is to be known that my actions were vol-
> untary and that I was not obliged to make any moves of opposition.
> Sgt. Gerald E. Sorensen
> U.S.A. Air Force
> A.S.N. I9095816

However, at the time that Jerry wrote this letter, the Secret Army was not yet ready for Jerry and Mac. At that point in July, Roger was engaged in activities in Brussels that were best performed by Belgians who knew the city and who spoke French and Dutch. It made no sense for Jerry and Mac to act on their desire to join the Resistance, or for the Secret Army to allow them to act, until the call to combat would come, and their skills could be best employed. As Jerry's note said, that time would come as the Allies approached Belgium.

Moreover, Arthur was not keen on the idea of Jerry and Mac joining the Resistance. When he took them into his home, Arthur had pledged to the Comet Line that he would keep Jerry and Mac safe. Engaging in Resistance activities was anything but safe. In fact, Arthur was not all that happy about Roger's plans to engage in combat when the time came either. After all, Roger was Arthur's only son. However, Roger was committed to the Secret Army, and Jerry and Mac were adamant that they were going to join Roger in the Resistance. As Jerry said to Arthur, "your struggle is my struggle, too." As a father, Arthur did not like the young men's plans. As a patriot, Arthur would acquiesce to those plans when the time came.

Then there was Jenny. Jerry, Roger, and Mac did the things that brothers would do with little sisters. They taught her things about the world. They did the household chores together. They played games together. They talked about all kinds of things that they could never talk about with their parents, like relationships between boys and girls. As older brothers are known to do, the young men relentlessly teased teenage Jenny. Roger had called her "Phatty" even before Jerry and Mac entered their home. The Americans picked up the nickname and corrected the spelling to "Fatty," which was what Roger really meant. At one point, Mac started calling Jenny "pug nose," and Roger soon picked up on that one. Of course, Jenny protested that she hated the teasing. However, deep down inside she enjoyed the attention from the young Americans, and they knew she did. The teasing was meant affectionately, and the affection was genuine. They had become a family. Before Jerry left the Abeels household, he wrote Jenny a small note that said:

> Dear little Sis,
> I always said you were a very good girl (when asleep), but I can't help but like you even when awake. Indeed you have been a grand sister. Remember your promise to be the guardian angel over my children.
> Affectionately,
> Jerry

Jenny took advantage of the opportunity that Jerry and Mac's presence in her home provided for her to improve her English. However, even that

Roger (left) and Jerry above; Mac and Jenny at bottom (courtesy Jenny Abeels).

could become a source of teasing. One day, Mac was downstairs with Jenny, helping her with her English, while Jerry was upstairs in the bedroom in the landing. Mac told Jenny that the expression "You Son of a Bitch" was a special greeting that good friends in America said to each other. He made her practice the phrase until she could say it with just the right American accent and tonality. He then told her to go try it out on Jerry and see how happy it would make him. Jenny proudly walked up the stairs to the bedroom, opened the door, looked Jerry in the eye and said "You son of a bitch!" The startled Jerry shouted something to the effect of, "What? I can't believe you would say such a thing!" He jumped up and said that he was going to spank her for her bad language. As Jerry lunged to grab Jenny, she ran down the stairs and into the living room. Jerry followed in hot pursuit and chased her around the house, while Mac laughed hysterically in the background. Jerry quickly realized that Mac had set her up, and gave up the chase. Jerry couldn't believe that Mac had taught a young girl to say something like that. Mac thought it was hilarious. Jenny claimed to be furious with Mac, but everyone knew that this was not true.

Jenny was a fourteen year old girl in puberty who was now interested in boys. Jerry was older and married, and Jenny thought of him only as her stable, wise, big brother. Mac, on the other hand, was younger, handsome, fun, and full of jokes. Jenny was clearly smitten by Mac, and that was pretty much obvious to everyone else in the household. Jenny was far too young in 1944 for anything to happen between the two of them. Besides, Mac insisted that he had a girlfriend in America, even though this girlfriend's name seemed to change from time to time. However, Mac clearly enjoyed the attention that he received from the young teenage girl, and he did nothing to discourage her puppy-dog like affections. Mac was a little flirtatious with Jenny, and Jenny ate up every moment of the attention that Mac paid her, but it all remained very innocent. Until the end of her life, Jenny remembered the summer of 1944 as the happiest days of her life.

• 8 •

Brothers in Arms

By the beginning of August 1944, it was obvious to everyone in Belgium, Belgian and German alike, that it was only a matter of weeks before the Allies would reach Brussels. The American, British, and Canadian armies had broken out of the bocages of Normandy and were sweeping their way across occupied France. German military resistance to the Allies in France crumbled over the course of the month, and Paris was liberated on August 25. Everyone knew that Brussels would be next, and that defeat for the Nazis in Belgium was now inevitable. In the face of this pending defeat, one would think that the Nazis would have eased up on their oppression of Belgium. In fact, they did just the opposite. As the Allies advanced rapidly across France, the Nazis intensified their exploitation of Belgium, and the Gestapo stepped up its activities against the Resistance.

Since their grip on Belgium was nearly lost, the Nazis decided to extract all that they could from Belgium while they could do so for use in the struggle that would continue in the German heartland. This extraction included Belgium's young men who could serve as laborers in German factories. Summonses to report for the labor draft intensified, as did the arrests of those who failed to report. Sometimes, the enforcement of the labor draft occurred in dramatic ways. On the first Sunday in August, the Gestapo staked out a local football game, and watched the fans enter the stadium to cheer their teams on. When the game was in full swing, they swept in and arrested all of the young men of labor draft age who were present. They packed the football fans into trucks and sent them away to Germany.[1]

Actions against the Belgian Resistance likewise intensified. The Gestapo made even greater efforts to infiltrate the Comet Line, particularly by sending English-speaking agents to pose as downed Allied airmen. These agents always posed as fighter pilots, since there would be no other crewmembers to contradict their identity. This forced Mme. Brusselmans and other Comet Line leaders to screen even more carefully the airmen who appeared looking for assistance. This created a new set of problems for the Comet Line. Not

150

realizing the danger, some legitimate Allied airmen resented the questioning they were subjected to, which they perceived as a slight to their character and honesty. It was truly a perilous time for the Comet Line.[2]

Nazi armed action against the Secret Army and other Belgian Resistance organizations likewise increased in the summer of 1944. In the area around Leuven, a Flemish SS officer named Robert Verbelen established a *Veiligheidskorps* (or Security Corps) that was given *carte blanche* by Reichsführer of the SS Heinrich Himmler to murder Belgians suspected of Resistance activities. Verbelen was so effective in this position that he was promoted to SS captain and awarded the German War Meritorious Cross.[3] In turn the armed Belgian Resistance organizations stepped up their attacks against the collaborators. In July, the Resistance killed 217 collaborators in 286 attacks.[4] On August 17, the Resistance assassinated the Rexist mayor of Charleroi, Oswald Englebin. In revenge, the *Rexists* murdered 27 innocent civilians.[5] In effect, a miniature civil war was now taking place between Belgian collaborators and the Belgian Resistance. Although the Allies were on the way, the war in Belgium was far from over.

On July 28, Nazi collaborators arrived at the Abeels home. They were not looking for Jerry and Mac, nor did they have any idea that there were two American airmen sheltering in the Abeels home. Rather, they were looking for Roger in order to serve him his third and final summons to report for labor duty. Clémy convinced the collaborators that Roger was not home and, in fact, he was not. However, Jerry and Mac were hiding in the attic. Although the Nazis left without Roger, the incident put everyone in the home in extreme danger. If Roger failed to report for labor duty in response to that third summons, he would be classified as a *réfractaire*, and the Nazis could seize him and send him to Germany. There would be no way for Arthur and Clémy to talk their way out of a house search if the Gestapo came to the Abeels home to look for Roger. Like Jerry and Mac, Roger too was now a fugitive. None of the three young men could remain at the Abeels home.[6]

In response to this development, Odette moved Jerry and Mac to the home of a Monsieur Goris in the community of Anderlecht on July 29, where they stayed for a couple of days. She then moved them back to the home of Marie De Stobbelier in Koekelberg, who had sheltered Jerry in May. Mme. Stobbelier's home was closer to the Abeels home, and Roger went to stay there as well. While they were there, the three young men devised a plan for what they would do next.[7]

In July, Jerry and Mac had vowed to join Roger in the Secret Army

The Three Musketeers, left to right, Jerry, Roger and Mac (courtesy Jenny Abeels).

when the time came. The time had now come, but they would need to find a place where Jerry and Mac could operate more openly and where Roger did not have to worry about the Gestapo turning up at his home to look for him. Jerry had an idea. In May, he had spent a week at the farm of Charles Lepoivre near the village of Gondregnies in the area around Enghien. Lepoivre had told Jerry that he was welcome to stay with them at any time if he ever found himself in need of refuge. The area around Enghien was also an important center of activity for the Secret Army, and Roger could transfer to the Refuge of the Secret Army that was operating there. The three musketeers therefore vowed to go Enghien and join up with the Secret Army unit operating in that area.[8]

On August 2, they returned to the Abeels home to inform Arthur of their intentions and to prepare to depart. Arthur was filled with conflicting emotions about the young men's decision. On the one hand, he had promised the Comet Line that he would protect the American airmen, not send them off to fight with the Resistance. He now regarded Jerry and Mac as sons, too, and he did not want to see all three of his sons put in harm's way. On the other hand, Arthur knew that it was not possible for Jerry, Mac or Roger to remain at home. He himself was active in the Independence Front and committed to the Resistance. He was a patriot who was firmly committed to the ideals of duty to country and duty to resist the Nazi oppressors. So, Arthur also felt a certain pride in the decision that the young men had made. In his heart, he knew that they must serve, and he agreed to help them despite the danger.

Because of the increased German surveillance and repression, it was far too dangerous for Jerry, Roger and Mac to risk traveling to Enghien by train. Arthur did not have a car, nor could he borrow one. So, Jerry, Roger and Mac would have to get to Enghien on their own foot power. Bicycle seemed like the best way to go. Roger owned a bicycle, and Arthur asked the neighbors if he could borrow two more. The neighbors knew better than to ask questions. They simply agreed with an obliging smile. It was then time to say goodbye. Being young and not fully realizing the danger, Jenny was filled with pride at that moment. Her three brothers were going off to fight for the liberation of Belgium! One of the last things that Roger said to her was that he was going to Enghien to kill some Germans in revenge for what they had done to Belgium. The last words that Jerry said to the Abeels family were in French: "*Je vous remercie beaucoup*" (I thank you very much). The three musketeers jumped on their bicycles and pedaled off toward Enghien. It was the last time that Arthur, Clémy, and Jenny would ever see Roger and Jerry alive. The date was Thursday, August 3, 1944.

The three young men pedaled about thirty miles (fifty kilometers) to the home of Monsieur Fourmanoir in the village of Silly. Coincidentally, when Jerry jumped from the *Wolverine* three months earlier, he had landed just outside of Silly, not far from Fourmanoir's home. Fourmanoir was a schoolteacher and a member of the Secret Army. Since Roger was already a member of the Secret Army in the Brussels area, it was decided that he would stay with Fourmanoir for the time being while Jerry and Mac would go to the Lepoivre's home. Jerry and Mac left their borrowed bicycles behind, and Fourmanoir walked with them to the Lepoivre family's farm in Gondregnies, which was about forty-five minutes away.[9]

The next day, Arthur and Jenny travelled by train to Enghien to collect the two borrowed bicycles. Fourmanoir met them near the station. Roger did not accompany him to the meeting, since the presence of a young man of labor draft age may have aroused suspicions if the Germans had seen him. Fourmanoir and Arthur had never met each other before. They had a small chat about the situation in the area in general and about what lay ahead for Roger, Jerry, and Mac in particular. Fourmanoir impressed Arthur as a decent and a sensible man. Arthur was reassured about the arrangements, and he felt that his sons would be safe there. Arthur and Jenny got on the two borrowed bicycles and pedaled back to Ganshoren. It was safer than trying to take the bicycles on the train. By now, the Germans were confiscating bicycles from civilians in public places for use in their pending retreat from Belgium.

When Jerry and Mac arrived at their home, Charles and Sylvie Lepoivre greeted them with open arms. Lepoivre's offer in May to shelter Jerry if he ever needed it was indeed sincere. The family genuinely liked Jerry and they were happy to see him again. They were also impressed that Jerry had managed to pick up some French in the intervening three months. For Jerry, staying with the Lepoivres brought a small taste of home. Not only was he living on a working farm again, but he was also able to ride a horse, probably for the first time since he had left Idaho. Meanwhile, with Fourmanoir's help, Roger began integrating himself into the local section of the Secret Army, and he began laying the groundwork for Jerry and Mac to join him.

Roger now belonged to Zone I, Sector D, of the Secret Army. This section was rather unique in the Secret Army for several reasons. Originally, it was not organized as a Secret Army unit at all. Rather, it was the personal creation of its Commandant, Émile Nerinckx, who remained the driving force behind its activities throughout the war. In his soul, Nerinckx was a patriot in the same sense that Arthur Abeels was. He was a sergeant in the reserve of the Belgian Army's medical corps, but he was not in active service when the Germans invaded Belgium in May 1940. Shortly after the capitulation, Nerinckx decided to create his own Resistance army in the area around Soignies-Enghien, and he began recruiting volunteers. Among the earliest volunteers were Gustav Culot, Albert Degauquier, and Guy Andrieux, who would serve as his lieutenants. Both Culot and Degauquier were veterans of the First World War, and Culot had been wounded sixteen times in that war. By August of 1941, the three had already recruited about 200 volunteers. This fact brought the force to the attention of the (then) Belgian Legion, which contacted him in October. Recognizing that he had a viable Resistance movement, the Belgian Legion asked him to join forces, and appointed him as the head of their command group at Soignies.[10]

However, in the first years of the war, Nerinckx ran his force in a rather independent fashion. He saw his duty as working for the liberation of Belgium, not necessarily as working for any particular organization. Therefore, he did not limit his activities to working for the Belgian Legion. Nerinckx's force was an important source of information to the intelligence services *Zéro* and *Marc*. He had direct links with the British SOE that were independent of the Belgian Legion. It appears that he supplied intelligence to and engaged in acts of sabotage in support of Group G. In fact, Nerinckx operated so independently of the Belgian Legion in the early days that in 1942 the Independence Front approached him to ask if he would bring his Resistance force into their organization. Nerinckx flatly refused their offer. He did not trust the Independence Front because of its links with the Communist Party.[11]

As the links between the government-in-exile and the Belgian Legion improved, the Belgian Legion became the Army of Belgium and ultimately the Secret Army. It became clear that the Secret Army was the official military instrument of the government of Belgium that was on the ground in Belgium. Therefore, Nerinckx began working more formally within the organization. When the Secret Army rearranged its territorial organization at the beginning of 1944, Nerinckx was given command of Sector D of Zone I, with a geographic responsibility covering the area roughly bordered by Enghien, Soignies, Silly, and Brain-le-Comte. Sector D consisted solely of his forces, which he grouped together in one refuge, called *Tarin*. (Tarin is a type of bird that is known as a siskin in English.) The fact that Nerinckx used only one refuge was another reason why his force was unique in the Secret Army. Most sections consisted of several refuges.

The *Refuge Tarin* was also known as the *Maquis de Saint-Marcoult*. Maquis is a French term that loosely translates as scrub or brush. It was a name that Belgian and French Resistance fighters used to describe the Resistance in general and their individual combat units in particular. Members of a *maquis* were called *maquisards*, a label that they wore with pride. Members of Nerinckx's command used the terms *Refuge Tarin* and *Maquis de Saint-Marcoult* interchangeably. The surviving veterans of the unit continue to do so to this day.

It did not take long for Nerinckx to come to the attention of the Gestapo, which actively searched for him throughout the war. On February 7, 1944, Nerinckx narrowly escaped arrest by jumping out of his bedroom window when the Nazis came to the front door to arrest him at 6:00 a.m. However, his number two at the time, Félix Ghislain, was less lucky and was captured. Nerinckx acquired a lot of experience in evading the Nazis, and this became even more important as the Nazis strengthened their grip on Belgium in August. Even the small village where Jerry and Mac were staying was no longer safe, as a fresh round of arrests threatened to compromise Lepoivre's home. Nerinckx agreed to take over responsibility for Jerry and Mac from the Lepoivre family, and they were moved to the home of Gisbert Van Delft in Saint-Marcoult. A few days later, the Gestapo arrested Charles and Sylvie Lepoivre and their children. They were sent to a prison in Mons.[12]

Monsieur and Madame Van Delft were the first people to shelter Jerry when he fell from the sky the previous May. Before the war, Van Delft was a colonial administrator in the Belgian Congo and his official residence was in Kasango in the Congo. He was a convinced Belgian patriot who believed that his country was doing good things in the Congo. Van Delft also owned a chateau-farm in Saint-Marcoult that served as the family home when they were visiting Belgium. As (bad) luck would have it, Van Delft, his wife, and their five children were visiting Belgium in May of 1940 when the Germans invaded. It was impossible for them to return to the Congo, and so the family was forced to spend the rest of the war at their Belgian residence. However, the family considered the Congo to be their real home, and they dreamed of the day when they could return there. In the meantime, Van Delft decided to serve his country in Belgium as he served his country in the Congo. He voluntarily placed his farm at the service of Nerinckx and the Secret Army.[13]

Saint-Marcoult and the Van Delft's chateau-farm were located in an isolated area. In fact, Saint-Marcoult could not even be described as a village at the time. It was a hamlet like Rose, Idaho, where Jerry was born. Only two roads intersect in Saint-Marcoult. One road leads through the hamlet and the other leads from the hamlet to a dead-end in a forest. There was (and is) no particular reason for anyone from outside of the area to go there. The chateau-farm itself was surrounded by fields, which provided an open clearing in the middle of the forest when seen from the air. It was for all of these reasons that Nerinckx decided to establish his headquarters there at the end of 1943. The isolated position of the village meant that his men could come and go without attracting a lot of attention from the Nazis. The farm's fields provided an excellent location for parachute drops. The only downside was that Saint-Marcoult was fewer than 9 miles (15 kilometers) from Soignies, where the Luftwaffe had an airbase. For that reason, London was initially unwilling to approve it as a site for parachute drops. However, Nerinckx eventually persuaded the SOE that the overall advantages of the location more than outweighed that one disadvantage, particularly since the effectiveness of the Luftwaffe was rapidly diminishing in the course of 1944.

Van Delft's chateau-farm became a major source of supplies for the Secret Army. Between March and September of 1944, the SOE parachuted over forty tons of armaments, ammunition, explosives, communications devices and other materials into the fields. These materials were initially stored and sorted in the chateau-farm. They were then transported to other sections of the Secret Army, including refuges that were as far away as Ghent and Bruges. This transport was often done by farmers who hid the armaments under bales of hay or grain in their horse drawn carriages. In one famous incident that the veterans of *Refuge Tarin* still talk about to this day, one of their wagons shipping arms to Mons got stuck in some mud near the village of Masnuy in May of 1944. As the farmer was struggling to free his wagon from the mud, a German patrol passed him on the road. Calmly and coolly, the farmer asked the Germans to help him dislodge his wagon from the mud. The Germans agreed, and they pushed the wagon out of the rut, not realizing that there was a cache of weapons underneath the hay. The farmer went on to deliver his arms to a Secret Army refuge in Mons, thanks to the help of the Germans.

On June 1, 1944, the BBC broadcast the following coded message to *Refuge Tarin: La fondraison des arbres nous cache le vieux moulin*, or "The foliage of the trees hides the old mill." This message was a code to signify that the *Refuge Tarin* was to become the command center of the entire

Zone I of the Secret Army, as it moved into its Phase Two orders. For Commandant Nerinckx, this meant that he and his men were now to provide the headquarters support for the Commandant of Zone I in addition to their normal responsibilities. Originally, the Commandant of Zone I was a Major Leurquin. However, the Nazis arrested Leurquin on July 23, and he perished in the Nazi concentration camp of Neuengamme in January of 1945. His replacement was Colonel, and soon to become General, Vandezande.

Vandezande remained in command of Zone I through the liberation. His authority extended throughout the Provinces of Hainault and Namur, a large geographic area that covered half of Wallonia. Exercising command of an underground army over such a large geographic area in an occupied country was not easy. The Germans could intercept any orders or communications that Vandezande would send to the refuges if he used the telephone, telegraph, radio or post office. So, Nerinckx and his men created an elaborate system of clandestine postal boxes and drop points throughout the zone that they used to deliver Vandezande's orders to the other sections.

Consequently, although Saint-Marcoult looked like a sleepy little hamlet on the surface, beneath that surface it was a fortified military encampment. It was a command headquarters for an entire zone of the Secret Army. It was a center for parachute drops to supply Secret Army refuges across the country. It was also a base from which Nerinckx's own *maquisards* would commit sabotage and combat the Nazis. By August, Nerinckx's command had swollen to over 400 men, who had come from as far away as Brussels, Namur and Dinant. Every home in the tiny hamlet was used to lodge Resistance fighters, or to store arms and ammunition, or to serve as a communications center or meeting point. The citizens of Saint-Marcoult hosted all of this infrastructure at considerable personal risk, under the noses of the Germans with their airbase just 9 miles (15 kilometers) away.

Thanks to Roger, Jerry and Mac were now at the center of this underground military encampment. From the moment that Roger first met Commandant Nerinckx, Roger pleaded with him to allow his American friends to join the Secret Army. Nerinckx was open to the idea, but he wanted to find out what the Americans were all about for himself. Since he was staying with the Van Delft family, putting Jerry and Mac under the same roof would allow him to get to know them. Nerinckx recorded his first impressions of Jerry and Mac. He thought that Jerry was a good man who was serious and mature. Nerinckx noted that everything that Jerry did, he did well and in a self-assured manner. However, Nerinckx noticed that Jerry's eyes were sometimes melancholy. Undoubtedly, these were the moments that he was missing Nora Lee. On the other hand, Nerinckx thought that Mac acted like a big brat and had a character that was as "wild as a young fox." However, he thought that Mac also had an "electrifying laugh" and a sense of humor that charmed him.

As they were talking on the morning that they met, an American bombing mission passed overhead. Jerry, Mac and Nerinckx stepped outside to watch. Nerinckx offered them a cigarette, which Mac accepted but Jerry, of course, refused. As they were watching the various planes fly over, Nerinckx asked Jerry and Mac what they knew about the various aircraft. Learning about the different military airplanes used by Allied and enemy forces was an essential part of their training in gunnery school. So, Jerry and Mac proceeded to give Nerinckx a detailed explanation of the different characteristics of each plane with an analysis of each plane's strengths and vulnerabilities. Nerinckx was impressed. Following lunch, Mac improvised a game of croquet in the courtyard with some items that he found on the farm. He then taught the Belgians how to play the game, and everyone, especially Van Delft's children, had a great time playing. For a moment, Nerinckx thought, Mac had managed to help them forget that there was a war going on.

Jerry with the Van Delft family's children (courtesy DeLoy Larsen).

Over the next two nights, Nerinckx went off on missions. When he returned to the home, Jerry and Mac would welcome him back and badger him with questions about what he had done. However, by now the Nazis were becoming suspicious that not everything was as it seemed in the sleepy area around Saint-Marcoult. They intensified their patrols and surveillance of the area. Collaborators became more active, too, and arrests were made. The Secret Army issued a red alert to be vigilant. Although the precise date is not clear, one evening a messenger was sent to the Van Delft home warning them that they may have been compromised.[14] It was possible that the Gestapo would arrive at any time. Roger, Jerry, and Mac sat together in the *grand salle* (great hall) of the chateau-farm contemplating the situation, while the Van Delfts withdrew to another room to discuss their options.

Commandant Nerinckx returned at around 11:00 p.m. It had been a difficult night and he had evaded several German patrols while tending to his tasks. As he approached the chateau-farm, he noticed that a small ray of light coming out of the window of the *grand salle*. This was highly unusual. Nerinckx silently crept up to the window and peered through a small gap in the shutter. He saw that the light was on and that Jerry, Mac and Roger were sitting in the room. Fortunately however, there were no Germans about. So, he entered the house to find out what was going on. Jerry, Roger, and Mac told him about the messenger, and said that the Germans could arrive at any moment. Nerinckx asked them, "What are you planning to if the Germans arrive?" They replied, "Run away." "Where to?" Nerinckx asked. They answered, "We don't know."

At that moment, Commandant Nerinckx turned to the two Americans and asked them to stand. "From this moment, you are members of the Secret Army. You must obey me blindly and without discussion. You will not return home before the liberation of Belgium. Any misconduct will be punished by execution without trial. You are to swear loyalty to the King, to the flag, and to me." Without hesitation Jerry and Mac raised their arms and said, "We agree, and we so swear." Jerry and Mac were now official members of the Secret Army, Zone I, Sector D, *Refuge Tarin*. Jerry was issued the Secret Army ID number of 112078; Mac's was 112079. Jerry, Roger, and Mac got their wish. All three were now officially brothers-in-arms in the Secret Army.

Nerinckx then spoke to Mme. Van Delft and informed her that he would send a woman later that night to take her and her children to a home where they would be safe. He led Jerry, Roger, Mac, and Monsieur Van Delft to the home of Emile Lemaire, who lived on the edge of the nearby woods. Nerinckx established a temporary headquarters there and found lodging for the other men for the night. The next day, the Germans continued to reinforce their search for the *Maquis de Saint-Marcoult*, and Nerinckx was feeling the enemy's noose grow tighter and tighter. It became too dangerous for the *maquis* to continue to operate from people's homes in the hamlet. Therefore, Nerinckx decided to create a military encampment in the nearby woods. He chose a strategic location literally in the middle of the woods. From this position, sentries could see danger approaching from any side, and the terrain was defensible in the event that the enemy found them and attacked.

Nerinckx decided to build a command post in the woods to house his headquarters and equipment, as well as to provide shelter for the men. Drawing on his colonial experience, Van Delft suggested the construction of a very large Congolese hut like the ones he knew from the forest dwellers of the Congo. The hut would be covered in ferns and other vegetation for camouflage. Nerinckx embraced the idea, and put Van Delft in charge of the construction of the hut. The first task of Jerry and Mac in the *maquis* was to work on the construction of this hut, along with Roger and seven other *maquisards*. There is no doubt that Jerry's experience on the farm in a small rural community in Idaho was very helpful in constructing the hut. For the city boys Mac and Roger, it was a case of on-the-job learning.

Construction occurred primarily at night and was conducted with the utmost secrecy. Particular care had to be taken when felling trees to ensure that the Germans would not hear anything out of the ordinary if a patrol came within listening distance. They also had to also be careful to leave no traces of their work behind should the Germans pass through the woods during the daytime. Van Delft's idea was brilliant. When the hut was finished, it was perfectly camouflaged and indistinguishable from the woods surrounding it.

While they were constructing this hut, Van Delft got to know Jerry rather well. In 1947, he wrote a letter to Nora Lee in which he reminisced about this time he spent with Jerry. In it he said:

> I used to have long chats with Jerry. He loved to talk about you, and his home, about the lovely time you spent together in Florida. One day he showed me some clouds that looked just like the mountains you can see from Pocatello. We used to make plans for when we would visit you in your little farm. Jerry used to get quite excited and say "When I have a car, I'll take you to Yellow Stone Park." He used to tell me about the Indians and their customs, and about his religion. He used to talk a lot about religion. I have never met a young man with such a very pure mind. I often used to think how I would like my boys to grow up like Jerry.[15]

Everyone who knew Jerry spoke about him in such terms.

With his new command post completed, Nerinckx turned the full attention of the *Refuge Tarin* on the preparation for *Jour-J*, the day of the liberation when the Secret Army was to move to Phase Three and engage the Nazis in combat. The SOE accelerated the parachute drops of arms and other supplies to the *Refuge Tarin*, and working on these parachute drops now became the most important task for Jerry, Roger, and Mac. At 7:15 p.m. each night, the BBC would broadcast the coded messages of when and where the parachute drops would be made in Belgium. A message like "*Tarin ouvre la porte*" (or "Siskin open the door") would be an instruction that a drop would be made to the *Refuge Tarin* later that evening. Nerinckx would then have about three hours to assemble a team and prepare the drop zone to receive the supplies. By 11:00 p.m., everything would need to be in place. Armed sentries would be posted in strategic positions around the zone, both to guard against Germans and to keep innocent civilians away. The men who were to recover the materials were to be ready in their positions. One man was posted at each corner of the drop zone. Each prepared a fire so that the four together would form the outline of the letter L when lit, signifying the direction and location of the drop. However, the fires would only be lit at the last moment.

British Lancaster bombers would make the drops, following a circuitous route from England in order to avoid giving away the location of the drop zone to the Germans. A typical route to Saint-Marcoult would see a Lancaster fly southeast from England to Paris, then northeast to Luxembourg, then turn left and fly back west to Saint-Marcoult. When the plane was about eight kilometers from the drop zone, the pilot could communicate directly with Nerinckx or one of his deputies, via the S-phone, a radio communications device whose transmissions were difficult for the Germans to intercept. Nerinckx would give the pilot the coordinates of the point he should travel towards, and warn the pilot about any obstacles or threats that may be present.

When the Lancaster drew within visual distance, Nerinckx would use a battery-operated lamp to send a Morse code signal to the bomber, which would respond with an identical signal. Nerinckx would then give the order to light the fires outlining the drop zone. The Lancaster's bombardier would drop the packages into the box outlined by the fires, and then the pilot would turn north to return to England via the Netherlands. As soon as the packages were dropped, the fires were extinguished while the other men rushed out into the field to collect the packages.

Normally a drop would consist of 12 to 16 large canisters, each weighing about 250 kilograms. The canisters contained a wide variety of objects, such as radio transmitters, grenades, dynamite, detonators, anti-tank weapons, and especially guns, particularly Sten and Brent guns as well as Thompson and Colt submachine guns. Given the weight of the containers, it took several men to move each package into the nearby woods. They put the packages on carts with rubber tires so that they would not make noise as they were moved into the compound in the forest. Meanwhile, another set of men ensured that there were no traces of the fires, packages or parachutes remaining for the Germans to find the next morning. It was always possible that Germans would be able to hear the airplane or see the fires, which made the operation very dangerous. It was indispensible that Nerinckx's team worked as quickly and silently as possible.

At the command post, the packages were then opened and sorted. This was when Jerry and Mac could really lend their expertise to the *Refuge Tarin*. The guns that the SOE dropped were not ready to use. They needed to be assembled, cleaned and prepared for combat. If there is one thing that gunnery school taught Jerry and Mac, it was how to assemble, clean, and prepare a gun for use under any condition. Therefore, Jerry and Mac spent hours of each day in mid–August assembling, cleaning and preparing the guns for their new comrades-in-arms to use on *Jour-J*. It was Nerinckx's special job for them. Jerry, Roger, and Mac also participated in acts of sabotage. The Brussels-Paris, Brussels-Lille, and Soignies-Le Roeulx train lines were favorite targets of the *Refuge Tarin*. The *Refuge* attacked facilities for the construction and repair of railway locomotives and wagons at Enghien, Tubize and Haine-St.-Pierre. Telephone and telegraph lines were likewise frequent targets. Occasionally, *maquisards* from *Refuge Tarin* would encounter German patrols and firefights would ensue. It is not known if Jerry, Roger and Mac participated in any such firefights.

César Van Herreweghen participated in the parachute drops and acts of sabotage with Jerry, Roger and Mac. César was from the village of Labliau. He was eighteen years old at the beginning of 1944 when the Gestapo came to serve his third summons for the labor draft. Like Roger, he chose to become a *réfractaire*. Also like Roger, he initially took refuge in the home of a local teacher who was active in the Secret Army. That teacher arranged for César to join the *Refuge Tarin*. Initially, César's father was unhappy with his son's decision to join the Secret Army. Earlier in the war, the Communist Partisans had assassinated some German soldiers near Labliau, and in retaliation the Nazis executed some innocent civilians from the village.

César's father could not forgive the Partisans for their actions. By that point, it was known that the Nazis were executing civilians in retaliation for the killing of German soldiers, and the Nazis certainly made no secret about the fact that they would do so. César's father could not accept that the act of killing Germans was worth the price in innocent civilian blood. So when César told his father that he was joining the Secret Army, his father made him promise that he would never engage in killing Germans. César kept his promise to his father. However, that did not prevent him from serving as a full member of the Secret Army by participating in parachute drops and sabotage operations.

César Vanherreweghen leaning on the roof of a German automobile captured by the *Maquis de Saint-Marcoult*, May 6, 1944 (the other *maquisards* pictured are unknown) (courtesy Louis Darbé).

César and the other *maquisards* formed some opinions about the characters of Roger, Jerry and Mac. Roger struck them as a patriot and a natural born soldier. Roger was very serious, disciplined, and always followed orders to the letter. Roger was clearly in the *maquis* because he believed in Belgium, and he believed in what they were fighting for. Jerry likewise impressed them as serious, responsible, and dedicated to the cause. Jerry never complained about the tasks he was assigned, even if those tasks involved endless hours of cleaning guns. The *maquisards* were also impressed that Jerry had learned enough French to carry on conversations. Jerry was very open and outgoing and he made a point of trying to converse with them. Mac's French was not as good as Jerry's. He spent most of his time with Roger and Jerry, and did not really reach out to the other members of the *maquis*. He was friendly enough, but he just didn't interact much. Mac also made no secret of the fact that he grew bored from time to time when cleaning and assembling guns became monotonous and boring.

In the evenings, the three musketeers would get together and talk about home, the Abeels home that is. Messages and notes could be exchanged between the young men and the Abeels via intermediaries. At one point, Arthur and Clémy were even able to send their boys a package containing some sweets and a "bottle for Mac, with something special." In turn, their now three sons wrote notes back to the family. Jerry wrote a note to Jenny in both English and French that said:

> Dear Jenine [*sic*],
> How are you today my little cousin? I hope you have not been bothered lately by any troublesome boys. Please tell your mom, pop, and your aunt hello for me. I am getting along quite good. I have missed you lately. Perhaps we will have a chance to see you again soon.
> Your Cousin,
> J.S.[16]

One evening, while Jerry, Mac and Roger were listening to a radio show featuring Jack Benny, Gary Cooper, Bing Crosby, and Glenn Miller, Mac wrote to Jenny:

> Dearest Pugnose!
> Roger, Jerry and I are sitting here listening to the radio. I guess the music makes the three of us rather homesick but we enjoy the music very much. Honey we miss you very much, but will be seeing you again soon. Say hello to mother, dad, auntie, and Janine be a good girl.
> Love and many kisses,
> Forever and always
> Mac[17]

When he was in a contemplative mood on August 24, Roger wrote a letter to his parents that he left with Nerinckx with instructions to deliver the note in the event that he were to be killed in action. The note said:

My Dear Mother and My Dear Father,
    We have just learned that we are going to leave on a mission. I hope that I will have the luck that I have enjoyed until now. If something bad happens to me, do not let it trouble you too much. Do not think of me as selfish. I love both of you tenderly. If my outward appearance is sometimes rude, at the center of my heart I adore you. I thank you again for everything that you have done for me until now. I am sorry if I have caused you any problems. Every time I did so, I regretted it. Think of me as a soldier. I only do my duty and I am happy to be able to. Above all else think of me as happy. You would have maybe better understood and accepted it if I had gone to battle in a uniform. Know well that a uniform does not protect against the bullets of the enemy. Be courageous. I am happy to not be an only child. Give the love that you give to me to my dear Phatty. I only ask one thing; that you will make sure that all of the traitors are punished. That is my only political wish. I die so that Belgium can become bigger and stronger. Do not laugh. These are not words said in vain, for me, that is the reality. Have courage, my dear parents. Think about Janine. Do not blame me. I send you the tender love that only a son can send.
    Long live the King!
    Roger[18]

At the same time, he wrote this note to his sister:

My Dear Little Janine,
    I love you very much more than you know. I wish that you will be very happy later on. As the good patriot that you have always been, and if you one day have children raise them to love their country and their King. I die for an ideal. You already know that. Know that the causes for which we die do not die. I love you very much.
    Your Brother,
    Roger[19]

One day later, on August 25, the Allied armies liberated Paris. It was now only a matter of days before the Allies would enter Belgium. The Secret Army was ordered to finalize their preparations for combat. *Jour-J* was at hand. Commandant Nerinckx organized his *maquis* into combat teams. Jerry, Mac, and Roger were placed in a team under the command of Captain André Brent. The other members of the team were Richard Decroës, Ghislain Duhainaut, Jean Colin, and Father Venquier, a priest who belonged to the Secret Army. César was also formally a member of this team, although everyone knew that he would sit out the combat when the day came in order to honor his promise to his father.

Then another American fell unexpectedly from the sky. On September 1, Lt. Frank A. Forsyth, Sr. of the USAAF 359th Fighter Squadron, 356th Fighter Group, was flying a P-47 Thunderbolt when he spotted a German ammunition train not far from Saint-Marcoult. Frank's nickname was "Fearless Fosdick" and, living up to that name, he moved in close and strafed the train, causing the ammunition to explode. Unfortunately, Frank was too close and the explosion heavily damaged his plane and forced him to crash land near Saint-Marcoult. A person named Frank Weiland found him and brought him to his home. The next day, he took Forsyth to the *Refuge Tarin*. There he met his fellow countrymen Jerry and Mac. It must have been a surprising turn of events for all of the Americans involved. Forsyth was the first American that Jerry and Mac had encountered in months, and they were probably happy for the taste of home. Forsyth was impressed with the decision of Jerry and Mac to join the Secret Army and carry on the war. Forsyth decided that he wanted to fight with the underground, too. Unlike Jerry and Mac, Forsyth never officially joined the Secret Army. However, Captain Brent allowed him to come along with his team when they went into combat the next day.

On Sunday, September 3, 1944, the Nazis were in full retreat across Belgium. The long-awaited *Jour-J* had arrived. Commandant Nerinckx ordered Captain Brent's team to go to the village of Marcq-Les-Enghien and take up positions along the *Chaussée d'Ath*, a major road connecting the city of Ath with Brussels in a southwest to northeast direction. The Germans would undoubtedly use this road for their retreat toward Brussels. Captain Brent's orders were to attack and to try to capture any Germans they encountered on this road. As expected, César asked to be excused from the operation in deference to his father. However, Forsyth asked to go along. Captain Brent and the eight men under his command departed for Marcq by bicycle.[20]

The team approached the village of Marcq on a small street called the *rue de Petits Marais* that intersects the *Chaussée d'Ath*. Just before that intersection, the bicycle of either Jerry or Roger developed a mechanical problem. It is not clear whose bicycle developed the trouble or exactly what the issue was. However, Jerry and Roger stopped to fix the bicycle while the others went ahead. Captain Brent and the other members of his team made a right turn onto the *Chaussée d'Ath* and took up their positions without Jerry and Roger on the southeast side of the road near a school. It was about 1:15 p.m.

From where Jerry and Roger were standing on the *rue de Petits Marais*, they could see the *Chaussée d'Ath* directly in front of them. However, the *Café Blanche* and some other buildings at the intersection obstructed their view of any traffic traveling along the *Chaussée d'Ath* approaching the intersection from the left. As Jerry and Roger were working on the bicycle, they saw a slow-moving German vehicle with officers on board pass in front of them on the *Chaussée d'Ath* in the direction of Brussels. They did not think about what they should do. This was the moment they had been waiting, training, and hoping for. It was their chance to strike back at the hated Nazis and bring Belgium one step closer to liberation. Jerry and Roger instinctively grabbed their submachine guns and opened fire.

The decision proved to be a mistake. What Jerry and Roger could not see from where they were standing was that this was the lead vehicle of a column of about 300 SS men. The vehicle containing the officers continued down the road, but a detachment of the Nazis that were following that lead vehicle came running around the corner. They were determined to hunt down and kill whomever had opened fire on their officers.

Jerry and Roger immediately knew that they were in trouble and badly outnumbered. Like a pair of rabbits pursued by a pack of dogs, they ran a short distance back down the street from where they had come with the Nazis chasing them. Bullets pockmarked the pavement around them as the Nazis opened fire on the run. Fortunately, a small road, the *rue Rouge*, appeared on the left. Jerry and Roger turned into it, temporarily taking them out of the aim of the deadly fire.

They both knew that the Nazis would follow them and that they would be shot in the back if they continued to run. Surrender was not an option, as they both also knew that the Nazis would show no mercy. Without discussing the issue, they decided to make a stand. Nearby was a farmhouse with a rabbit hutch that would provide some cover. They jumped to the ground, and using the wall of the hutch to protect their backs, they positioned themselves for their final defense. As the SS men rounded the corner in pursuit, Jerry and Roger opened fire. Bullets flew in both directions as the home of the bewildered and terrified rabbits became a battleground. If Jerry and Roger felt the same way, they did not show it. They remained calm and cool as they fired their submachine guns, determined to defend themselves as long as their ammunition lasted.

The well-armed and battle-hardened Nazis surrounded the rabbit hutch. One of them crept in close enough to throw a grenade into Jerry and Roger's defensive position. The grenade exploded, sending shrapnel into Roger's back and into Jerry's head and neck. Life slipped away from their bodies as they lay together side-by-side, guns still in hand. The blood of Jerry and Roger mingled as it flowed into the soil of a Belgium that would soon be free.

• 9 •

Farewell

As they turned onto the *Chaussée d'Ath,* Captain Brent's team came across some local citizens who warned them that there were still Germans in the school a short distance away. Eager to attack Germans, the team headed down the road toward the school. They reached an abandoned house just before the school when they heard vehicles coming down the road behind them. It was a column of the hated SS. The team dropped their bicycles on the side of the road. Brent, Decroës, and Duhainaut went into the abandoned house to take up their positions. Colin jumped behind the hedge in front of it. Mac and Forsyth went behind the wall of the adjacent garden. Farther Venquier, with a .45-caliber gun in his hand but wearing his cassock, took up a position on the side that would help protect the others from being outflanked. Although he would not personally participate in the attack, he stood ready to defend the others in a counterattack.[1]

As the first vehicle drew close, Colin saw that it contained three German officers and a driver. Although Colin and the other members of Brent's team did not know this, it was the same car that Jerry and Roger had fired on a few minutes before. Colin and the men in the abandoned house opened fire, hitting the officer in the front seat. The car continued for a few more meters before reaching the garden wall. Mac and Frank leaned over the wall and fired their submachine guns into the car, killing all of the occupants. The team continued to fire at the German trucks that followed the lead car, and the Germans returned fire. Brent's men managed to disable one of the trucks with a grenade. However, the Germans kept coming and the ones who were in the school opened fire on the *maquisards* as well. Brent realized that they would quickly be outnumbered and overrun, and he gave the order to retreat. The team withdrew out of the back of the house and the garden. They jumped over a fence and ran across a field before they found a ditch where they could take cover. The Germans chose not to pursue them. They had already lost time hunting down Jerry and Roger and they were apparently worried about getting out of the way of the approaching British Army.

Captain Brent and his men remained in the ditch for about a half hour after the gunfire of the Germans stopped, but everything was quiet. They then walked back to the *Chaussée d'Ath*, arriving just as the British army was entering the village. The liberation had arrived. Mac and Forsyth talked to the commander of the first British tank in the column. The commander allowed them to jump on board, and they got a free trip back to Brussels riding on the front of a British tank. Neither Mac nor anyone else in Brent's team was aware at the time of what had happened to Jerry and Roger.

Gustav Van Meus was a teacher at the nearby school. He witnessed Jerry and Roger's initial exchange of gunfire with the Nazis near the intersection, and he saw them run down the *rue de Petits Marais*. After the German column had left the village, he walked down that street to find out what happened to them. When he came to the *rue Rouge*, he found Edouard Vandercappelen and Alphonse Smoes standing next to Vandercappelen's rabbit hutch. Vandercappelen and Smoes had witnessed Jerry and Roger's final stand from their homes, and they were now staring at the two lifeless bodies. They reported that the Nazis had rifled through their clothes and taken everything of value.[2]

Van Meus brought the two bodies to his school and put them in his classroom. He cleaned the bodies as best he could, and he put bandages on the wounds to collect the blood. He called the Red Cross. By now, news of what happened to Jerry and Roger had spread through the village. Captain Brent and his other team members came to the school and identified the remains. Around 5:00 p.m., a Red Cross ambulance arrived and took the bodies to the hospital at Enghien. Mac was still on the way to Brussels, and he had no idea that his two friends were dead.

In 1944, embalming was not widely practiced in Belgium and the Enghien hospital had nothing like a modern morgue. It was necessary to bury the bodies quickly, even if the bodies would soon need to be exhumed and moved. To prepare a body for transport in Belgium in those days, it was first put inside of a coffin made of zinc, and then the zinc coffin was placed inside of a wooden coffin for aesthetic reasons. The authorities in Enghien knew that Roger was Belgian and they assumed that his family would come to claim the body. So, they put him in the zinc coffin first, and then put the zinc coffin in a wooden coffin. However, Jerry was an American, and the authorities in Enghien had no idea what the Americans would do with him. They did know that the British tended to leave their war dead in the cemeteries where they were initially buried, and so the authorities guessed that the Americans would do the same. Since zinc coffins were more expensive, they decided to place Jerry directly in a wooden coffin.[3]

Before the burial in Enghien the next morning, a small ceremony for Jerry and Roger was held. By now, Van Delft had heard the news about Jerry and Roger and he came to Enghien for the ceremony. He later wrote to Nora Lee: "I shall never forget that terrible morning, when I knelt beside his body and kissed him on the forehead for his wife and mother. He looked so very peaceful, and had a slight smile on his lips. I felt quite sure that his soul was in heaven already."[4]

That same day, Mac brought Forsyth to the Abeels home to introduce him. Mac, Forsyth and the Abeels still did not know about what had happened to Jerry and Roger. Everyone assumed that they were still alive and with the other members of the *Refuge Tarin*. Mac told the Abeels about their experiences in the *maquis* and their combat with the Nazis in glowing terms. Since everyone expected Jerry and Roger to return at any time, Mac and Forsyth decided to spend the night at the Abeels home to wait for them. In the meantime, Odette informed the Abeels family that the USAAF and the RAF had set up an office at the *Hôtel Metropole* in Brussels to register the American and British airmen who had been in hiding in Belgium. She said that Jerry and Mac would have to report there as soon as possible. There was still no news about Jerry and Roger on Tuesday morning, so Mac and Forsyth decided to go to the *Hôtel Metropole* without him. Jenny led them to the hotel and expected to bring them back home that afternoon. However, the USAAF wanted to debrief them, and they required Mac and Forsyth to spend the night there. Jenny went home without them.[5]

A couple of representatives of the Belgian Red Cross arrived at the Abeels home at around 7:00 p.m. that evening. When Arthur and Clémy opened the door for them, they immediately knew that something must be terribly wrong, and their hearts began to sink. They invited the Red Cross officials into the house, and they learned about what happened to their two sons. To say that they were devastated would be an understatement. Arthur and Clémy had lost two sons and Jenny had lost two brothers. The reality was just too much to take, and everyone melted in tears and hysterical grief. It was impossible for anyone in the family to sleep that evening.

The next morning, Mac arrived in his new USAAF uniform, still unaware of what happened to Jerry and Roger. Arthur informed him, and Mac's immediate reaction was one of disbelief. The magnitude of what Arthur was saying was just too great. Mac argued that there must have been some kind of mistake. After all, Mac was in Marcq and he took part in the combat. He knew that no one from Captain Brent's team had died. So, Arthur and Mac decided to go to the Red Cross's offices on the *Chaussée de Vleurgat* to confirm if the news was really true. As had become the practice during the war, the Red Cross posted a list outside of the office of those who they could confirm to be deceased. There, in black and white, stood the names Roger Abeels and Gerald Sorensen. The news was true. With their last ray of hope crushed, they went inside to get the details about where Jerry and Roger were buried.

At some point that day, Arthur turned to Mac and asked him to avenge the deaths of Jerry and Roger. Mac pledged that he would, and he apparently fulfilled his promise to Arthur. He wrote the following in a letter to Nora Lee in 1947, "Nora Lee I can truly say that their deaths were avenged to the utmost. I'd rather not go through the details of it, but should we ever meet, I promise that you will know and realize to the fullest extent how for him vengeance was carried out."[6] No one alive today knows what Mac did to avenge their deaths. Whatever it was that Mac did, the event must have occurred at some time over the next seven days.

On Thursday afternoon, Arthur, Mac, Forsyth, and an American journalist whom Mac had met went to Enghien to arrange to bring the bodies home. Jacques Wathoz, the mayor of Ganshoren and a personal friend of Roger's, accompanied them to help smooth any bureaucratic problems that might arise with the local authorities. There were no such problems. The bodies were disinterred on Friday morning. Jerry's wooden coffin was placed inside of a zinc coffin for transport, and then inside of another wooden coffin for aesthetics. It was therefore much larger than Roger's coffin. An American flag was draped over Jerry's coffin and a Belgian flag was draped over Roger's. The bodies were loaded into two hearses, and a few members of the Secret Army joined them for the trip back to the Abeels home in Ganshoren. A priest came to the house to bless the coffins after they arrived. By now, the news of the tragedy was spreading, and flowers were arriving at the Abeels home. On Saturday, the bodies of Jerry and Roger laid in repose in the Abeels home. Friends, relatives, veterans, and members of the public came to pay their respects and give their condolences.

The burial was scheduled for 3:00 p.m. on Sunday, September 10. By now, everyone in Ganshoren was aware of what had happened, and the occasion became a moment of great patriotic outpouring as well as grief. Jerry and Roger left the Abeels home for the last time that day at 2:30 p.m., and they were taken to the cemetery in a grand procession. The chief of police of Ganshoren led the procession followed by policemen, resistance fighters, and youth associations of Ganshoren. All carried wreaths, flowers, and other tokens of respect for the grave. Roger's hearse followed. His coffin was covered with the Belgian flag. On top of the flag was a cross, an arrangement of white flowers with a ribbon that said "Papa, Maman," and a cushion made of the same flowers with a ribbon that read: *A mon cher frère, Janine* (To my dear brother, Janine). Members of the Secret Army and the Independence Front formed an honor guard surrounding the hearse. Mac, Forsyth and an army captain representing the American military followed Roger's hearse, and behind them was the hearse containing Jerry's body. His coffin was draped with an American flag. On top of the flag were the same cross and flowers as on Roger's coffin. However, the inscriptions on the ribbons of the flowers were a little different. The ribbon on the flowers from Arthur and Clémy said "Pa, Ma," and the ribbon on the little cushion said "To My Dear American Brother, Jenny." Members of the Secret Army likewise formed an honor guard surrounding Jerry's hearse. Arthur, Clémy and Jenny walked sullenly behind Jerry's hearse, followed by other relatives. Behind the family came the mayor and city council members of Ganshoren. They were followed by delegations from the Red Cross, the Ganshoren Veterans Association, other patriotic organizations, Roger's fencing club, and finally the general public.

When the procession arrived at the cemetery, Roger's coffin was brought in first, followed by Jerry's. A bugler played "Last Post," the Belgian equivalent of "Taps," and then everyone entered the small cemetery. Once everyone was assembled at the graves, the coffins were lowered into the ground and soldiers of the Secret Army fired a twenty-one rifle volley salute. Mac and Forsyth participated in the firing of the salute. Mayor Wauthoz, and a Lt. Poelman, who represented the Belgian military, gave speeches in honor of Jerry and Roger. As was the practice in Belgium, Arthur, Clémy, and Jenny each threw a flower into the grave, as did Mac and Forsyth. The ceremony was over. When the five of them returned to the Abeels home, they found it very, very empty.

On Monday, the family went with Mac and Forsyth into the city where they met up with Pompon. Despite their grief, they tried to do some sightseeing for the benefit of Mac and Forsyth, and they visited Saint Michael's Cathedral as well as the Grand Place. Jenny used her French to help Forsyth with some business he needed to do at Lloyd's Bank. Forsyth then went to the *Hôtel Metropole*, where he had been ordered to check in. Meanwhile

Mac and Jenny went to the *Hôtel Bedford*, which the U.S. Army was occupying. Mac and Jenny had realized that Nora Lee and the Sorensens had probably had no news about Jerry since he was reported as missing in action. They met with an American colonel and told him the whole story. The colonel promised to contact Jerry's family and tell them what had happened.

On Tuesday, September 12, a funeral mass was held in the National Basilica for Roger. Since Jerry was a Mormon, it was not officially a mass for him. However, Jerry was honored at the mass, and for those in attendance it felt like a religious service for both. The Abeels had a friend named Georgette who was a relatively famous singer in Belgium, and she sang at the mass. Georgette was young, attractive, and had a beautiful voice. Mac noticed all three things. After the mass, the Abeels and Mac walked over to the cemetery. Clémy took the ribbons from the flowers that had been left at Jerry's grave. She handed them to Mac, and asked him to deliver them to Jerry's family. Mac said that he would do so. That evening Mac spent his last night at the Abeels home, at least in 1944. The USAAF had told Mac and Forsyth that they were leaving for England the next day.

Jenny took Mac and Forsyth to the *Hôtel Metropole* the next morning. Mac and Forsyth had said that they would be busy in the morning, but that

The coffins of Jerry and Roger just before departure for the cemetery (courtesy Jenny Abeels).

they would be free at lunchtime. So, Arthur and Clémy came downtown so that they could all share a going-away lunch together. Madame Van Delft also came to Brussels for the occasion. At some point that day, Mac took Jenny off to the side. He told her how much he really liked her, but that he had a girlfriend at home. He said that if he got home and found out that

Mac and Jenny in downtown Brussels on September 5, 1944 (courtesy Jenny Abeels).

his girlfriend had been unfaithful, he would come back to Belgium for Jenny. It is hard to say what Mac's intentions were in saying such a thing. Given his sense of humor, he may have intended it as a joke. However, for a teenage girl, this was heavy stuff. Jenny had a wild crush on Mac, and this lit a flame of hope in the candle of her secret dreams. In any event, Jenny did not mention the conversation to her parents.

At 2:15 p.m., the Abeels walked with Mac and Forsyth to the *Hôtel Metropole*, and they said their goodbyes. Mac and Forsyth were supposed to leave that afternoon for England with a group of twenty other aviators. After the Abeels returned home that afternoon, they heard a plane pass overhead. They imagined it to be Mac and Forsyth on their way to England. However, something very strange happened that night. At about 10:00 p.m., the doorbell rang. It was Mac and Forsyth. Mac said that he wanted to hear Georgette sing one more time. So, Jenny took them to Georgette's home, and she sang "Ave Maria" for them. It was now 11:00 p.m., and Mac and Forsyth said that they had to get back to the *Hôtel Metropole*. They said goodbye again, and left. This time it really was goodbye.

It was a strange time for the Abeels family. On the one hand, they were drowning in grief over the loss of Jerry and Roger, as well as the departure of Mac. On the other hand, they were now free of the Nazis, and all three young men had played a role in their liberation. For both reasons, they passed their time over the next few weeks attending the various patriotic ceremonies and commemorative events that were now taking place throughout the city.

During one of these days, Arthur and Jenny passed a group of German POWs who were being held in a courtyard behind a fence. Arthur was smoking a cigarette, and they stopped to look at the prisoners. Arthur simply looked at them in silence, while Jenny began to say insulting things about them in French. One of the Germans made a gesture to Arthur to ask for a cigarette. Arthur and the German soldier spoke for a moment in German. Arthur handed him a cigarette through the fence and struck a match to light it. Jenny was furious with her father. The Germans had destroyed her country and murdered her two brothers. She screamed at him, "How could you do such a thing for a *Boche*?" Arthur looked at Jenny and simply said, "I was once a prisoner, too."[7]

While all of this was taking place, Nora Lee was unaware of where her husband was or what had happened to him. She was living with Jerry's parents in Tyhee, where she had remained following her marriage.[8] It was there that she received on May 16 the dreaded Western Union telegram announcing that Jerry was missing in action. Outside of some correspondence with the Army's Quartermasters Corps concerning Jerry's personal effects, she had heard nothing more since May. On November 4, 1944, a letter arrived from a Lt. Harold Cherniss of the U.S. Army. Cherniss was writing in a personal capacity, not an official one, and was undoubtedly acting upon the promise that the American colonel had made to Jenny and Mac at the *Hôtel Bedford* in Brussels in September. The letter from Cherniss informed Nora Lee about what had happened to Jerry. It told her about his experience with the Abeels family, his service in the Secret Army, and how he died. It also gave her Mac's address; by now he was back in Flint, Michigan. Nora Lee was in shock. The Army had not yet officially informed her of Jerry's death, and the letter from Cherniss was the first news that she had had.

Three days later, Nora Lee wrote to Mac asking for information about Jerry's last days and his friendship with the Abeels family. Mac apparently replied rather quickly, and told her all about the Abeels family. Although she knew her husband was dead from her correspondence with Mac and Cherniss, she had still not received official notification from the Army about it. So, on November 16, she wrote to the Army asking for additional information and inquiring about the remainder of his personal effects. She then decided to return to her parents' home in Texas, and she resolved to get in contact with the Abeels family.[9]

Contacting Nora Lee was also the highest priority for the Abeels family. The Abeels had heard so many stories about Nora Lee and Jerry's family that they felt that they knew them personally. However, they recognized that Nora Lee and the Sorensens probably knew nothing about them or the experiences they shared with Jerry in the summer of 1944. The Abeels wanted to tell them everything, but they could not make contact. Although Belgium was liberated in September of 1944, the war in Europe was very much still raging. Thousands of lives would still be lost in Operation Market Garden, the Hürtgen Forest, the Battle of the Bulge, the Alsace, and other bloody contests before Europe would be free. Winning the war remained the Allies' overarching objective, and that objective trumped all others. Civilian mail service, telephone calls, telegraphs and other forms of communication between Europe and America had to wait until the war was over in both Europe and Asia.

In Europe, that day came on May 8, 1945, which was also Jenny's fifteenth birthday. Transatlantic civilian links were partially restored that summer, but it was not until after the surrender of Japan that things began to return to normal. In August of 1945, the Abeels were able to contact Nora Lee by post. They invited her to Belgium for a ceremony to inaugurate a new monument in honor of Jerry and Roger near the place where they were killed in Marcq. Nora Lee wrote the following in response in a letter dated September 1, 1945:

> My Dear Mr. and Mrs. Abeels and Janey [sic],
> I hope that by this time you have received my wire that I could not be present with you on September 3 for the ceremonies which you wrote to me about. I wish very much that I could have been there. It would mean so much to me. However, I shall be thinking of you, and I hope that you will write to me soon and tell me all about it. In order to get transportation to Europe, I had to have authority from the War Department. They would not grant the authority at this time, but it is said that within six months or one year or perhaps even sooner I will be able to travel to Europe. Mother and Dad Sorensen also wish to come to Belgium as soon as they can make arrangements. I hope that we may come at the same time. I have not heard from Mac recently, but I understand that he also wants to return to Belgium. August has been a great month for us here in the U.S.A., as well as for all the whole world, for the war with Japan has ended, and that means that peace has once again returned to us, after so many long bitter years. I believe that we are all more aware than ever before of the brotherhood of man, and I sincerely pray that peace may remain in the world. Then our loved ones shall not have died in vain. You will notice that I now have a new address. My parents have moved to Amarillo and I live with them. I hope to hear from you soon. My greatest desire is to visit with you as soon as possible. I close with my best wishes and love, and with prayers for God's blessing to be yours.
> Sincerely your friend,
> Nora Lee Sorensen[10]

It appears that Nora Lee was quite actively seeking ways to get to Europe in the autumn of 1945. Arthur wrote to Nora Lee on November 21, 1945:

> Dearest Nora,
> It is with a very great pleasure, that we have received your very nice and sweet letter from October 22nd, that we have waited with impatience. It is always a great joy to receive memos from our dear Nora. We have not answered you sooner, because I had not a recent photo of me, and I have made one immediately. All what you ask us, we try to do it, because we will that our very dear Nora be happy. Everyday, we speak of you, and we say: "In a few months, Nora will be here at home." We have lost two sons, and God gave us a daughter, and to Jenny a great and nice sister. You can't understand, dear Nora, how much we love you. You are the dear wife of our beloved Jerry. We have love [sic] him the first day he came at home. We have never met a better boy than him. When he called us Pa and Ma, we were so happy. Roger and Jerry were like brothers together. It is for that rea-

son that they are stayed together [*sic*], and that they died together. It will be a beautiful day for us, when we'll can tell you it yourself [*sic*] Jenny has told you all about the ceremony of November first, and she has said you [*sic*] that we have put the flowers that you prefer for the birthday of our dear Jerry. The graves were so beautiful, and many, many persons have prayed before. We send you, dear Nora, four photos of us, and we hope you will be happy of it. Now, you know us a little better. We have not received memos from Mother and Father Sorensen. We hope that they are all in good health, and you also, like we are. As I am a collectionner of post stamps, may I ask you to keep the stamps that you receive of our letters. Thank you very much. We hope to hear from you again very soon, and we send you, dearest Nora, our love and many kisses. God bless you always.

Your Belgium Papa and Mama

A. Abeels[11]

Jenny carried on a separate set of correspondence with Nora Lee. In a December 1945 letter she wrote:

My Dearest Nora,

Many thanks for your nice letter I receive one week ago. Excuse me, Nora, for not writing quicker, but I was ill when I received it and I am always ill, but getting better. I could not answer you cause I had a stupid eye ache and when I began to write, my eyes made me suffer much. And you? I hope you are enjoying the best of health. My parents have just received your letter and they are answering you. As you want, I'll continue always to send you photos in my letters but sometimes could you not do the same and join some photos of yourself, Jerry, and your family. I know nothing about you except the information by Jerry or by your letters. As you know, I am making an album with all the photos. When you come here you'll see them and the pictures you haven't. When you'll come in Belgium, if you will we'll speak French together and I'm sure that you'll know it quickly. Jerry understood very much of French but it was more difficult for him to speak. I have found after his death, in the bedroom a dictation that Jerry did and it is splendid to see how he already wrote after two months of studied. When you'll come I'll show you all those things. If you knew how many souvenirs we have to tell you or show you. We have all which is ready, there is just one thing we haven't it is "You!" So arrive as soon as you can dear Nora. Sometimes when I think to that "D Day" I believe it will be always a dream … so far. But I hope and pray that it will soon be real and it will be won't it? It is the only thing I wish, to know you and to have you as long as possible at home. My ideal is to be a nurse. My parents don't like that job for me, but I am sure that it will be in nursing the others and in seeing all those human sufferings, I'll no more have time to think at mine. Every night I pray and ask two things: to see you and to be a nurse. In French we say "The prayer is always heard and hearkened to, but the answer makes it sometimes wait a long time or may disconcert." The answer of my first wish I'll wait it for next spring or perhaps before, and the answer of my second is my own

work. I hope that now your brother is again in your home. I think I'll no
more hear about Mac 'cause he doesn't like to write says his wife, except if
one day I go to the U.S.A. Yes, Nora, I should like very much to come once.
It is my second country and a part of my heart is there with you and Jerry's
family, with Mac, and with many others. Now, my dearest Nora, I must
close because my eyes begin to be tired. I wait news from you quickly and
send you much love and kindnesses from ma, pa and myself. May God
always bless you.
  With many affectionate kisses from you adopted sister,
  Jenny[12]

They continued to correspond over the next few months, but the bud-
ding relationship between Nora Lee and the Abeels experienced a small
crisis in the spring of 1946. The United States government caused the crisis,
and the issue was the final disposition of Jerry's remains. American soldiers
and airmen who died during the war were initially buried in temporary
cemeteries near where they fell. Sometimes these were hastily created battlefield cemeteries. Sometimes the graves were in existing civilian cemeteries, like the one in Ganshoren where Jerry was buried. Where a soldier or
airmen was initially buried depended upon the circumstances under which
he perished. Shortly after the war, the U.S. Army Graves Registration Service
began exhuming the remains from these temporary cemeteries, both battlefield and civilian, and consolidating them into larger American military
cemeteries. The families of the deceased were then given a choice. If they
so wished, the remains of their loved ones would be repatriated to America
at the expense of the United States government. Otherwise, the fallen would
be buried in one of the new permanent American military cemeteries
abroad, and cared for in perpetuity by the American Battle Monuments
Commission. In Belgium, there are three American military cemeteries.
The Flanders Field American Cemetery in Waregem contains the graves of
servicemen who were killed in the First World War. Those who perished
in the Second World War are buried in the Ardennes American Cemetery
in Neupré and in the Henri-Chapelle American Cemetery, which bridges
the communities of Welkenraedt, Aubel, and Plombières.

  In April 1946, without prior announcement, the U.S. Graves Registration Service arrived at the Ganshoren cemetery to exhume the body of Jerry
and move it to one of the new American military cemeteries. The Ganshoren cemetery staff alerted Arthur, who left work and rushed to the cemetery. Arthur pleaded with the American major who was in charge of the
project to not exhume the body. He explained the whole story of how Jerry
came to be buried in Ganshoren and he said that Jerry's family wanted the

body to remain where it was. It helped that Arthur spoke English, and that he had enough experience with Americans to say all the right words. The major stopped the exhumation, but he told Arthur that he would need proof that Jerry's family wanted the body to remain there. Arthur asked the major to give him a couple of days. He went immediately to Western Union and sent a telegram to Nora Lee explaining what was happening. He asked Nora Lee to send a return telegram stating that she did not want the body to be moved.[13]

Nora Lee sent the telegram on April 25. In those days, Western Union would call to arrange for delivery of a telegram, and Jenny answered the phone when the call came. When the Western Union employee said that the telegram was from Nora Lee, Jenny asked the man to read her the telegram. She could not wait to know what Nora Lee said. The Western Union employee, who apparently spoke some English, began reading the telegram verbatim. He said, "Family Sorensen requests body..." Jenny slammed down the phone on the man before he had finished talking and she burst into tears. She could not believe that Nora Lee was asking for Jerry to be repatriated! She told her parents, and they all cried. It was a sad night in the Abeels household. The next day Western Union delivered the telegraph itself to Arthur and he read it. What the telegraph actually said was, "Family Sorensen requests body remain Ganshoren." Jenny had over-reacted with the man on the phone who had not had time to finish reading the telegram. For the rest of their lives, Jenny's parents would remind her of this story as an example of what happens when one overreacts.

Arthur took the telegram to the United States Embassy and saw the major. The major agreed not to exhume the body. However, this was only the first stage in what turned into a rather protracted paperwork battle to leave Jerry's remains in Ganshoren. The United States Army did not like the idea of leaving its deceased in isolated graves outside of the American military cemeteries. The reason for that is that the Army knew that the American Battle Monuments Commission would take care of the graves of its dead in perpetuity in the American cemeteries. However, it would be up to the Abeels family and Belgian civilian authorities to take care of Jerry's grave if it remained in Ganshoren. The Army feared that as the war faded in memory, the grave would cease to be cared for, and the Army encouraged Nora Lee to reconsider her decision. Several rounds of paperwork on this issue were exchanged among Nora Lee, Jerry's parents, the Abeels family, the City of Ganshoren, and the United States Army. It was not until January of 1949 that the Army finally agreed to leave Jerry's remains undisturbed.[14]

Shortly after the incident with the American major, Jenny wrote a letter to Nora Lee to reassure her that the grave would be cared for. It said:

> My dearest Nora,
>   I can't tell you how much I thank you from the bottom of my heart. I already imagine the day we'll receive a telegram from Mrs. Nora Sorensen" announcing us: Arrive tomorrow and be in Belgium at.... Yes Nora, I will receive one in two or three months and you, you will send it won't you? On May 1st, there was two years Jerry was fallen in Belgium. I put him lily-of-the-valley. I send you the little branches which has been on his ground, it's no more nice but it has been. On May 8th, I put red roses on the graves. The first of the Season. I also send you two petals. My dearest Nora take courage and hope. We shall ask to the Ambassador of America in Belgium to help you to come this summer. So take patience and you in America continue to hope you will come once in Belgium at GANSHOREN (remember it). Nora I join at this letter another branch of lily of the valley. It is longer than this of Jerry. It is one of myself. I received it on my birthday. It is the flower I prefer. I send it for two reasons: The emblem of this flower is Bracelet (bringing happiness). The signification is the love as flower can speak better than paper. I wish lily of the valley tell you my great love for you. The graves are all recovered of Forget-me-nots and white pansies. I join you a little forget-me-not of Jerry, and I wish that all these flowers will bring a smile on your wonderful face....
>   My respects to all of yours,
>   Jenny[15]

Jenny's prayer finally came true in 1947 when Nora Lee came to Belgium. At the time, Nora Lee was working as a secretary for an attorney in Amarillo named A.O. Ward, and she was receiving a small government pension from Jerry's death. Thus, she had some income. However, the trip to Belgium was much more expensive in relative terms in those days than it is today. More importantly, traveling to Belgium would mean giving up her job, with absolutely no guarantee of finding work when she returned. This fact was important because the demographic forces that allowed Nora Lee to enter the labor market in 1943 were now reversed as millions of young men left military service and rejoined the civilian labor market. Coming to Belgium would mean sacrificing everything she had. However, it was a sacrifice that she both wanted to make, and felt that she had to make. Officially, Nora Lee stated in a letter to the War Department: "I feel that I am obligated to visit Belgium because of the feelings of the Belgian people towards the United States. They feel that the United States was their liberator and the monument and grave of my husband over there is a memorial to them of all the American soldiers who died in Belgium and all over the world. That is what they write to me, and in every letter they ask me to please come as soon as possible." Unofficially, there was another, more personal reason why she knew that she had to make this trip. Nora Lee was still in love with Jerry, and Jerry was in Belgium. She had to say farewell.[16]

At 6:15 a.m. on Monday, January 13, 1947, Nora Lee boarded a train that travelled from Amarillo to Chicago. In Chicago, she changed to a Pacemaker train to New York City and she arrived in the city on Wednesday. She had a few days to spend in New York City before her boat would leave for Europe, and the experience made a real impression on the farm girl from Texas. Nora Lee had lived in New Orleans so she knew what a city was all about, but New Orleans was nothing like New York. From her arrival at the cavernous Grand Central Station to her departure a few days later, Nora Lee used every moment of her time in New York to experience the city. She saw a couple of shows on Broadway, which turned her into a fan of the theater. She visited the Empire State Building, the Statue of Liberty, and the other tourist sights. However, she also saw the less wholesome side of New York when she nearly fell into a trap.

Nora Lee met a young man in New York who said his name was Jerry and who said that he had been in the service, too. She told this new Jerry all about her deceased husband and the purpose of her trip. He seemed sympathetic and respectful, and he offered to show her around the city for a day. Nora Lee thought that he was such a nice man to make such an offer to a heartbroken widow from Texas who was alone in the big city. It was a pleasant enough day. However, when he tried to take her back to his apartment, Nora Lee figured out what this guy was really all about. As a good Christian young woman, she would have nothing to do with it. The man began to get angry about her refusal to go to his apartment, and she ran away from him with her honor intact.

On Sunday, January 19, Nora Lee set sail aboard the *Queen Elizabeth*, which was under the command of Captain Charles M. Ford. She shared a cabin with three other women. One was a fellow war widow and the other two were unmarried. Like New York City, the *Queen Elizabeth* left her with both positive and negative impressions. She wrote:

> The Queen Elizabeth is a very grand ship and beautiful, but I don't like to ride in ships! I did not get very seasick but was nauseated a great part of the time. However, I had a very pleasant trip on the boat. Even before we sailed I met a very nice English girl who had visited three months in Canada with her husband's people. Her husband also is killed. We found a couple of Yankee wolves and fed them a terrific line—all in fun. They helped the days pass more quickly for us. There was a movie each day and music in the "Winter Garden" by the orchestra each evening and afternoon. The ship had

good food, but after the second day it became tasteless. However, I ate every meal except two breakfasts when I would rather sleep. Thursday night as we were entering the harbor at Southampton everyone went on the deck and sang together—English, American, Canadian, and all. There were many English people aboard and I liked them very much.

Nora Lee arrived in England on Friday morning, but she did not have time for sightseeing. She was supposed to take a plane to Belgium that evening. Upon arrival, she took a bus from Southampton to London, and then a taxi to the Victoria Station. This was a mistake, because what she really needed was the Victoria Air Terminal, which was not located any where near Victoria Station. After several hours of confusion and running from place to place, she finally arrived at the Victoria Air Terminal at 5:30 p.m. for her 7:05 p.m. flight, only to learn that it had been cancelled because of bad weather. There was a silver lining to the cloud because it allowed her to spend a night in a hotel room in London and get a good night's sleep on solid ground.

On Saturday morning, Nora Lee was able to board a flight to Brussels. It was the first time in her life that she had ever been on an airplane, and it was a beautiful experience. There were no clouds in the sky. England was covered in snow, but Belgium looked beautiful in the sunshine. She realized then why Jerry loved flying so much. She arrived at 11:42 a.m., and Arthur and Jenny were waiting for her at the National Airport at Haren, just outside of Brussels. Nora Lee wrote in her diary: "Jenny and her Dad met me at the airport with lots of kissing and a huge bouquet of beautiful pink roses. They were all very happy that I am here and shower me with every attention. They treat me as if I were a tiny baby. They don't want me to wish for anything. I will be very spoiled when I come back from Brussels." The Abeels were surprised by the amount of luggage that Nora Lee brought with her. They remarked that it looked as if she was moving to Belgium permanently.

The next day, Nora Lee, Arthur, Clémy, and Jenny visited the graves of Jerry and Roger. Arthur and Clémy invited Georgette the singer and her family over for dinner to meet Nora Lee. They lived across the street from the Abeels and Georgette's parents were good friends of Arthur and Clémy. Georgette herself was twenty-three and Nora Lee had just turned twenty-four. They got along splendidly together. Nora wrote: "The man and wife came first and brought me a nice little bouquet of yellow flowers. Then a little later the beautiful daughter came bringing a large bouquet of red and white tulips. She is a professional singer and she sang several beautiful songs—some English and some French. She has a beautiful and cultured voice…. You can see that I receive many flowers which I like very much. Flowers, singing, and music—they are the things I love—and they are plentiful here." Georgette and her family visited frequently while Nora Lee was there.

Throughout Nora Lee's stay, Clémy went out of the way to make her feel at home. Clémy was always worried about whether or not Nora Lee had enough to eat, and was constantly trying to feed her. Nora Lee's stay in Belgium coincided with an unusually cold winter in Belgium. To keep Nora Lee warm, Clémy prepared hot milk for her every day and a hot water bottle to take to bed at night. Clémy kept her house decorated with fresh flowers the entire time that Nora Lee stayed there.

Arthur ensured that Nora Lee could meet as many people who had known Jerry as possible. In February, Nora Lee fell ill and Arthur fetched the same doctor who had treated Jerry's ankle to come to the house and treat her. Odette came over for dinner in March with Victor Schreyen's widow. They gave Jerry's dog tags to Nora Lee, which the Comet Line had kept. Commandant Nerinckx came to Ganshoren to visit with her, and Mme. Brusselmans came over for dinner along with her husband. Both brought more mementos of Jerry. Bertha Fillée came to the house to meet Nora Lee as well. Arthur also invited Pat Algoet to the house for dinner. Algoet did not know Jerry, but he was a war reporter who had captured film footage of the American crossing of the Rhine at Remagen. Nora Lee found his story to be fascinating.

Nora Lee and Jenny developed an especially close relationship. Jenny volunteered to be Nora Lee's guide for everything. She showed her all of the sights of Brussels, like the Grand Place, the Congress Column, the Royal Palace and Saint Michael's church. Jenny also took her to see the *Mannekin Pis*, but Nora Lee could not really understand what it was all about and why it was so popular. Nora Lee and Jenny took train trips to Antwerp, Ghent, and Bruges, which Nora Lee thought was beautiful. They visited the battlefield of Waterloo together, which Nora Lee described in her diary as thrilling. They went to the *Théâtre Royal de la Monnaie*, and saw a performance of *The Barber of Seville*. Nora Lee had never seen an opera before, but she fell in love with the art form. In fact, Nora Lee fell in love with Belgium. It was all so new and exciting for her.

Jenny was still only seventeen in 1947, so Nora Lee took upon herself the role of Jenny's big sister. Part of that meant helping Jenny mature into a decent and respectable woman. Before she left for the airport to meet Nora Lee for the first time, Jenny had painted her fingernails bright red. Nora Lee thought that it "didn't look quite natural" on Jenny, but she kept quiet about it at first. As she got to know Jenny better, however, she asked Jenny about the bright red nails. Jenny told her that she did it especially for Nora Lee to help her feel at home. Jenny was convinced that all American girls painted their nails that way. Nora Lee corrected her, and that was the end of the bright red nail polish. Once early on during the stay, Jenny offered Nora Lee a cigarette. Jenny said that she knew that American women smoked, and thought it was sophisticated. Nora Lee quickly and very firmly disabused her of both ideas, and rebuked her for even thinking about taking up smoking. For the rest of her life, Jenny never touched a cigarette again. Jenny truly looked up to Nora Lee and internalized everything that she said. Nora Lee was the big sister that Jenny always wanted and her female role model.

The only point of contention during Nora Lee's stay at the Abeels home was religion. The Abeels were Catholic, but they did not go to church often and they did not regularly practice their faith. They believed in God. However, they also believed that the church was a human institution and that humans, not God, developed the precepts of the church. As a Protestant, Nora Lee agreed with that, but the Abeels took the logic one step further. Arthur said that men wrote the Bible, not God, so it must contain errors and human biases. In fact, Arthur summarized his views about religion with one sentence: "Why should we believe in what a man says about God?" Arthur's views on the Bible troubled Nora Lee greatly. Nora Lee was deeply religious and a devout member of the Church of Christ. She could not accept that the Bible was anything but the Word of God. In letters home, she said that she prayed every night for the Abeels to see the truth. However, her discussions with the Abeels family about religion were never heated. Although both sides would present and defend their beliefs, neither side tried to force the other to accept their beliefs. Religion was a point of discussion, not discord, in the relationship.

Nora Lee's primary reason for coming to Belgium was to learn more about her husband's days there and especially to grieve his loss. Each day, Nora Lee and Jenny would visit the graves of Jerry and Roger. Each day, Jenny would share a new story about Jerry, or show Nora Lee a new picture or memento of him. What would have been the third wedding anniversary of Nora Lee and Jerry came on Thursday, March 20. Nora Lee ordered a special plaque to be made to mark the occasion. On the anniversary, she and the Abeels family held a small private ceremony to put the plaque on the cross that marks Jerry's grave. The plaque is still there to this day. It reads, "In Loving Remembrance, Nora Lee and Ma Sorensen."

Ten days later, the community of Ganshoren organized a special commemorative event in Nora Lee's honor. A procession formed at the town hall. Led by the police, it included the mayor, aldermen, and town council officials of Ganshoren, representatives of the Secret Army and various veterans' organizations, and Major Bouhon and Lt. Col. Moore, who represented the United States Embassy. It stopped at the Abeels home where the mayor invited Nora Lee and the Abeels family to join the procession. They proceeded on to the cemetery.

At the graves, Joseph Perreboom, the mayor of Ganshoren, gave a speech in honor of Jerry and Roger. A priest from the Basilica and a Belgian military chaplain offered prayers. A representative of the Belgian military posthumously awarded to Jerry and Roger the *Croix de Guerre*, a Belgian military honor for those who distinguished themselves in acts of heroism. Roger's medal was pinned to Arthur's chest. Jerry's medal was pinned on Nora Lee. The assembled dignitaries and patriotic organizations laid wreaths and flowers at the graves, and a bugler played "Last Post." The procession then re-formed and moved to the city's community center, where the city hosted a banquet in honor of Nora Lee.

During the banquet, Mayor Perreboom declared Jerry and Nora Lee honorary citizens of the community of Ganshoren. The mayor also announced that the town council had decided to rename one of Ganshoren's streets, *rue Sergent Sorensen*, or Sergeant Sorensen Street, and that another street would be renamed *rue Roger Abeels*, or Roger Abeels Street. Col. Cuvelier, representing the Secret Army, posthumously awarded Jerry and Roger the Medal of the Armed Resistance, which was awarded to all veterans of the Resistance. Major van den Stichelen, representing the National Federation of Veterans, posthumously awarded Jerry the Cross of the National Federation of Combatants of Belgium. Jerry's medals were pinned on Nora Lee, next to the *Croix de Guerre*. The banquet lasted for the entire afternoon. Clémy put on a brave face throughout it all, but when she got home, she broke into uncontrollable tears.[17]

About one month later, on the morning of April 27, Nora Lee and Jenny boarded a train for Enghien. Commandant Nerinckx met them at the train station and took them to Marcq-lez-Enghien, the village where Roger and Jerry had died. They went to the village school near where Jerry and Roger had encountered the German column. Nora Lee met the Lepoivre family, who had sheltered Jerry, and Monsieur Fourmanoir who had sheltered Roger. The Van Delft family wanted to be present as well, but they were now back in their home in the Congo and it was not possible. However, they did send a letter to Nora Lee to mark the occasion. Commandant Ner-inckx escorted Nora Lee and Jenny into a large room that was filled to capacity with representatives of the Belgian government, the armed forces, the Secret Army, various patriotic and civil organizations, and ordinary private citizens from the local community. The mayor declared Nora Lee an honorary citizen of Marcq-lez-Enghien. Then Commandant Nerinckx gave a speech in which he said the following:

> Sorensen, a young aviator who fell to the soil of Belgium after accomplish-ing his mission above Germany, found that his duty to the world was not yet finished, voluntarily and officially joined the Secret Army. With his young Belgian comrade Roger Abeels, who had sheltered him from the claws of the enemy, he led the dangerous life of a Resistance Fighter. Together, they fervently worked to prepare for our deliverance. Together the two fought vigorously side-by-side together, and it is side-by-side that they fell and touched death, with the same peaceful smile of someone who had died at peace knowing that they accomplished their duty. Our task is to guard the precious heritage of these heroes if we do not want patriotism to perish. That is the only real wealth of a country.

Commandant Nerinckx presented Nora Lee with a small oak box containing soil from the ground where Jerry was killed, and a piece of a parachute embroidered with the symbol of the Secret Army. The parachute from which that piece of cloth had been cut had been used by the British to drop sup-plies to the *Refuge Tarin*. Commandant Nerinckx gave the same gifts to Jenny in honor of Roger.[18]

Following that ceremony, the assembly left the school in a procession. School children led the procession, followed by veterans of the Secret Army and other patriotic organizations. They led Nora Lee and Jenny to the place where Jerry and Roger had made their last stand and died together. Nora Lee and Jenny both placed flowers on the spot. They then proceeded a short distance away to a nearby crossroads where a monument to the Secret Army had been erected in 1945. The monument is inscribed with the names of Jerry and Roger, as well as a third member of the *Refuge Tarin* who was killed on a different occasion. The assembled dignitaries and civic organ-izations laid wreaths at the monument and "Last Post" was played. Follow-ing the ceremony, the veterans of the *Refuge Tarin* hosted a reception and a lunch in Nora Lee's honor, and she received flowers. When the day was over, Commandant Nerinckx took Nora Lee and Jenny back to the train station.

The longer that Nora Lee remained in Belgium, the more she knew that she belonged in Belgium. In fact, Nora Lee loved living in Belgium so

Jenny and Nora Lee at the ceremony in Marcq-lez-Enghien (courtesy Louis Darbé).

much that she decided that she wanted to stay there. It was so different than the life she knew in Texas, and there were so many more things to do in Belgium that she could not do at home, like go to the opera. She now felt that she was part of the Abeels family, and her beloved husband was buried nearby. Nora Lee did not want to leave all of that behind, and she began looking for a job to support herself in Belgium. She went to the United States Embassy to see if they would hire her. However, the embassy said that they needed people who spoke French, and Nora Lee did not. Although she had

Nora Lee wearing the medals awarded to her husband (courtesy DeLoy Larsen).

learned some French from Jenny, it was not nearly enough to work in a professional environment. She heard the same message over and over again at other places where she looked for employment.[19]

Over the month of May, reality set in. Although Arthur and Clémy made it clear that Nora Lee could remain in their home, the fact was that she had already been living there for four months. She knew that she was doing little financially to support the family, and this bothered her. Her mother was sending a constant stream of letters asking her when she was coming home. Jerry's mother was writing, too, and had invited Nora Lee to visit her in Idaho. In her heart she wanted to stay in Belgium, but her mind told her that she would have to return to America and put her life back together. If nothing else, Nora Lee understood the meaning of the word responsibility. If she could not support herself in Belgium, she would have to support herself in America. She decided to do the responsible thing and return home.

Before she did so, there was one last patriotic duty in honor of Jerry to attend to. Nora Lee had already received the Purple Heart that the United States of America had posthumously awarded to Jerry. At the ceremony in Ganshoren in March, she accepted in Jerry's name the Belgian *Croix de Guerre*, the Medal of the Armed Resistance, and the Cross of the National Federation of Combatants of Belgium. At some point during Nora Lee's stay, Jerry was also posthumously awarded the Commemorative Medal of the War, which was given to everyone who served the cause of Belgian freedom and unity during the war. One last award awaited. On May 28, Nora Lee was ushered into the office of Belgian Minister of Defense, Raoul de Fraiteur. In the name of Charles, Regent of the Kingdom of Belgium, de Fraiteur posthumously promoted Jerry to the rank of Commander in the Order of Leopold II, with gold palm. This is the medal that is awarded for meritorious service by the sovereign of Belgium as a token of the sovereign's personal good will. This means that Jerry's sacrifice for Belgium had even reached the attention of the acting king, who was personally moved enough by the story to honor him.[20]

On Wednesday, June 4, Arthur, Clémy and Jenny took Nora Lee to the airport at Haren. They said their tearful goodbyes. Jenny hoped that the separation would be only temporary, but Nora Lee knew better. She boarded a Douglas DC-4 airliner that belonged to the Belgian national airline Sabena and flew to New York City. It was a historic occasion. She was on the very first commercial transatlantic flight ever between Belgium and the United States. In January, Nora Lee had arrived in Europe on a ship, and in June she left for America on an airplane. Nora Lee and the world were entering a new era.

• 10 •

The Legacy

The new era was one about moving on and building a better life for one's children. Jerry's generation had fought and won the Second World War. This was an accomplishment with far-reaching consequences, and one of which they could be proud. But those who served in the war were not interested in celebrating victory. Rather, they wanted to celebrate the peace and security that this victory had brought them. They wanted to raise families, pursue their careers, serve their communities, and live to the fullest the lives they had so recently risked. Some members of that generation tried to move on by forgetting about the war. Others found a place for it by remembering the lessons they learned. Still others never recovered and were haunted by the war for the rest of their lives. The people who knew Jerry in his brief life fell into all three categories.

The Crew of the Wolverine

All of the members of the crew of the *Wolverine* returned to America after the war except Jerry. However, some had an easier trip home than others. Lt. George Smith and Sgt. Lester Hutchinson had it the "easiest." The Comet Line sheltered them in a number of safe houses from May to August of 1944. Unlike Jerry's experience in which he could stay with one family for a long period of time, periodic betrayals and arrests required the Comet Line to move Lt. Smith and Sgt. Hutchinson often. However, the Comet Line was always one step ahead of the Gestapo in their cases, and kept them both safe from the Nazis. Both were still safe when the liberation came. Lt. Smith and Sgt. Hutchinson reported to the *Hôtel Metropole* in September as Mac had done, and they returned to active duty in the USAAF.[1]

After bailing out of the *Wolverine*, Lt. James MacConnell, Sgt. Vito Champa, Sgt. John Glass and Sgt. Otto Stange were quickly captured by the Germans. They were sent to Stalag Luft IV in Gross-Tychow in Pomerania,

191

which at the time was part of Germany but is now in Poland. Members of Group G initially sheltered Sgt. Smith, then turned him over to the Comet Line. However, on July 14 he was passed on to another escape line, and at some point after that the Nazis took him prisoner. He, too, ended up at Stalag Luft IV.[2] The conditions at Stalag Luft IV were horrible. The basics of human hygiene like toilets and showers were inadequate. Food was scarce, and Red Cross packages were not delivered as they should have been. In short, Stalag Luft IV did not meet the standards for the treatment of POWs that Germany was obligated to meet under international law. It was not much different from a concentration camp.[3]

As the Soviet Red Army was bearing down on the camp in early 1945, the Nazis decided to close it and move the prisoners to the interior of Germany. On February 6, the Nazis started the prisoners on what would become a ninety-day forced march in the middle of winter, which was also one of the coldest winters in the twentieth century. They slept in the open on the march, regardless of winter weather conditions. Their already meager food rations were cut dramatically, resulting in starvation. The prisoners were subjected to beatings if they failed to keep up with the others, and in some cases, they were simply bayoneted. After two months of forced marches in these conditions, the POWs arrived at Fallingbostel.

However, by then the American army was closing in from the west. After only ten days at Fallingbostel, the Nazis marched the POWs back out of the camp and toward the east, the direction from which they had come. The starvation and physical toil of the previous two months left the POWs so weak that they could only walk fewer than five miles (eight kilometers) per day. On May 2, the British Army found the emaciated prisoners near the city of Lauenburg on the Elbe River. They had walked over 500 miles (800 kilometers) over three months. Fortunately, Lt. MacConnell and Sgts. Champa, Glass, Smith, and Stange had survived the ordeal. They returned home at the end of the war and did their best to put it all behind them.

Lt. Eugene Dingledine and Lt. Denuncio Street also had a difficult trip home. Like Jerry, Dingledine and Street were recovered by the Comet Line after they were shot down, and they initially stayed with some of the same families that Jerry did. As was the case with Jerry, the Comet Line was able to find a relatively stable place for them to spend most of the summer. In June, they were lodged with Jean-Louis Meysmans, who had a farm near the village of Opwyck. They spent the rest of the summer with Meysmans and became close to the family. However, at the very end of August, just before the liberation, the Flemish collaborator and SS Captain Robert Vebelen and his *Veiligheidskorps* raided the Meysmans farm. They arrested ten people, including Dingledine and Street. All were beaten, and Verbelen himself personally tortured Dingledine and Street. Verbelen then sent Dingledine and Street to the Nazi concentration camp at Buchenwald, where they remained until they were liberated by elements of the American Third Army in April of 1945.[4]

When the Allies reached Belgium in September, Verbelen and his men in the *Veiligheidskorps* fled to Germany. Verbelen regarded this as only a temporary setback, and he did not believe that the war was over. In Germany, Verbelen set up a police battalion of fellow Flemish SS men who had also fled Belgium. He intended to use this force to re-establish Nazi control of the Belgian population after the reconquest of Belgium. To reward Verbelen's initiative, Himmler appointed him the head of the police of the fascist government-in-exile of Flanders that the Nazis had set up in Germany. Of course, the concepts of a fascist government-in-exile and a Nazi reconquest of Belgium were self-delusions. However, the fact that Verbelen believed that these delusions were plausible is a testament to the depth to which he clung to his belief in the Nazi cause at that time. As the Allies liberated Germany from the Nazis and the war drew to a close, Verbelen fled to Austria.

In the end Verbelen proved to be an amazing opportunist. During the Allied occupation of Austria, he offered his services to the United States Army's Counter Intelligence Corps, and the American government employed him as a spy for the next eleven years. He identified former Nazi colleagues who might potentially undermine the American occupation. He also helped identify individuals who were working for the communists. He must have performed his tasks well. Verbelen claimed that when the Americans withdrew from Austria in 1955, they offered to take him to America and grant him citizenship. However, he preferred to remain in Austria. By then, Verbelen had well-placed friends in the Austrian government. He applied for Austrian citizenship and the request was granted. However, while all of this was taking place in Austria, Verbelen was a wanted war criminal in Belgium. The Belgian judiciary tried him *in absentia* in 1947. He was convicted of sixty-seven charges and sentenced to death. When the Belgian government learned that Verbelen was living in Austria, the government asked for his extradition to face justice back home. However, by then Verbelen was an Austrian citizen and the Austrian judiciary refused to turn him over to Belgium.

In January of 1984, the *New York Times* broke the story of Verbelen's Nazi past and his links with the United States government. The story was picked up in February by NBC television news, which interviewed Dingledine. Dingledine told the reporter about what Verbelen had done to him and Street, and their plight even reached the attention of the United States Senate, which investigated the story in a hearing. Although a small political tempest was unleashed, nothing ever resulted from the investigations. Verbelen was never brought to justice for his deeds, and he spent the rest of his days living in peace in Austria. Unfortunately, the story of Verbelen was not unique.

The strategic necessities of the Cold War led the American government to hire other Nazis with blood on their hands. For example, Wernher von Braun, the primary developer of the V-2 rocket for the Nazis, knew that his weapon was constructed with slave labor, and even twice visited the Dora concentration camp where it was made. So cruel were the working conditions at Dora that more people died in building the V-2 than were killed by the weapon itself. Von Braun did not care about the slave labor, and he even believed it to be expedient to the cause. However, that did not stop the American government from bringing von Braun to America after the war. The logic was that it was better for the United States to put von Braun's engineering talents to use for themselves, rather than allow him fall into the hands of the Soviet Union. Von Braun later led the development of the Saturn rocket that took the astronauts to the moon.[5]

The Cold War was filled with such compromises, which if not moral, were at least comprehensible in the circumstances of the times. However, the logic of the Cold War never impressed the victims of the Nazis like Dingledine. In his television interview, Dingledine said that he could never understand why the United States government would employ a man like Verbelen.

The same year as this interview was broadcast, Dingledine came to Belgium. He stayed with the Meysmans family and visited with the Lepoivre family. He visited the monument in honor of Jerry and Roger in Marcq-les-Enghien that lies near the spot where they were killed. Although there is no documentary record of this, he probably visited Jerry's grave in Ganshoren as well. As for Lt. Street, he used the GI bill to attend Harvard Law School. Street met Nora Lee in New York City in 1947 when she returned from her trip to Belgium, and she learned a great deal about Jerry's experiences during the war.[6]

The *Wolverine* itself landed on its belly in Lanquesaint with most of the bomber exposed above the ground. The Nazis carried off parts of it and Belgian civilians took the rest, looking for scrap metal and parts. Fragmentary evidence of the bomber was found in October 2010.[7]

After the war, the USAAF asked the crewmembers of the *Wolverine* to complete a questionnaire to explain what they knew about Jerry's fate. All of them had learned about what Jerry had done, and all were impressed with the decision that he had made to join the Belgian Resistance. As one crewmember wrote, "Sorensen died because he firmly believed in what we were fighting for. He would rather fight with the Belgians than to return home in safety. Only those who knew him can understand this."[8]

The Maquis de Saint-Marcoult

Following the liberation of Belgium, Commandant Émile Nerinckx was not finished with the war. He organized a company of volunteers from Enghien to serve with the American Army in the clearance of the Siegfried Line and in occupation duty in Germany. He then returned to civil life as a commercial agent after the war was over. Ironically, the man who had survived so many clandestine engagements without a scratch and who had so successfully evaded capture and certain death at the hands of the Nazis ultimately met a violent death. He and wife were killed in a traffic accident on the *Chaussée d'Enghien* at Saintes (Tubize) on January 27, 966.[9]

The veterans of the Secret Army's *Refuge Tarin* with whom Jerry had fought formed themselves into a *Fraternelle* or association to keep in contact with each other and to keep the memory of their deeds alive. They gather each year on the weekend closest to September 3 at the monument in Marcq-les-Enghien to hold a small ceremony in honor of Roger, Jerry, and Armand Vanderschueren, another *maquisard* who was killed on a different occasion. They lay flowers at the monument. They play both the U.S. and Belgian national anthems, as well as the *Chant des Partisans*, which was adopted as the anthem of all Resistance fighters. By tradition, the most senior of the surviving members of the *Refuge Tarin* is the president of the association, and the president gives a small speech at the ceremony. In September of 2009, the president was Max Robert. The mayor of Enghien is often present for the ceremony, as are other city officials. After the ceremony, they go to a nearby home where the City of Enghien offers the veterans, their families, and their friends a small aperitif. They then retire to a restaurant for a lunch that lasts all day long and during which they reminisce.

Each year, the number of veterans dwindles as old age takes its toll. In 2014, there were only three left: Léon Allard, Maurice Leclerq and César Van Herreweghen. Maurice Leclerq and his wife live in Saint-Marcoult in a farmhouse that overlooks what was the Van Delft's chateau-farm, the same house where he lived during the war. Every day he sees the field where the SOE dropped its supplies to the *maquis*, and the woods where Commandant Nerinckx established his headquarters in the Congolese hut. César Van Herreweghen is the youngest of the four surviving veterans. In October of 1944, he joined up with the American Army, and he participated in the crossing of the Rhine at Remagan. César is the guardian of the original flag of the *Refuge Tarin*, which he proudly carries when he represents the *Refuge Tarin* at official commemorations.[10]

Although the veterans are passing away, their children and increasingly their grandchildren are keeping the Veterans' Association of the *Refuge Tarin* alive. After Max Robert passed away in 2010, the surviving veterans asked Bernard Deherder, a son of one of the deceased veterans, to take on the mantle of president. He agreed, and he pledged to reach out to young people to teach them about the deeds of the Secret Army. In 2013, a small museum in honor of the Belgian Resistance was opened in the former church of the village of Saint-Marcoult. The memory of the *Refuge Tarin* and their ceremony at the monument in Marcq will outlive the remaining veterans.[11]

The Comet Line

The United States Army liberated the founder of the Comet Line, Andrée de Jongh, from the Mauthausen concentration camp in 1945. She was awarded several American, Belgian, British, and French military honors and was made an honorary lieutenant colonel in the Belgian Army. However, Dédée was not one to stop serving the cause of humanity and rest on her laurels. She spent the rest of her adult life after the war working in leper hospitals in the Congo and in Ethiopia. She eventually retired to Brussels, and was elevated to the status of Countess in 1985. She passed away in 2007 and was buried with full military honors in the presence of British and American officials.[12]

Anne Brusselmans moved to Canada after the war. She was made a Member of the British Empire and was awarded the Medal of Freedom with Silver Palm by U.S. General Dwight D. Eisenhower. She published her diary that she had kept during the war, which her daughter re-released in 2001.[13]

No one in Belgium today who was associated with Jerry's story is sure what happened to Odette Gryspiert. Her father's electronics store and home have long since disappeared. Jenny Abeels believed that Odette married an English aviator whom she had sheltered during the war and that she then moved to England.

After their arrest on August 11, 1944, the Lepoivre family was sent first to a prison in Mons, and then to the prison of Saint Gilles, one of the nineteen communities of Brussels. On September 2, they were packed aboard what would become known as the "Phantom Train." At that moment, the Allies were rapidly approaching Brussels. Everyone knew the British would be in Brussels the next day, or the day after at the latest. So, the Nazis tried to ship one last trainload of prisoners to the concentration camps in the east. However, employees of the Belgian railroad conspired to ensure that the train would never leave Belgium. The Nazis packed 1,500 men, women, and children into cattle cars, only to find that the train's locomotive would not function. A few hours passed as a new locomotive was found and attached to the train, but by then the engineer had gone missing. He was home sick, and escaped arrest by having a doctor vouch for the story. It took the railway authorities a while to find another engineer. When they finally did so, that new replacement engineer had an accident on the way to the station that delayed his trip to work. By the time the replacement engineer arrived, the train was over six hours behind schedule.

The train began to move but it soon developed engine problems because the steam engine had not been filled with enough water. It appears that the station in Brussels had run out of water, or at least that's what the Germans were told. The engineer told the German guards that he would take the train to Mechelen, north of Brussels, to fill up with water. The engineer knew full well that the water pump at Mechelen was broken, but the Germans did not know that and they agreed with his plan. It took the train eight hours to travel the 20 kilometers (13 miles) to Mechelen. The engineer blamed the slow speed on the lack of water, which he said forced him to stop frequently to avoid overheating the locomotive. There was no water at Mechelen, of course, but the railway employees at that station pretended to be surprised that the pump did not work and pretended to try to fix it.

At 5:00 a.m. the next morning, with the British now only hours away, the frustrated Germans ordered the train to return to Brussels. When they got back to Brussels, they arrived at a train station that was crowded with people. The engineer jumped out of the locomotive, and disappeared into the crowd. The British were now just outside of the city, and no one could be found who could drive the train. So, the Germans decided to escape before the British arrived, and they left without their prisoners. Thanks to the delaying tactics of the employees of the Belgian railway, the phantom train never left Belgium. They saved the lives of 1,500 civilians, including the Lepoivre family.[14]

Two other families that had sheltered Jerry were not so fortunate. Victor Schreyen was arrested the day before Jerry moved into the Abeels home. For two months, the Gestapo questioned and tortured him. However, it appears that Schreyen never revealed any information that compromised the Comet Line, as no one else was arrested as a result of his capture. In August of 1944, the Gestapo sent him to the Buchenwald concentration camp in Germany, where he died about a month before the camp was liberated. Schreyen was twenty-eight years old.[15]

A collaborator denounced Gilbert Tedesco and his wife Elise, who had sheltered Jerry in May. On June 22, 1944, the Gestapo arrested them along with two British airmen they were sheltering. In addition to serving as a safe house for the Comet Line, Tedesco was a section chief for the Independence Front. The Nazis found arms and clandestine newspapers at his home. He was tortured and eventually murdered at the Fort Breendonk concentration camp in Belgium. Elise was sent to the Ravensbruck concentration camp in Germany and then to the Sachsenhausen concentration camp outside of Berlin. At Sachsenhausen, she was unspeakably abused. She was alive but in a horrible condition when the camp was liberated. She died of the wounds she had suffered at the camp in July of 1945, two months after the war had ended. Gilbert was thirty-six years old. Elise was twenty-nine.[16]

The Sorensen Family

Jerry was Ephraim's only son and Ephraim needed help on the farm when Jerry left for the service. He invited Kenneth Whyte, who had just married his niece Evelyn, to come to Tyhee to manage the farm with him. (This was the same Evelyn who had been the maid of honor in Jerry's wedding.) However, it was always Ephraim's dream that Jerry would take over the family farm when he returned from the war. Nora Lee stayed with Ephraim and Louella after her wedding with Jerry, and they got to know her well. Her employer, Western Union, allowed her to work in Salt Lake

City that summer. From Salt Lake City, she maintained regular contact with Jerry's family. Ephraim knew that Nora Lee would be a great mother for his grandchildren. The future looked bright.[17]

Those dreams were shattered on the day that the letter from Lt. Cherniss arrived announcing Jerry's death. Making matters even worse, Ephraim and Louella's daughter Thora died in childbirth five months later. Ephraim was a man of deep faith. He knew that these deaths were God's will, and his faith taught him that his family would be reunited after death. Although this consoled him, it did not change the fact that he had lost his only son and a daughter, and that his dreams for the future were shattered. Ephraim decided to give up farming altogether, and he went to work as a field representative of the Bannock County Agricultural Extension Service. He left the care of the farm to Kenneth and Evelyn. He gave them one-half of everything that was produced on the farm, which was a generous deal by the standards of the day.

In September of 1946, Ephraim entered the hospital complaining of a digestive problem. It turned out to be appendicitis. While the doctors were operating to remove the appendix, they found a hard lump in his stomach. Apparently, Ephraim had swallowed a fish bone years before that had become stuck in his stomach lining. His body had built a cyst around it. The doctors removed the cyst at the same time that they removed the appendix. Ephraim seemed to be recovering well. However, one day while he was recovering in the hospital, he got up to go to the bathroom and just fell over dead. The doctors said it was a blood clot. However, Louella suspected that there may have been a deeper reason. In correspondence with the U.S. Army concerning the final resting place of her son's remains, Louella wrote, "My son died on September 3, 1944. My daughter on March 23, 1945, and my husband on Oct. 3, 1946 with a broken heart."[18]

It was Louella whose heart was broken. In the space of two years, she had lost her only son, a daughter, and her husband. It is hard to imagine how hard this must have been to take. Like her husband, Louella was a devout member of the LDS Church. She drew her strength from her faith, believing that God must have had some higher purpose in all of this tragedy and knowing that her family would be reunited in the afterlife. But faith doesn't pay the bills when you still have a have a thirteen-year-old daughter at home. She did her best to make ends meet, working at odd jobs where she could with the help of the family. She eventually met and married William Lorenzo Green. However, this was a marriage of economic necessity, not romance, and Green knew that too. Louella was sealed to Ephraim.

Louella died on November 11, 1956, and was buried next to Ephraim in the cemetery in Groveland, Idaho.

Jerry's sister Aletta and her husband Leo Larsen owned a farm in Groveland. They raised a family of ten children: Donald, DeLoy, Claudette, Henry, Gwen, Sandra, Gerald, Jeanette, Dianne, and Sharon. Their seventh child Gerald was born two months after Jerry died and was named after him. Aletta and Leo have forty-seven grandchildren, 113 great-grandchildren and two great-great-grandchildren. Leo died in 1974, and Aletta passed away in 2003.

Jerry's sister Thora was married to George Facer, also a farmer. They had one daughter, Sharlene, before Thora died in childbirth with their second child, who did not survive either. Sharlene would go on to give Thora three grandchildren and two great-grandchildren, although Thora never knew them. Incidentally, Facer remarried a woman named Melba Hokanson, a school teacher who lived in the basement apartment of Ephraim and Louella's home. Jerry's sister Shirley married Hugh Hatch, who was also a farmer. Sadly, Shirley suffered from diabetes and was not even forty years old when she passed away. However, she and Hugh had three children together, and those three children produced five grandchildren.

Darwin, Jerry's cousin and best friend while he was growing up in Rose, moved to Salt Lake City. He spent thirty-nine years as a firefighter for the city. He was happily married to Ruth Schrader, and they raised a family of five children. Darwin worked hard to support his family, and sometimes worked a second job to ensure that his family enjoyed the standard of living that he wanted them to have. Ruth in turn devoted her life to raising their children. Their children gave Darwin and Ruth twenty grandchildren and thirty-eight great-grandchildren. Ruth passed away on December 27, 2003, with Darwin at her side. Darwin lives in a retirement community near Salt Lake City.

Darwin's younger sister Evelyn and her husband Kenneth stayed on Ephraim's farm in Tyhee until 1949. They then moved to Groveland, where Kenneth farmed for awhile, and at the same time they owned a sewing machine and fabric store, called "Sewfari." Ken later went to work as the secretary-manager for the Eastern Idaho State Fair, while Evelyn ran a kindergarten out of their home. Having had enough of the Idaho winters, they moved to Phoenix, Arizona, in 1969, where Kenneth went into the real estate business. Kenneth and Evelyn have devoted much of their lives to the LDS church. Kenneth served as a bishop in the Groveland area and was a sealer in the Mesa Arizona Temple. They had five children, fourteen grandchildren and twenty great-grandchildren. Kenneth passed away in 2012, and Evelyn still lives in Phoenix, Arizona.

All of Jerry's family members remain actively involved and influenced by the teachings of the Church of Jesus Christ of Latter-Day Saints. They are all proud of Jerry, and Jerry would certainly be proud of them.

Mac

Mac never came to terms with what happened in the summer of 1944. On the surface, he was proud of his service in the Secret Army, and he liked to talk about it. He even gave an interview to a Flint newspaper that hyped his story into something that bears little relationship to the reality that he experienced. However, beneath that bravado was a tortured man who blamed himself for the deaths of Jerry and Roger. He believed that if only he had stayed with Jerry and Roger to help with the bicycle on the day that they were killed, everything would have been all right. Of course, nothing could be further from the truth. Jerry and Roger were badly outnumbered by the Nazis when they made their final stand. If Mac had stayed with them, there would have been three dead young men that day instead of two. Although everyone who knew Mac tried to convince him of that fact, and although he, too, probably accepted the logic of the argument in his mind, in his heart he did not believe it. He blamed himself for not being there at the moment of combat. He blamed himself for living while his friends died.[19]

In December of 1944, Mac returned to Michigan. He married Irma Kiss on December 30 at the Sacred Heart Church in Flint. It was Christmas-time, and the church was richly decorated. It was a storybook romantic wedding, with the proud war hero in uniform and the blushing bride in white. Unfortunately, the marriage itself did not live up to the promise of the ceremony. After he left active duty, Mac joined the Reserves of the U.S. Army Air Forces, which soon became the United States Air Force. Mac functioned well enough when he was doing his military service with the Reserves. However, he had difficulties holding jobs in the civilian world, and he was frequently depressed. Today, we can surmise that Mac was suffering from Post Traumatic Stress Disorder. In 1945, no one had ever heard of that. By Mac's own accounts, he was a war hero, and to the outside world he looked fine. Inside of himself, Mac was tortured. His condition took its toll on the marriage and he and Irma were divorced in 1947.

Mac and Nora Lee were corresponding with each other at that time.

He decided that he wanted to visit Belgium like Nora Lee had done. However, he did not have the money for the trip. Thinking that it would help Mac recover and get over the war, his mother and other members of the family scraped the money together to send him to Belgium. He made the trip in the spring of 1948, and Arthur and Clémy warmly welcomed him as a son returning home. As with Nora Lee's visit the year before, Arthur and Clémy went out of their way to make Mac feel at home and loved. They showed him the historic and cultural sites of Belgium. They introduced him to people they knew, and reintroduced him to people he knew during the war.

However, it was obvious that Mac did not have the same enthusiasm that Nora Lee had for meeting people and for learning about Belgium's historic and cultural treasures. Mac came to Belgium looking for something else, namely Jerry and Roger. He visited the cemetery almost daily. He visited Marcq and the places he, Jerry, and Roger had fought together. Unlike Nora Lee's visit to Belgium, Mac did not visit those places in order to reconnect with people he knew or to attend ceremonies of remembrance. Mac's visits were the visits of a man looking for ghosts and for answers to questions that could not be answered. Unfortunately, the trip did little or nothing to alleviate the guilt that Mac felt.

However, the visit did have one unintended consequence. When Mac was living in the Abeels home in the summer of 1944, Jenny had a very obvious crush on him, and Mac was a natural-born flirt. However, at that time Jenny was fourteen, and Mac was twenty. Both were under the very watchful eyes of Arthur, Clémy, Roger, and Jerry. Jenny's crush on Mac remained just a teenage crush, and Mac just enjoyed the attention. However, by 1948, Jenny had matured into an eligible eighteen-year-old woman. Mac was single again, and he remained a flirt. Romance between the two blossomed. It remained all very innocent. Jenny was living with her parents and Mac was staying in their home. Arthur and Clémy ensured that their daughter's honor remained intact. Nevertheless, Jenny fell deeply in love with him.

It is difficult to discern what Mac's feelings were for Jenny. On the one hand, pictures from that visit show a Mac who seemed happy in Belgium. The pictures also show Jenny and Mac as a happy couple, and his notes to her are dotted with terms of endearment. Mac's sister Lorena once told Jenny that when Mac was in America, all he would talk about was how much better life was in Belgium and how much he missed Jenny. On the other hand, when he was actually in Belgium with Jenny in 1948, all he wanted to talk about was how much better everything was in America, and how much he missed the people back home. Mac did not know what he wanted. The fact that Jenny was so closely associated with the traumatic events in his life may well have caused this ambivalence.

In a letter to Nora Lee written shortly after his visit in 1948, Mac said that all Jenny wanted to do was to talk about the war. He said that he had had enough of it.[20] However, although he said that he did not want to talk about the war, it was clear to everybody that Mac was still living in the war. After staying with the Abeels for three months, Mac decided to return to America. He told Jenny that he loved her and that he might one day send for her. However, he also said if he ever met and married someone else instead, he would name his daughter after her. When Jenny kissed Mac goodbye at the airport, something in her heart told her that she would never see Mac again. She was heartbroken.

A year or so later, Mac was at a dance at a convention and conference center in Flint that was called the IMA. He met a woman named Frieda McGill, who was from a small town near Flint. Frieda and Mac started dating and were married in 1950. They set up a home in Davison, which was near Flint. On March 2, 1951, a daughter was born. Mac and Frieda named the baby girl Janine, which was Jenny's original name before the war.

By then, the Korean War was underway, and the United States Air Force needed trained personnel. Mac was still in the reserves, and he was called into active duty. Mac did not want to go to Korea, and he had a very bad feeling about it. When he said goodbye to his mother for the last time, he turned around as he started to leave the house and came back inside. He told his mother, "I know that I am not going to come back. I just feel it."

Mac was assigned to the 13th Bomber Squadron of the 3rd Bomber Wing that was based in Japan. He was now a tail gunner on a B-26 C Invader bomber. On September 2, 1951, the squadron flew from Japan on a night intruder mission. The squadron encountered heavy anti-aircraft fire. Mac's plane was hit, and it crashed in flames. Mac was initially listed as missing in action, and after the war he was declared to be presumed dead. Although his body was never recovered, it is almost certain that Mac died that night. It was almost exactly seven years to the date after Jerry and Roger were killed.

His widow Frieda and their baby daughter Janine went to live with her grandmother. Frieda now had to raise a young child as a single mother in an era when such things were uncommon. Frieda's grandparents were very supportive and took care of Janine while her mother worked. When Janine was six, her mother remarried a man named Raymond Gover, who adopted Janine. Janine Park now lives in Camp Hill, Pennsylvania. In 2009, she learned about Jenny Abeels for the first time, and she corresponded with her namesake.

The Abeels

Arthur and Clémy lost two sons on September 3, 1944. One of those sons was the keeper of the family name, and Arthur's hope for the future. It was Roger who was to follow in his father's footsteps, bring him grandchildren, and carry on the family legacy. All of that was lost now. One day shortly after the war, Arthur and Clémy were talking with a family friend about how horrible they felt about the loss of Roger. In an effort to cheer them, the friend looked at Jenny, who was standing with them and said that they needed to remember that they had a wonderful daughter, too. With Jenny standing next to him, Arthur said, "Janine can never replace Roger." The words cut through Jenny's heart like a dagger. However, they do convey the depth of the loss that Arthur felt.[21]

The ever youthful, cheerful, and playful Clémy that everyone had known also died with Roger and Jerry that day in September of 1944. Clémy became more quiet, serious, and somber, even in her choice of wardrobe. Melancholy cast a shadow over her personality for the rest of her life. She simply was not the same person anymore.

Arthur strove to keep the memory of his sons alive. He remained active in the Ganshoren Veterans Association and other patriotic organizations, where he could commemorate the sacrifice of Roger and Jerry. In 1952, Arthur commissioned a special monument that still lies at the foot of the gravesite of Jerry and Roger. Although Arthur purchased the stone, it was sculpted for free by a friend of Roger who was a member of his fencing club. Arthur and Clémy visited the graves of their sons nearly every day. Arthur passed away in 1970 and was buried between his two sons. After his death, Clémy continued the tradition of visiting the graves daily. Clémy passed away ten years later in 1980. It was Clémy's wish that her body be cremated and her ashes spread.

Of all of the people in this story, Jerry, Roger, and Mac had the greatest personal impact on Jenny. She was too distraught to return to school in the autumn of 1944. When she did return her grades suffered, especially in

Clémy (left) and Jenny (right) at the graves of Jerry and Roger (courtesy Jenny Abeels).

mathematics. Roger had always helped her with her math homework. Without him, she did not know what to do. Although Jenny had wanted to study nursing, Clémy talked her out of it. Clémy convinced Jenny that it would be too sad to work in a profession around people who were sick and dying. Jenny changed her studies to teaching, but she still struggled in school. She was traumatized by her brothers' deaths, and more interested in visiting and caring for their graves than she was in studying.

Of course, Jenny wrote to Mac immediately after the war, but she received a letter back from his wife Irma. Irma wrote that Mac said that he did not like to write much, and so Jenny should not expect much contact. However, Mac and Jenny did begin more regular and direct correspondence after his divorce. Jenny fell hopelessly in love with Mac during his visit in 1948. She would have moved to the U.S. for Mac if he had asked her to. He never did, and she knew that he never would. However, she kept her flame for Mac alive. While other young women her age were going to dances, parties, and dating young men, Jenny stayed at home and spent a lot of time visiting her brothers' graves. As Nora Lee said, "Jenny never married because she was in love with Mac. No other man than Mac would do."[22] Mac stopped corresponding with Jenny again after he met and married Frieda McGill. It was a couple of years after the fact that Jenny learned that Mac had been killed in Korea. It was not until 2009 that she learned that Mac had named a daughter after her.

In the meantime, Jenny herself had changed her own name. At birth, she was christened "Janine Constance Abeels." However, she insisted on being known as Jenny from the moment that Jerry called her that after arriving at her parent's home. About 30 years after the war, she went one step further and had her name legally changed to "Jenny Roger Jerry Abeels," which she was known as for the rest of her life. Jenny claimed that she never liked her given name.

When Jenny finally did enter the labor force, it is not surprising that she looked to the sky for her employment. Roger had wanted to be a pilot. Jerry and Mac were airmen. So, Jenny wanted a job that had something to do with aviation. Her first real job was with the Air Traffic Control Services (Services de Contrôle d'Aérien) at Belgium's military airport in Evere. It was 1953. Jenny was now 23 years old and one of the first group of women to be hired by this service. At the time, radar was still in its infancy and could only detect planes in a two-dimensional sense: its position and direction of travel. It could only imperfectly detect speed and could not detect altitude at all. So, her job involved watching the skies for aircraft coming into the airport and reporting on their positions as a double check of the readings that the controllers received coming from the radar.[23]

It was Expo 58 (the World's Fair in Brussels in 1958) that opened the door to Jenny's ideal job that she would hold for the rest of her professional career. The Belgian national airline, Sabena, was hiring both hostesses for their pavilion at the Expo and stewardesses to staff the flights that were bringing people to the Expo from all over the world. Originally, Jenny was hired as a hostess for the pavilion at the Expo, but her supervisors soon noticed that Jenny spoke excellent English and interacted very well with the English-speaking visitors of the pavilion.

After the Expo, Jenny was offered the job of a stewardess, and she was soon promoted to serving on the transatlantic route. This was a coveted "plum" job among the stewardesses at Sabena, and to land that job meant that Jenny leaped above many other colleagues with more seniority, but whose English was less good. Although the assignment won her no friends among her colleagues at first, she did not mind. She also did not mind the fact that she would have to wait to have a husband. When Jenny began working at Sabena, it was a different era of air travel. Sabena did not allow married women to serve as stewardesses, and a stewardess had to give up her job if she got married. This was not a problem for Jenny. The only man who she ever wanted was the now-deceased Mac. Moreover, working as a stewardess for Sabena was Jenny's dream job that allowed her to visit her beloved America hundreds of times, and to stay in touch with those people who she now considered to be family in America.

Jenny corresponded with Mac's sister Lorena after his death. She also corresponded with Jerry's sister Aletta, and then with Aletta's daughter Claudette. In May of 2001, Claudette and her husband Kent visited Belgium to meet Jenny and visit her uncle's grave. However, Jenny's most intensive efforts to stay in touch were reserved for Nora Lee. Ever since Nora Lee's visit to Belgium in 1948, Jenny considered her a sister. She wrote to Nora Lee often, and sent cards on all of the holidays. Jenny telephoned Nora Lee when she was in the U.S., and she also called Nora Lee from time to time from Belgium, which says a lot in an era when international telephone calls were very expensive. On more than one occasion, Jenny telephoned Nora Lee in the middle of a Texas night. It is likely that those calls were made at the moments when she was missing Nora Lee and Jerry the most, and she simply did not think about the time difference.[24]

In 1968, Nora Lee invited Jenny to visit her in Dumas, Texas. Nora Lee remarried in 1947 and had given birth to three boys. By 1968, the boys were old enough that Nora Lee could travel. Jenny had dreamed of visiting the American "Wild West" ever since Jerry had lived with her family. She had a rather stereotypical vision of what it was all about, forged by the popular media, television and movies. Accompanied by her eldest son, Nora Lee did her best to show Jenny what Jenny had come to Texas for. They took her to see the Palo Duro Canyon near Amarillo, which Jenny mistakenly believed was the Grand Canyon. They took her to the outdoor performance of *Texas*, a show steeped in frontier lore that is still performed in the canyon to this today.

Jenny especially wanted to see an Indian chief, so Nora Lee and her son took Jenny to the Taos Indian Reservation in New Mexico. They found the chief and introduced him to Jenny from Belgium who had travelled from across the ocean to see him. It was a disappointing encounter for Jenny. Jenny had envisioned that she was going to meet a tall muscular man adorned in feathers, war paint, and the traditional clothing of the plains Indians. Instead, the chief was a rather ordinary looking individual, wearing the normal clothing that one would see on the streets of Amarillo.

That aside, Jenny's visit went very well. Nora Lee enjoyed showing her Belgian friend around Texas and New Mexico. Jenny left a charming impression on Nora Lee's husband and children. The only time things became a

Left: **The graves in 1947.** *Top right:* **The graves today.** *Bottom right:* **Jenny laying the AOMDA wreath at the Memorial Day ceremony, May 25, 2009 (left, courtesy Jenny Abeels, and bottom right, courtesy Chris Dickon. Top right photograph by the author).**

little uncomfortable was when Jenny wanted to talk about the war and Jerry. For Nora Lee, life had moved on.[25]

For the rest of her life, Jenny continued to live in the house where she was born and raised, the same house that sheltered Jerry and Mac during the war. It was a virtual museum. Photographs of Jerry, Mac, Nora Lee, Roger, Arthur, and Clémy filled the walls. Cabinets were stuffed full of scrapbooks, photos, and souvenirs of the war. Every award, honor, and certificate that the family received in Roger's honor was proudly displayed. Memories were everywhere. The attic where Roger practiced his gymnastics looked the same in 2011 as it did in 1944, with Roger's gymnastic equipment still in place. Her parents' bedroom likewise looked the same as it did on the day that her mother died in 1980. The dress that Nora Lee wore the day she got engaged and that she gave to Jenny in 1947 hung in one of the closets. The house was frozen in another time and era. As Jenny said, "I live with Roger and Jerry every day." Jenny Abeels never moved on from the tragedy that befell her on September 3, 1944. She passed away alone at home on November 5, 2011, surrounded by her memories.

Nora Lee

When Nora Lee returned to America in June of 1947, her first stop was to visit Louella Sorensen in Pocatello. She told Louella all about what had happened during her trip to Belgium, and what she had learned about Jerry's life there. She showed Louella her photos from the trip, her souvenirs, and the various medals and other honors that she either received personally or posthumously in the name of Jerry. It was obvious that she was proud of Jerry, and that she was still in love with him, despite the fact that he had been dead for almost three years. Louella knew that this was not good for Nora Lee. Nora Lee was still young at twenty-four years old, and had her whole life ahead of her. However, Nora Lee was still looking to the past, and she was still in love with a dead man.

Louella had had more than her own share of recent tragic experiences in life, but her faith encouraged her to move on. The fact that she was Jerry's mother entitled Louella to say the things that Nora Lee needed to hear. It was probably Louella who finally brought Nora Lee to accept that it was time to get on with her life. Being ever responsible, Nora Lee decided to go home to Texas. She gave Louella some items that she received in Belgium, like the medals that Jerry had been posthumously awarded. However, she kept the items that had been given to her as a personal gift, like the piece of parachute that was embroidered with the emblem of the Secret Army. Nora Lee then boarded a Greyhound bus and travelled home to Amarillo, Texas.[26]

Jim Ed Morton was patiently waiting for Nora Lee in Amarillo. Jim Ed was born on September 13, 1925, and he grew up in a farm in Moore County Texas. In 1945, he was drafted into the Army. However, Jim Ed was an only child and his labor was needed on the family farm. The Army granted him a family deferment from service to help with the farm. During the period of this deferment, the war ended so Jim Ed never had to serve. After the war, Jim Ed used to joke with his family and friends that he wanted to marry a rich war widow. One of Jim Ed's cousins took that joke seriously. She knew Nora Lee, who was then teaching Sunday school at the Church of Christ in Amarillo. Jim Ed sat in on one of Nora Lee's Sunday school classes in 1946, and the cousin introduced them afterwards. They began to date.

For Jim Ed, it was love at first sight, but Nora Lee was not yet ready for a relationship. She thought that Jim Ed was a nice man, but her heart was still with her dead husband. When Nora Lee left for Belgium in 1947, she formally broke off the relationship. However, Jim Ed was a patient man. Although it was not easy for him, he understood what Nora Lee was going through. Jim Ed wrote to Nora Lee while she was in Belgium. They were kind letters, ones that reflected empathy and understanding that Nora Lee needed to do what she was doing. Nora Lee was worth waiting for.

When Nora Lee returned to Amarillo from Pocatello, she packed her memories of Jerry into a box and resolved to move on.[27] She and Jim Ed began dating again. This time, she gave the relationship a chance to work, and she, too, was soon in love. Jim Ed and Nora Lee married on November 28, 1947. They bought a house in Dumas, Texas, where Jim Ed was working in a garage. It was a model marriage, and they never had a fight in over sixty years. Jim Ed passed away on October 21, 2011. Nora Lee is still alive today, but she is in a rest home and her health is seriously failing. Nora Lee and Jim Ed had three sons: James E. (Jed) Morton, Jr., born in 1949, Darwin Lewis Morton, born in 1950, and William James (Jones) Morton, born in 1954. Jed served in Vietnam. Jim Ed liked to joke that he succeeded in his goal of marrying a rich widow, since Nora Lee was drawing a government pension of $32.10 per month.

Nora Lee did not talk a lot about her marriage to Jerry, or her experiences during the war. However, the story would surface in bits and pieces from time to time in conversations with her children. She named her second son after Jerry's cousin and childhood friend Darwin. Every now and then, Nora Lee would receive a letter from the Sorensen family. More often, she would receive a letter, card, or telephone call from Jenny. When she had to discipline her children, she would sometimes use some of the French that she picked up while living with the Abeels family.

Jenny's visit to Texas in 1968 briefly brought discussions of the war into the open as Jenny told stories of her wartime experience with Jerry and Nora Lee's postwar visit to Belgium. However, when Jenny went home to Belgium, the stories went home with her. Nora Lee's marriage with Jerry was not a topic of conversation in the Morton home. Only Nora Lee knew about the existence and contents of the box containing her memories of Jerry in the attic, until it surfaced in the summer of 2008 just before a couple of strangers from Belgium came to visit her.[28]

Three hand-painted flags made of wood and suspended from the porch rail greeted the visitors from Belgium as they arrived at the Morton home in August 2008. The first was a flag of the United States of America. The second was a flag of the State of Texas. The third was a flag of the Kingdom of Belgium. Nora Lee had made the flags and hand-painted them shortly after the terrorist attacks against the United States on September 11, 2001. She hung them on the porch as a simple act of patriotism. She did not talk about what she had done, nor did her husband and children ask about it. They did not need to. Everyone understood why Mom did that.

Jerry's Legacy

It is telling that in the wake of the worst attack against America since the Second World War, Nora Lee linked her patriotism for America with a symbol of a small nation in Europe. She did not think too much about it when she did so. In the Second World War, America and Belgium fought together side-by-side against a tyranny that threatened all free and demo-cratic nations in the world. She had lost a husband in that cause. Sixty years later, the free world faced a new form of tyranny. Nora Lee instinctively knew that all free and democratic nations in the world must stand together to defeat this new tyranny, too. She probably also thought about the Nora Lees of today, whose husbands would be called upon to fight that tyranny and who would never return home.

Like the members of the armed forces who defend our freedom today, neither Jerry Sorensen nor Roger Abeels wanted to die. Jerry dreamed of returning to Idaho, owning his own farm, and raising a family with his beloved Nora Lee. Roger dreamed of becoming a pilot, meeting his "Miss Right," and raising a family of his own as his father had raised him. Neither Jerry nor Roger was forced to fight and die either. In 1944, all that Roger was required to do was to hide from the labor draft and wait for the inevitable liberation, like almost all of the other young men in his situation had done. Instead, Roger volunteered for the Secret Army. All that Jerry was required to do in Belgium was wait in hiding until the Allied armies liberated him, like almost all of the other airmen who were sheltered by the Comet Line had done. Instead, Jerry volunteered to join Roger in the Secret Army. Had Jerry and Roger simply done what they were required to do, they might both still be alive today. Instead, both men freely chose to continue the fight for liberty in the Resistance, a decision that ultimately cost them their lives.

Why did they make that decision? Both Jerry and Roger wanted the world that their children would grow up in to be a world where people were free. They wanted a world where citizens chose their leaders. They wanted a world where people would enjoy freedom of speech, freedom of the press, freedom of assembly, and freedom of religion. They wanted a world where people could live their lives and raise their families in peace and security. They wanted a world where all people were equal under the law. In short, they wanted a world for their children that would be like the world that they had known growing up in America and in Belgium before the war. They wanted a world that would look like the one we live in today.

However, the Nazis had annihilated that world in Belgium, and they threatened to do the same to America. Passivity in the face of that threat would mean the continued enslavement of Belgium, and the eventual enslavement of America. Jerry and Roger knew that they had a responsibility to combat the threat to liberty that their countries faced, and not expect others to do it for them. They believed that this is the responsibility of all citizens in a free society. They also believed that this duty transcended national boundaries. For Jerry and Roger, fighting for the liberty of Belgium was fighting for the liberty of America and fighting for the liberty of America was fighting for the liberty of Belgium. They were committed to the principle that all free peoples must stand together when the values that they believe in are threatened. That is why Jerry and Roger died.

The cross that marks Jerry's grave in Ganshoren bears a simple inscription. It reads:

Gerald Sorensen (USA)
Mort Pour La Belgique
1919–1944

In English, *Mort Pour La Belgique* means "Died for Belgium." Attached to this cross is the plaque that Nora Lee placed there on their wedding anniversary in 1947. The cross that marks Roger Abeels' grave likewise carries a simple inscription:

Roger Abeels
Mort Pour La Patrie
1924–1944

Mort Pour La Patrie means "Died for the Country." Between the graves of Jerry and Roger is a third cross, marking the grave of Arthur Abeels, who passed away in 1970. At their feet is a monument that Arthur commissioned for the graves shortly after the war. It bears a picture of Jerry in his U.S. Army Air Forces uniform and a picture of Roger in the uniform of the Secret Army. Between the photos is the emblem of the Secret Army, a lion's head in an inverted triangle. Beneath that emblem is a relief of the *Croix de Guerre*, which both Jerry and Roger were posthumously awarded. The graves lie in a section of the cemetery that is a place of honor, reserved for those who died fighting the Nazis.

The graves tell the story. Roger and Jerry fought together side-by-side, died together side-by-side, and were buried together side-by-side. At their feet are symbols of their comrades-in-arms, the Secret Army, and the recognition of a grateful nation, the *Croix de Guerre*. Between them lies Arthur. He was Roger's natural father and Jerry's adopted father. Arthur's patriotism inspired both young men. The plaque that Nora Lee left on Jerry's headstone states, "In Loving Remembrance, Nora Lee and Ma Sorensen."

The cemetery is now closed to new burials and it is largely neglected. If the gates are unlocked, they creak when opened. Inside are the untended tombs of hundreds of Belgians who passed away years ago and whose memories are largely forgotten. Many of the tombs are overgrown with vegetation. The solitude and stillness of the place are almost overwhelming. The visitor's ears are filled with silence. Yet if one listens with one's heart instead of one's ears, one can hear Jerry and Roger speaking to us today. From their graves, they are calling out to us to remember why they died.

Epilogue

Triumphalism is normal for victors in a war, particularly after a long and bloody war. However, triumphalism can take many forms. After the First World War, it took the form of vengeance. The victorious Allied Powers imposed the Treaty of Versailles on Germany, a treaty that was highly punitive and designed to ensure that the German nation would pay for its perceived crimes. Ultimately, however, the vengeance backfired, as the harshness of Germany's treatment unleashed even greater forces of nationalism that led to the destruction of Germany's nascent post-war democracy and the rise of Adolf Hitler. The result was the Second World War, which dwarfed the one that came before it in its brutality, physical destruction, and cost in human lives.

Following that war, there was a well-deserved sense of triumph in the hearts of Americans and their allies. After all, the generation that fought and won the Second World War had simultaneously defeated two anti-democratic totalitarian empires in two different hemispheres. However, the war had been so horrific in its cost of human life, so destructive in terms of economic wealth, and so evil in the depravity of the behavior that it unleashed that this same generation of citizens wanted nothing more than to put it all behind them. They were not interested in taking revenge on those they had been at war with, nor did they wish to celebrate their victory. Instead, they wanted to marry, raise families, pursue their careers, practice their religion, serve their communities, and live normal lives. All that they really cared about was ensuring that their children would not have to suffer what they had suffered.

That is why the Second World War was a different kind of triumph. Rather than punish and lord their victory over the losers, the Allies chose to champion their own values. They nurtured the emergence of democracy and freedom in their former enemies, and they continuously gave their former enemies the economic and political support that was required to allow that freedom and democracy to blossom. The Allies ensured that the Second World War would stand for a triumph of ideals, not a triumph of peoples.

The former Axis powers in turn seized the opportunity that the Allies gave them. Led by Konrad Adenauer, the Federal Republic of Germany rebuilt itself from the ground up. It created a true democracy with strong protections for human rights and the rule of law. It did not hide from or deny the crimes that Germany had committed during the war. On the contrary, Germany apologized for its crimes and taught its youth the truth about its history.

To ensure that this history would never be repeated, Germany and the other free nations of Western Europe bound themselves together in system of international institutions designed to support, to promote, and to defend their values. In 1952, six nations formed the European Coal and Steel Community. Economically, this organization evolved over time into a customs union, then into a single market, and then into economic and monetary union with a single currency. Politically, it evolved into a family of nations united in a commitment to freedom, democracy, and the protection of human rights. Today, it is known as the European Union (EU), an institution that economically and politically binds its member states together into a system of values under the rule of law.

By economically tying its member states so closely together, the EU made war among its member states economically impossible. By politically tying its member states together on the basis of shared values, the EU made war politically unthinkable. Because war among the EU member states is economically impossible and politically unthinkable, European nations today settle their differences over the bargaining table rather than over the battlefield. In a very real way, the EU removed the basis of war among its member states. Thanks to the EU, it is safe to assert that the EU's member states will never, ever, go to war with each other again.

However, at its origins, this emerging new Western European political and economic reality was threatened by a new menace. Although the Soviet Union was an ally in the Second World War, it was an ally that was rooted in the old adage of "the enemy of my enemy is my friend." The Soviet Union and the Western democracies that were "allied" with it shared nothing in common. Once their common enemy was gone this fact became blatantly evident. Indeed, the Soviet Union had a completely different vision of what Europe should look like after the war, and it imposed that vision on its satellites in Central and Eastern Europe. While the Western democracies embraced individual freedom, the Soviet Union enslaved its satellites in a dictatorship under the banner of equality of condition. That "equality" would not include freedom of speech, freedom of press, freedom of assembly, freedom of thought, freedom of religion, or any of the other freedoms that Western democracies enjoy today.

Western democracy was again threatened after the Second World War. America, Canada, and most free nations of Western Europe bound themselves together in the North Atlantic Treaty Organization (NATO) to safeguard their freedoms. Militarily, NATO remained vigilant against the threat from the Soviet Union and its Warsaw Pact satellites, and it stood prepared to defend its members at every level. Politically, NATO projected a stability that allowed Western values and the EU to develop under the protection of its military might. NATO was, and is, the military and political commitment between North America and Europe to defend our common values.

After the fall of the Berlin Wall, the EU and NATO became more, not less, relevant. Both reached out to their former communist adversaries in Central and Eastern Europe. The EU gave those former adversaries the possibility to develop into free market economies and Western democracies. NATO provided the security that allowed this economic and political development to occur, and a model for the reform of military and security structures to Western norms. NATO also brought an end to the wars in former Yugoslavia, which were brutal wars with atrocities against civilians that rivaled those of the Nazis. In short, what the U.S. and its Allies did for the Axis powers after the Second World War, the EU and NATO did for the countries of Central and Eastern Europe after the collapse of communism.

This was a completely different type of world than the one that Jerry Sorensen and Roger Abeels grew up in, but it was the type of world that they had fought for and died to create. Of course, Jerry and Roger did not know anything about the international institutions that would emerge after the war to protect the freedoms they fought for. They just knew that they wanted those freedoms to be safeguarded. They wanted their children to be so secure and free that their children could take that freedom and security for granted. Jerry and Roger got the type of world they wanted for their children.

Unfortunately, however, threats to freedom, peace, and prosperity still exist in the world today. It is not always popular to point out this fact, but enemies of Western democracies do exist. Terrorist organizations are capable of inflicting thousands of deaths and terrible amounts of damage, as the events of September 11, 2001, demonstrated. The same is true of various states that have particular grievances with the West. At the moment, none of these threats are organized enough or strong enough to challenge the Western way of life in the way that the Nazis challenged that way of life in the Second World War.

However, the fact that the current enemies of Western democracy are relatively weak today does not mean that potential enemies will always be so weak in the future. New powers based on different values can arise and can challenge the West. In fact, if history teaches anything, it is that new powers will arise and will challenge the West in the future. The fact that the West must continue to defend its values and remain vigilant against potential adversaries is as important today as it was during the Cold War.

For the moment, however, the real threat to the transatlantic Alliance comes from within. A public that takes its freedom, peace, and security for granted can forget what it took to earn that freedom, peace and security. It will not want to recognize the threats that do exist, and it will pretend that these threats do not exist. In democracies, governments respond to what their voters perceive and want. Societies that take their liberties for granted become inward looking. Spending on defense and security becomes unpopular. Economic considerations trump principles. Anti-democratic governments are treated with kid gloves. Actual security threats are perceived as someone else's problem.

Such patterns of behavior weaken the international institutions that were put in place after the war. Disparities emerge among the contributions of member states to the institutions themselves and to the missions that they carry out. Disparities breed resentment, as nations that contribute their share of the burden grow exasperated at nations that do not. Resentment grows when governments seek to score short-term political points with their public by breaking ranks with their allies over difficult long-term decisions. Politicians find it expedient to exaggerate the differences among allies in order to achieve perceived domestic political gains, rather than to remind voters of the commonalities that bind allies together.

Today the voices in America who doubt the utility of NATO and the transatlantic alliance are growing in strength. Many, if not most, Americans like to believe that the United States simply does not need Europe anymore. Many Europeans likewise believe that Europe does not need the United States, particularly when maintaining the transatlantic alliance requires governments to make sacrifices that cost voters money and put their citizens in harm's way. These trends are threats to the institutions that tie the transatlantic alliance together. These threats come from within.

Institutions are important. NATO is the only institution that ties America and Europe together to discuss and plan for the defense of common values. The EU is the only institution that ties European nations together under the rule of law to support and sustain their common values. If NATO did not exist, there would be no other forum where North America and Europe could prepare for the common defense of their values. If the EU did not exist, there would be no other legally-binding forum that would ensure that European governments deliver on the commitments they have made to safeguard the rights and freedoms of their citizens. If these institutions are destroyed, they cannot and would not be re-created. Yet, the more they are taken for granted, the easier they are to destroy.

The end result would be a world that looks much different than the one today. If Western democracies do not stand together to sustain and support the spread of their values in the world, real threats to those values will emerge. People and countries that do not share those values will exploit divisions in the West in order to impose their vision of the world on today's Western democracies. If Western democracies do not defend their freedoms together, they will lose them individually. The freedoms that appear to be so secure to the average citizen of Europe and America today can, in fact, disappear tomorrow.

That is what Jerry and Roger are calling for us to remember from the silence of their graves. Jerry and Roger were quite different from each other. They shared nothing in common when it came to nationality, religion, upbringing, language and culture. Despite these differences, they shared the same values. They were true allies and brothers, and they were the very real, human, and personal embodiment of the transatlantic alliance. Sustaining that alliance today is what gives their sacrifice its meaning.

Appendix: AOMDA Belgium

Established in 1923, the American Overseas Memorial Day Association (AOMDA) in Belgium perpetuates the remembrance of the over 14,000 American servicemen who died in the two world wars and whose final resting place is in Belgium.

Each year, AOMDA organizes the Memorial Day ceremonies at the three American military cemeteries in Belgium, namely, the Ardennes American Cemetery in Neupré, the Flanders Field American Cemetery in Waregem, and the Henri-Chapelle American Cemetery, which straddles the communities of Aubel, Plombières, and Welkenraedt. Thousands gather at these ceremonies annually to honor the men who died for our freedom and who are buried far from home. Senior American and Belgian government officials, military officers, diplomats and other distinguished guests give testimonials in honor of the fallen. Chaplains offer prayers in the name of all faiths. American and Belgian military units salute their fallen forebearers with military honors. The presence of American and Belgian veterans of the Second World War, whose numbers are dwindling each year, are a poignant witness to the sacrifices made. Most of the attendees at the ceremonies are Belgians who come to remember what America did for their country. Many families bring their children to these solemn and dramatic ceremonies to teach them the true meaning of freedom and its cost in human life.

There are also several American servicemen who are buried in isolated graves outside of the American cemeteries in Belgium, like Jerry Sorensen. AOMDA preserves the memory of these servicemen, and it organizes annual Memorial Day ceremonies at each of their graves. When necessary, AOMDA also works to ensure that these graves are maintained and cared for into the future. Although the ceremonies at the isolated graves are much smaller than the ceremonies at the three American cemeteries, these ceremonies give Memorial Day a personal meaning by reflecting on the lives and sacrifices of individual servicemen.

A very important part of the mission of AOMDA Belgium is to engage in youth outreach to help young Belgians and Americans learn the value of remembrance. With each passing year, memories of the wars in Europe fade. Even those deceased servicemen who lie in graves marked with names are increasingly unknown by those alive today. But while the memory of the individuals who fought the war fade, the memory of why they fought and died must never fade. One of AOMDA's primary responsibilities is to pass the torch of remembrance to the next generation, and that is the meaning of the torch that appears in AOMDA Belgium's logo.

AOMDA has created programs to help young people learn about the wars and why remembering the wars is important, such as the Price of Freedom Award. It also organizes school visits in which children can meet serving members of the American armed forces, and learn why the defense of freedom today is just as relevant now as it was during the two world wars. Youth participation is also an integral part of the annual Memorial Day ceremonies.

In a tradition that began in 1923, the Belgian school children of the City of Waregem learn "The Star-Spangled Banner," which they sing each year at the Memorial Day ceremony at the Flanders Field American Cemetery. American and Belgian high school students also participate in that ceremony by reading John McCrae's poem, "In Flanders Field." In 2008, the school children of Rotheux followed in Waregem's footsteps by starting a new tradition of singing the American national anthem at the Memorial Day ceremony at the Ardennes American Cemetery. Meanwhile, the school children from the villages surrounding the Henri-Chapelle American Cemetery offer a unique and special tribute at each year's Memorial Day ceremony that they create themselves.

As an organization, AOMDA Belgium is a private-public partnership that brings together representatives of the United States Embassy to the Kingdom of Belgium, representatives of the American Battle Monuments Commission, and private citizens from the AOMDA Foundation for the shared mission of perpetuating remembrance. The AOMDA Foundation itself consists of private American and Belgian citizens who provide the coordination, impetus and financial resources necessary for AOMDA Belgium to accomplish its mission. Although its broad mission of perpetuating remembrance and our origins are similar, AOMDA Belgium is entirely independent of and not affiliated with AOMDA in France.

For information about AOMDA Belgium and how you can help to carry on this mission, please visit www.aomda.org.

Chapter Notes

Introduction

1. The full story of Jerry and Roger's combat with the Nazis and final stand is recounted in Chapter 8.

2. See Homer Hickam, *Torpedo Junction* (New York: Dell Publishing, 1991).

3. The Union of Soviet Socialist Republics bore a disproportionate share of the burden in defeating Nazi Germany. The Soviet Union destroyed more German armies and its citizens suffered and died in far greater numbers than the Western allies did. The Soviet Union was an ally in the liberation of Europe from Nazism. However, the Soviet Union certainly was not an ally for freedom. The USSR itself was a totalitarian empire that succeeded in imposing its own anti-democratic ideology on much of Central and Eastern Europe, and tried to do the same to the rest. The alliance with the Soviet Union was the classic example of the ancient adage that the enemy of my enemy is my friend.

4. Estimating the number of people who died as a result of the two world wars is fraught with difficulties. Given the conceptual, definitional, and census issues involved, it is impossible to provide a truly accurate number. The number of 95 million given in the text was often cited by Willy De Clercq, a well-known Belgian politician who served at various times as a Belgian minister of finance, a European commissioner and as a member of the European Parliament. As a "back of the envelope" calculation the author finds it useful for conveying the scale of the events that brought today's European Union and NATO into existence. However, the author does not recommend that the reader cite it as reliable.

Chapter 1

1. The Bingham County Historical Society provided the information about the origin of the name "Blackfoot."

2. The above information about Jerry's family and experiences growing up in Rose is compiled from interviews with and documents in the possession of Jerry's cousins Darwin Sorensen and Evelyn (Sorensen) Whyte, Jerry's nephew DeLoy Larsen and his niece Claudette (Larsen) Lundt. It is also drawn from the unpublished family manuscript "The John Cope Dean and Elizabeth Howard Dean Family of Woodruff, Utah and Groveland, Idaho," compiled by Deanne Yancey Driscoll of Blackfoot, Idaho.

3. *Doctrine and Covenants* (101: 79–80).

4. *Doctrine and Covenants* (134: 1–4).

5. Ephraim was responsible for the Sunday school in Rose, where he taught Jerry and the other children these lessons. Although Ephraim himself never served in the military, he did register for the draft in the First World War, and he was fully prepared to serve if the call had come.

6. The information in the preceding paragraphs concerning the beliefs, doctrines, and history of the Church of Jesus Christ of Latter-day Saints is a compilation of information drawn from official church publications and web sites, unofficial church web sites, conversations with members of the faith, and the book by Leonard J. Arrington and Davis Bitton, *The Mormon Experience: A History of the Latter-day Saints* (Urbana and Chicago: University of Illinois Press, 1992).

7. From the unpublished Dean family manuscript.

8. The information in this paragraph comes primarily from Darwin Sorensen, with additional input from DeLoy Larsen and Claudette Lundt.

9. Leonard J. Arrington, "Idaho and the Great Depression," *Idaho Yesterdays* 8 (Summer 1969), 2–8, accessed via http://imnh.isu.edu/digitalatlas/geog/demgrphc/depressn.pdf.

10. Clifton E. Anderson, *History of the College of Agriculture at the University of Idaho*, Chapter 4, undated, but probably 1989. Accessible via http://www.cals.uidaho.edu/centennial/history/CAgH_04.pdf.

11. *The History of Bannock County 1893–1993*, Betty Hale, ed. (Logan, UT: Herff Jones, 1993), pp. 279–285.

12. While Ephraim was doing so, he rented a small place on the Indian Reservation that Louella, Shirley, and he would make a temporary home.

13. The information in the preceding paragraphs concerning the move to Tyhee and Jerry's life in Tyhee is a compiled from interviews with and documents in the possession of Darwin Sorensen, Evelyn Whyte, DeLoy Larsen, and Claudette Lundt, as well as the unpublished Dean family manuscript.

14. The information about Jerry's experience at Pocatello High School was drawn from records in the archives of Pocatello High School and the school's yearbook, *The Pocatellian*, from 1937 and 1938.

15. This information was primarily drawn from the interview with Darwin Sorensen and records in the possession of DeLoy and Claudette Lundt.

16. The information in the preceding two paragraphs was from records in the archives of Pocatello High School, the school's web site, and the yearbook, *The Pocatellian*, from 1937 and 1938.

17. Anderson, Chapter 4.

18. This information is from Jerry's transcript from the University of Idaho.

19. The information about student cooperatives and the Idaho House was primarily drawn from an article by Bill Johnston, "Student Cooperatives at the University of Idaho," *The Improvement Era*, January 1942. It also contains information from an article by Sylvia Watterson, "Habib Always Held His Cards Close to His Chest," in *The Spokesman Review*, August 9, 1982, p. 6.

20. Information from Jerry's transcript.

21. The information in the preceding two paragraphs is from the University Of Idaho's yearbook for 1942 and from documents in the possession of DeLoy Larsen and Claudette Lundt.

Chapter 2

1. All of the general information about the Aviation Cadet program in this chapter is compiled from multiple sources, including but not limited to:
- *Aviation Cadet Training for the Army Air Forces*, a recruitment pamphlet published by the USAAF during the war.
- *Preflight Training in the AAF 1939–1944*, Army Air Forces Historical Studies No. 48, AAF Historical Office, Headquarters Army Air Forces, November 1946.
- *Initial Selection of Candidates for Pilot, Bombardier and Navigator Training*,

Army Air Forces Historical Studies No. 2, assistant chief of Air Staff Intelligence, Historical Division, November 1943.
- Charles A. Watry, *Washout! The Aviation Cadet Story* (Carlsbad: California Aero Press, 1983).
- Eugene Fletcher, *The Lucky Bastard Club: A B-17 Pilot in Training and in Combat 1943–1944* (Seattle: University of Washington Press, 1993).
- Raymond, George, and Fred Crawford, *Three Crawford Brothers: The WW II Memories of Three Pilots* (Bloomington, IN: AuthorHouse, 2008).
- Stephen Ambrose, *The Wild Blue: The Men and Boys Who Flew The B-24s Over Germany* (New York: Simon & Schuster, 2001).
- Interviews with General (ret.) Robert Bazley and Major General (ret.) Charles Wilson, both of whom were graduates of the USAAF Aviation Cadet program during the war.

2. All of the information about the dates of Jerry's enlistment and base assignments throughout this chapter are contained in a personnel record in his Individual Deceased Personnel File of the United States Department of the Army, which was supplemented with information in the records of the Larsen family.

3. *Initial Selection of Candidates for Pilot, Bombardier and Navigator Training*, p. 51.

4. The *Three Crawford Brothers* book describes what Thanksgiving dinner was like at Santa Ana that year.

5. *Aviation Cadet Regulations*, Santa Ana Army Air Base, Headquarters, Army Air Forces, West Coast Training Center.

6. Jerry's squadron assignment and commander are documented in the records held by the Larsen family.

7. The information in the paragraphs above concerning Thanksgiving, Christmas and New Year's at Santa Ana as well as the timing of events at the base throughout Jerry's time there was drawn from the *Three Crawford Brothers* book, Chapters 3–5. Like Jerry, George Crawford was in class 43-I and was at Santa Ana at the same time period that Jerry was. However, they were in different squadrons and there is no evidence that they ever met each other. Similarly, Eugene Fletcher, author of the *Lucky Bastard Club*, was also in Class 43-I at Santa Ana. However, he, too, was in a different squadron from Jerry and there is nothing that would indicate they knew each other either. Charles Watry, author of *Washout!*, likewise underwent classification and preflight training at Santa Ana, but he was there several months after Jerry.

8. This statistic is from an unnumbered table showing the results of Class 44-I at Santa Ana in the appendix to *Pre-flight Training in the AAF, 1939–1944*.

9. Much of the information below about Cal-Aero and its founder comes from Eugene Fletcher's book in Chapter 3. Like Jerry, Fletcher was sent from Santa Ana to Cal-Aero. However, because his squadron was subjected to a medical quarantine, Fletcher graduated from Santa Ana one month after Jerry did. Again, there is no reason to think that Jerry and Fletcher would have known each other at Cal-Aero either, but their experiences would have been similar.

10. The composition of Jerry's squad is documented in the records of Nora Lee Morton.

11. Jerry's Gold Star Flying Award is documented in records possessed by the Larsen family, which still owns the certificate and wallet with Jerry's name inscribed.

12. Jerry's experiences at Merced were common to all aviation cadets in their training at Basic Flying School. They are described in the sources discussed in endnote 1 above.

13. Jerry's ground-loop, washout, and weekend at Yosemite are documented in records of Nora Lee Morton.

14. This is documented by a caption to a photo that Jerry wrote in his photo album.

Chapter 3

1. Throughout this chapter, the information about Nora Lee's parents and her upbringing is based upon conversations with two of her sons, Jed Morton and Jones Morton, and extracts from her diaries.

2. This account of Clyde's service in the army was drawn from his discharge papers together with the following histories that explain the actions that the Fifth Artillery Brigade fought in:

- George B. Clark, *The American Expeditionary Force in World War I: A Statistical History, 1917–1919* (Jefferson, NC: McFarland, 2013).
- Edgar Tremlett Fell, *History of the Seventh Division, United States Army, 1917–1919* (Philadelphia: H. Moore, 1927).
- *The Official History of the Fifth Division USA: During the period of its organization and operations in the European world war, 1917–1919, the Red Diamond (Meuse) Division* (Society of the Fifth Division, 1919).

3. Edgar Jones, Ian Palmer and Simon Wessely, "Enduring beliefs about effects of gassing in war: qualitative study," *BMJ* 335, December 22–27, 2007, pp. 1313–1315. Within this quotation, the authors cite Tim Cook, "'Against God-inspired conscience': the perception of gas warfare as a weapon of mass destruction," *War and Society* 18, pp. 47–69.

4. "Limestone County," Texas State Historical Association, http://www.tshaonline.org/handbook/online/articles/hcl09.

5. "Borger History," City of Borger, http://www.ci.borger.tx.us/history.htm.

6. The description of training and classification at Amarillo is drawn from the *Army Air Forces in World War II, Volume Six: Men and Planes*, edited by Barry Leonard (Washington, D.C.: Government Printing Office, 1983), Chapter 16.

7. The economic impact of the war on Amarillo is explained by R. Douglas Hurt in *The Great Plains During World War II* (Lincoln: University of Nebraska Press, 2008).

8. The information in the preceding paragraphs about the courtship and romance of Jerry and Nora Lee is drawn from the author's interview with Nora Lee with additional details provided by Jenny Abeels.

9. The information in the preceding paragraphs about what gunnery school training was like is drawn primarily from Kelsey McMillan, "AAF Aerial Gunner Training," Bomber Legends eMagazine, Vol. 2, No. 2, accessible via http://www.bomberlegends.com/pdf/BL_Mag_v2–2-GunneryTrain.pdf.

10. This information was provided by Evelyn (Sorensen) Whyte.

11. The information about Jerry's base assignments is from his service record contained in his IDPF.

12. Jones Morton remembers his mother talking about her training for Western Union in Salt Lake City.

13. The information about Nora Lee's move to New Orleans and the motivations behind it was from the author's conversation with Nora Lee and records in her possession.

14. It can, however, be quite fun and exhilarating at low altitudes on a warm, sunny summer day. The information about what it was like to fly in a B-17 came from members of the Arizona Commemorative Air Force and from the author's personal experience as a passenger during a flight of a B-17 in July 2012.

15. The information about what training was like at Drew Field is a compilation from the same sources that are listed in endnote 1 of Chapter 2.

16. The information about Jerry and Nora Lee's engagement was drawn from the personal records of both Jerry and Nora Lee that are in Nora Lee's possession.

17. The information in the preceding two

paragraphs is based upon conversations with members of the Larsen and Morton families. However, the comments on the attitudes of the parents of Jerry and Nora Lee are largely the author's conjecture formed on the basis of those conversations, and the circumstances surrounding the eventual wedding.

18. The information about Jerry and Nora Lee's wedding is compiled from information provided by Evelyn (Sorensen) Whyte, their wedding announcement in the Pocatello newspaper, and their records that are in the possession of Nora Lee. The story about the flowers is from Jenny Abeels.

19. This information was drawn from the records of Jerry and Nora Lee.

Chapter 4

1. The preceding information is compiled from the same sources as endnote 1 of Chapter 2, plus Edward Jablonski, *Flying Fortress* (Garden City, NY: Doubleday, 1965).

2. In the preceding paragraphs, the crew responsibilities are explained in Edward Jablonski's book *Flying Fortress*, pp. 324–339. The composition of the crew is in Jerry's IDPF. The personal information about the other crew members was compiled from information collected by Philippe Connart, Michel Dricot, Edouard Renière, and Victor Schutters and can be found on the web site www.evasioncomete. org. It is also taken from information in the World War II Prisoners of War Data File of the National Archives and Records Administration (available via www.archives.gov).

3. The casualty information for B-17 tail gunners is in Charles W. McArthur, *Operational Analysis in the U.S. Army Eighth Air Force in World War II* (American Mathematical Society, 1991), p. 287.

4. Interview with Judge Maurice Braswell in December 2010.

5. The experience of a B-17 crew preparing for combat in the above two paragraphs is based on the same sources as endnote 1 above.

6. The information in the preceding paragraphs explains the normal northern route to the European Theater of Operations taken by B-17 crews departing from Hunter Field. From photographs and information in Jerry's album, and based on his crew's assignment in England, it is clear that Jerry's crew took the northern route with a new aircraft. However, it is possible that the itinerary was slightly different from what was described. For example, the crew might have stopped at Gander rather than Goose Bay in Newfoundland. Descriptions of the flight to Europe can be found in the sources

listed in endnote 1. A particularly good description is provided in an unpublished manuscript by Joel Punches that is simply entitled "B-17F Flight Log (5 Sept 1943–21 Feb 1944)." Punches was a B-17 navigator with the 385th Bomb Wing based in Great Ashfield, England. The manuscript was accessed via http://www. ferrer-aviation.com/public/B17log.pdf.

7. See Ron Macay, *The Last Blitz: Operation Steinbock, the Luftwaffe's Last Blitz on Britain, January to May 1944* (Red Kite, 2010).

8. All of the information about the Snetterton Falcons in the rest of this chapter is drawn from the book by Robert E. Doherty and Geoffrey D. Ward, *Snetterton Falcons II: The 96th Bomb Group in World War II* (Dallas: Taylor, 1996).

9. Jerry wrote an account of the events of May 1, 1944, that he left behind with the Abeels family. He writes about his friendship with Howe, Shirley and Meadows in that account.

10. In fact, the 25 mission rule was never as hard and fast as it was sometimes believed. In May of 1944, the 8th Air Force considered a completion of a tour of duty to occur between 25 and 30 missions, depending upon attrition and the availability of replacements. Later that year, the number was raised to 35, and by the end of the war it had reached 50. See Historical Studies Branch, USAF Historical Division, "Combat Crew Rotation: World War II and Korean War," unpublished manuscript prepared for the Aerospace Studies Institute, Air University, Maxwell Air Force Base, January 1968. Accessed via http://www.afhra.af.mil/ shared/media/document/AFD-080424-048. pdf. For bomber combat casualty information see:

- Eugene Fletcher, *The Lucky Bastard Club: A B-17 Pilot in Training and in Combat, 1943–1945* (Seattle: University of Washington Press, 1992).
- Mark K. Wells, *Courage and Air Warfare: The Allied Aircrew Experience in the Second World War* (London: Frank Cass, 1995), p. 161.
- James J. Carroll, "Physiological Problems of Bomber Crews in the Eighth Air Force in World War II," unpublished research paper submitted to the Air Command and Staff College, March 1997, p. 16, accessed via www.dtic.mil/cgibin/ GetTRDoc?AD=ADA398044_.

11. This letter is in the files of Evelyn Whyte.

12. Information about the bomber can be found on http://warbirds.wikia.com/wiki/B-17G-5BO_42–31132_/_42–31231. The photograph is in Jerry's photo album.

13. The information about how a B-17 flew into combat in the preceding paragraphs is a

compilation of information listed from the sources in endnote 1 as well as an excellent account on the web site "B-17 Queen of the Sky," http://www.b17queenofthesky.com/positions/bombardier.php.

14. The information in the above three paragraphs comes from the Doherty and Ward book *Snetterton Falcons*.

15. The information in the preceding paragraphs about Jerry's experience in the Snetterton Falcons and the mission of May 1 is drawn primarily from his own written account of the experience. The author supplemented that account with information found in the Doherty and Ward book *Snetterton Falcons* and the general sources of what it was like to prepare for combat found in the sources listed in endnote 1.

16. The author would like to thank Louis Darbé of Marcq for finding the location where the *Wolverine* crashed. Mr. Darbé took the author to the crash site with two other individuals who owned metal detectors, and small pieces of the *Wolverine* were recovered from the site in October 2010. Mr. Darbé also introduced the author to Madelaine Petit, who provided the account in the above paragraph. Madelaine's brother Henri was also active in the Belgian Resistance. He belonged to the *Partisans Armées* and was killed in combat with the Nazis on September 3, 1944, the same day that Jerry Sorensen and Roger Abeels lost their lives.

17. The above three paragraphs are based on Jerry's written account of the mission.

Chapter 5

1. The information in the paragraphs concerning the Comet Line is drawn from the following sources:
- Anne Brusselmans, *Rendez-Vous 127: The Diary of Madame Brusselmans, MBE*, translated by Denis Hornsey (London: Ernest Benn Limited, 1954).
- Airay Neave, *Little Cyclone* (London: Coronet Books, 1954).
- Peter Eisner, *The Freedom Line* (New York: HarperCollins, 2004).
- Information provided by Philippe Connart, Michel Dricot, Edouard Renière, and Victor Schutters, much of which can be found on www.evasioncomete.org.

2. From the frontispiece of Brusselmans' *Rendez-Vous 127*.

3. Brusselmans, p. 91.

4. This account of how Jerry came into the hands of the Comet Line was taken from Jerry's diary that he wrote while staying with the Abeels family and the account of Commander Emile Nerinckx discussed in the next note. The author speculates that the "English lady" whom Jerry referred to in his diary was Van Delft's wife, Marie Anne (de Crombrugghe) Van Delft. Mme. Van Delft was a Comet Line spotter who spoke English, and it stands to reason that she would have taken Jerry to her home. Two other individuals claimed to have found Sorensen. Maurice Husson, who served in Jerry's Secret Army refuge, told the author that he was the one who found Jerry and led him to the Van Delft home. However, neither Jerry nor Nerinckx make any mention of Husson or of a man being present when Jerry was found. Similarly, the son of Paul Vanhove told the author that his father is the person who found Jerry and that his father initially sheltered Jerry in his home. However, there is likewise no written evidence of Vanhove's involvement in either Jerry's or Nerinckx's accounts. Since the Comet Line spotters did work in teams, the author believes that Husson and Vanhove were part of the team that found Jerry. Moreover, since Vanhove did transport airmen in a hidden compartment of his wagon, Vanhove probably did play a role in transporting Jerry at some stage along the way.

5. The information in this paragraph was from an account of Jerry's experiences written by his Secret Army commander, Emile P. Nerinckx. It is an unpublished manuscript entitled "Comment Vecut et Mourut un Aviateur Américain en Belgique Occupée: Sorensen Gerald." It is dated April 27, 1947. Additional information was also provided by Lea De Vos.

6. The information about the Lepoivre family in the above three paragraphs is from René Cobaux, "Sauvetage des aviateurs allies en 1944: la bonne planque de Gondregnies," *Le Courrier de l'Escaut*, July 28, 1994.

7. From Jerry's account of his experience, information provided by Louis Darbé, and Smith's file on www.evasioncomete.org/fsmithjr.html. Madame d'Adam belonged to Group G, discussed in the text below.

8. From Jerry's account and information provided by Jenny Abeels.

9. The information about Victor Schutters was primarily provided by his grandson, who is also named Victor Schutters after his grandfather. Mme. Brusselmans also discusses Schutters in her book on p. 133.

10. The information about Odette Gryspeirt is from Jenny Abeels and files provided by Victor Schutters.

11. The information about the people who sheltered Jerry and the dates that he stayed with them is a compilation of information in

Jerry's account of his experience, files provided by Victor Schutters, and information that Philippe Connart, Michel Dricot, Edouard Renière, and Victor Schutters has made available on www.evasioncomete.org. However, there are contradictions in the dates and names among these sources. The author decided to rely primarily upon Jerry's account of his experience since he wrote this account shortly after the events occurred. However, it is possible that Jerry did not always understand where he was or when he was there. Therefore, there are some differences in the details of Jerry's movement from Schreyen's care to the Abeels home between this text and the details presented on www.evasioncomete.org. However, the differences are inconsequential. The families that Jerry stayed with and the people in the Comet Line who helped Jerry are the same in the two lists.

12. Brusselmans' diary provides a gripping account of the problems she and the Comet Line faced at that time. See for example p. 128.

13. The impact of Schreyen's arrest is described in Brusselmans' book.

14. Rival in the sense of taking credit for successes. The various Resistance organizations never came into conflict with each other.

15. The information about the Belgian Resistance in the paragraphs below is a synthesis of information from the following sources:

• Pieter Lagrou, "Belgium," in *Resistance in Western Europe*, Bob Moore, ed. (Oxford: Berg, 2000). This is the primary source of information relied upon.

• *Livre d'Or de la Resistance Belge*, a work commissioned by the Belgian Ministry of Defense and published in Brussels by Les Editions Leclercq, year of publication unknown.

• Hervé Gérard, *La Résistance Belge face au Nazisme (1940–1945)* (Braine-l'Alleud: J.M. Collet, 1994).

• Information from conversations with several different veterans of Belgian Resistance organizations.

16. The account of the Secret Army in the paragraphs below is primarily from Henri Bernard, *l'Armée Secrète 1940–1944* (Paris-Gembloux: Duculot, 1986). Additional information comes from Lagrou's book chapter cited above and conversations with the surviving veterans of Jerry's Secret Army unit.

Chapter 6

1. Albert Carreras and Cailla Josephson, "Growing at the Production Frontier: European Aggregate Growth, 1870–1914," working paper,

October 2009, Universitat Pompeu Fabra, Department of Economics and Business, p. 14.

2. Unless otherwise noted, the information in the seven paragraphs below concerning Belgium and the First World War is drawn from multiple sources, but especially:

• B.H. Liddell Hart, *History of the First World War* (London: Papermac, 1992).

• John Keegan, *The First World War* (London: Pimlico, 1999).

• Hew Strachan, *The First World War, Volume I: To Arms* (Oxford: Oxford University Press, 2001).

• Barbara Tuchman, *The Guns of August* (New York: Macmillan, 1962).

• Brand Whitlock, *Belgium* (New York: D. Appleton, 1919).

3. This quote appears in multiple references to the war, but the author has never been able to track down the original reference. The quote may well be apocryphal.

4. Found on the World War I Document Archive, http://www.gwpda.org/1914/papersc rap.html.

5. "German Dead 5000 in 3 Days," *New York Times*, August 9, 1914.

6. Strachan, p. 211.

7. "Albert Dares the Kaiser," *New York Times*, August 15, 1914.

8. Tuchman, p. 193.

9. The information about Arthur Abeels' military service in the paragraphs below was provided by Rob Troubleyn of the Belgian Royal Military Museum, who drew the information from the following sources:

• The military records of Arthur Henri Abeels.

• Archives returned from Moscow: history of the 11th Regiment and history of the Battle of Liège.

• The Directorate-General War Victims.

In addition, information about the 11th Line Infantry Regiment and the defense of Liège was also drawn from:

• Brevet Lt. Col. Tasnier and Brevet Major R. Van Overstraeten, *La Belgique et La Guerre, Vol. III: Les Operations Militaires* (Brussels: Henri Bertels, 1923).

• René Lyr, *Nos Héros Morts Pour La Patries, L'Epopée Belge de 1914 à 1918* (Brussels: Société Anonyme Belge d'Imprimerie, 1920).

• Professor Leon van der Essen, *The Invasion of Belgium and the War in Belgium from Liège to the Yser* (London: TF Unwin, 1917).

10. Unless otherwise noted, personal interviews with Jenny Abeels provided the information about Arthur's leg injury and its effects on Arthur's character in the paragraphs above.

The interviews with Jenny were also the source of all of the information in the rest of this chapter about Arthur's experiences, thoughts and feelings when he was a prisoner of war. Furthermore, she also shared all of the information about the Abeels family in the rest of this chapter.

11. The account of the German blitzkrieg in Belgium in the paragraphs below is primarily based on two sources:
• Brian Bond, *France and Belgium 1939–1940* (London: Purnell Book Services, 1975).
• An excellent web site entitled "The Campaign of the Belgian Army in May 1940" that sadly does not attribute an author. The web site can be accessed at: http://home.scarlet.be/vdmeiren/The%20Campaign%20of%20the%20Belgian%20army%20in%20May%201940.html.

12. Quoted on the web site "The Campaign of the Belgian Army in May 1940."

13. Quoted in Colonel Rémy (pseudonym of Gilbert Renault), *Le 18e Jour: La Tragedie de Leopold III, Roi des Belges* (Paris: France-Empire, 1976), p. 335.

14. Marcel Gruneer, Arthur Van Waeyenberghe and Jean-Jacques Coeymans were all members of the *La Rapière* fencing club who gave their lives in the Resistance.

15. The information about Mac in this paragraph is from an interview with his daughter, Janine Park.

16. This information is from the Missing Air Crew Report for Mac's plane and from the www.evasioncomete.org.

17. This information is from an excerpt from Jenny Abeels' diary that is in the files of Nora Lee Morton.

18. The information about Victor Schreyen and his role in the Comet Line is from Anne Brusselmans, *Rendez-vous 127: The Diary of Madame Brusselmans, MBE*, translated by Denis Hornsey (London: Ernest Benn, 1954), p. 133. The information about Odette and Mac's arrival in the home is from interviews with Jenny Abeels, as well as excerpts from her diary in Nora Lee's files.

19. This information is primarily from Jenny's diary excerpts in Nora Lee's files, but also from interviews with Jenny.

Chapter 7

1. All of the information in this chapter is a compilation of information drawn from:
• Personal interviews with Jenny Abeels.
• Excerpts from the diary of Jenny Abeels in the files of Nora Lee Morton.

• Photographs and records in the possession of Jenny Abeels and Nora Lee Morton.

In addition, important background information that help put these sources in context was drawn from
• Anne Brusselmans, *Rendez-vous 127: The Diary of Madame Brusselmans, MBE*, translated by Denis Hornsey (London: Ernest Benn, 1954).
• Peter Schrijvers, *Liberators: The Allies and Belgian Society 1944–1945* (Cambridge: Cambridge University Press, 2009).

2. The story of Thimister-Clermont is from Mathilde Schmetz of the Remember Museum.

3. In one of her conversations with the author, Jenny Abeels remembered that there were hard collaborators who lived across the street at No. 48, but these are all of the details that she could remember. Since that conversation, the author acquired a number of documents and examples of clandestine press from the Resistance that belonged to Alcide Hannequin. One of these documents contained a list of collaborators in which Nipper's name, address, and activity for the Nazis appears.

4. Jenny Abeels said that Mac and Jerry told her about television. However, it is highly unlikely that either Mac or Jerry would have had a television set, since there were only 5,000 sets in private homes in the United States at the time. Therefore, Mac and Jerry must have either seen a television set in some public setting at some point in their military careers, or they simply heard or read about the invention and told Jenny about it.

Chapter 8

1. Recounted in Anne Brusselmans, *Rendez-vous 127: The Diary of Madame Brusselmans, MBE*, translated by Denis Hornsey (London: Ernest Benn, 1954), pp. 156–157.

2. Brusselmans, p. 80, but also throughout the book.

3. Neal M. Sher, Aron A. Golberg, and Elizabeth B. White, *Robert Jan Verbelen and the United States Government*, report to the assistant attorney general, Criminal Division, U.S. Department of Justice, June 16, 1988, pp. 7–9. Accessible via http://www.justice.gov/criminal/hrsp/archives/1988/06–16–1988verbelen-rpt.pdf.

4. Martin Conway, *Collaboration in Belgium: Léon Degrelle and the Rexist Movement* (London: Yale University Press, 1993), p. 258.

5. Conway, pp. 270–272.

6. This information is from interviews with Jenny Abeels.

7. This information is based on records that were in the possession of Jenny Abeels. In the paragraphs below, there are discrepancies between the dates given below and other sources, such as the records of the Comet Line association, the records of the Lepoivre family, and Commandant Nerinckx's account, none of which agree with each other. The author chose to rely primarily on the records in the possession of Jenny Abeels. However, the author did not exclusively do so, depending upon the overall context of the documents. It remains very possible that the exact dates of the events leading to Jerry's entry into the Secret Army may be inaccurate by a day or two.

8. The information in this paragraph and the five paragraphs below is based primarily on records in the possession of Jenny Abeels and interviews with Jenny Abeels.

9. The author has no proof of this, but it is probable that Monsieur Fourmanoir was related to the Lepoivre family. Fourmanoir was the maiden name of Lepoivre's wife Sylvie.

10. The information on the Secret Army's Zone I, Sector D, in this paragraph and the three paragraphs below is from Henri Bernard, *l'Armée Secrète 1940–1944* (Paris-Gembloux: Duculot, 1986), pp. 173–178, and "Nos héros de la seconde guerre mondiale," unpublished manuscript from the Tourist Information Office of the community of Silly released in 2013.

11. Nerinckx would later write that, because of this rebuff, the Independence Front began a slander campaign against him, and he was threatened with being denounced to the Germans. This is reported in "Nos héros de la seconde guerre mondiale," Vol. 2, p. 7, an unpublished manuscript released in 2013 by the Tourist Information Office (Syndicat d'initiative) of the community of Silly.

12. René Cobaux, "Sauvetage des aviateurs allies en 1944: la bonne planque de Gondregnies," *Courrier de l'Escault*, July 28, 1994.

13. Unless otherwise noted, the information in the rest of this chapter concerning Commandant Nerinckx, the activities of the *Refuge Tarin*, and Jerry's service in the Secret Army is drawn from three sources:

• Émile P. Nerinckx, "Comment Vecut et Mourut un Aviateur Américain en Belgique Occupée: Sorensen Gerald," unpublished manuscript dated April 27, 1947.
• M. Andrieux, "Le Macquis de St-Marcoult," *Revue Trimestrielle du Relais des Patriotes*, July 1997.
• Henri Bernard, *l'Armée Secrète 1940–1944* (Paris-Gembloux: Duculot, 1986.
• André Berten, "Souvenirs d'un agent parachutiste." This manuscript was ob-

viously published in a periodical. However, it was given to the author by Louis Darbé, who did not record the name of the publication or the date of publication.

• Interviews with Max Robert, Maurice Leclerq, and César Van Herreweghen, veterans of the *Refuge Tarin*.

14. Nerinckx gives the date as August 5 in his account. However, it appears that Jerry and Mac were still staying with the Lepoivre family on that date. It seems more probable that event would have occurred around August 7 or 8.

15. This letter is in the records of Nora Lee Morton.

16. This letter is in the records of Jenny Abeels.

17. This letter is in the records of Jenny Abeels.

18. This letter is in the records of Jenny Abeels.

19. This letter is in the records of Jenny Abeels.

20. In addition to the Commander Nerinckx's manuscript listed in note 13 above, the account of Jerry's final combat and death below includes information contained in his Individual Deceased Personnel File from the United States Department of the Army.

Chapter 9

1. The information in this paragraph and the two paragraphs below is from Émile P. Nerinckx, "Comment Vecut et Mourut un Aviateur Américain en Belgique Occupée: Sorensen Gerald," unpublished manuscript dated April 27, 1947.

2. In addition to Nerinckx's manuscript above, the information in this paragraph and the next paragraph is from the legal deposition of Gustave Van Meus and Alphonse Smoes, for the Commune of Marcq, September 4, 1944.

3. This information is from interviews with Jenny Abeels.

4. This letter is in the records of Nora Lee Morton.

5. All of the information in the paragraphs below concerning the funeral, the memorial service, and the departure of Mac and Frank from Belgium is from records in the possession of Jenny Abeels. It has been supplemented with information from interviews with Jenny Abeels.

6. This letter is in the records of Nora Lee Morton.

7. This information is from interviews with Jenny Abeels.

8. Correspondence in the IDPF from July 1944 shows that she was in Texas at that time.

However, other correspondence in the IDPF shows that she was in Idaho before and after July.

9. This information is in the IDPF. Although the letter from Cherniss is not in the IDPF, Nora Lee references it in other correspondence contained in the file.

10. This letter is in the records of Nora Lee Morton.

11. This letter is in the IDPF.

12. This letter is also in the IDPF.

13. The information in this paragraph and the following paragraph is from interviews with Jenny Abeels and records in her possession.

14. This information is contained in the IDPF.

15. This letter is in the IDPF.

16. The letter is in the IDPF. Unless otherwise noted, almost all of the information in the rest of this chapter is from Nora Lee's personal diary, photographs, souvenirs, and other records in her possession.

17. The information about the ceremony in Ganshoren is recorded in two newspaper articles from 1947. One was given to the author by Mr. Darbé and is entitled "Un aviateur américain repose au cimetière de Ganshoren," and is dated April 1, 1947. However, the name of the newspaper is not recorded. The second article is in records in the possession of Janine Park and is entitled "Grootsche heldenherdenking te Ganshoren." However, neither the date of the article nor the name of the newspaper is recorded.

18. Nerinckx's speech and the gifts he presented to Nora Lee and Jenny are recorded in a 1947 newspaper article entitled "Manifestation patriotique à Marcq-lez-Enghien." The article was provided by Mr. Darbé, but the name of the newspaper and exact date of publication is not recorded. Nora Lee still has the piece of the parachute that she was given.

19. The information in this paragraph is from interviews with Jenny Abeels.

20. Nora Lee's diary and the newspaper articles record the circumstances of the awarding of four of the five medals mentioned in this chapter, but not the reasons for which those medals were awarded. The medals themselves are in the possession of the Sorensen family, and based on those medals, the author determined the reasons why the medals were rewarded.

Chapter 10

1. www.evasioncomete.org.

2. The fact that all five men ended up at Stalag Luft IV is recorded in the World War II Prisoner of War Data File, 12/7/1941–11/19/1946, of the National Archives, accessible via www.archives.gov. For Sgt. Smith, there is as of yet no documentary evidence of how he was captured. However, it is distinctly possible that the escape line he was handed off to was in fact was one of the fake escape organizations that the Nazis created to capture downed airmen, such as the one that was run by the infamous collaborator Prosper De Zitter. See Herman Bodson, *Downed Allied Airmen and Evasion of Capture: The Role of Local Resistance Networks in World War II* (Jefferson, NC: McFarland, 1995), Chapter 8.

3. The information about what happened to the five men is all drawn from John Nichol and Tony Rennell, *The Last Escape: The Untold Story of Allied Prisoners of War in Germany 1944–1945* (London: Penguin Books, 2002). However, the author was not able to determine which, if any, of the five were left at Fallingbostel and which, if any, continued on to Lauenberg. The fact that all five survived and eventually returned to the States is revealed in several of the official records, such as the Missing Air Crew report.

4. The information in this paragraph and below about Verbelen and what Dingledine and Street experienced at his hands is drawn from the following sources:

- Neal M. Sher, Aron A. Golberg, and Elizabeth B. White, "Robert Jan Verbelen and the United States Government," report to the assistant attorney general, Criminal Division, U.S. Department of Justice, June 16, 1988, pp. 7–9. Accessible via http://www.justice.gov/criminal/hrsp/archives/1988/06–16–1988verbelen-rpt.pdf.
- Hearing before the Subcommittee of the Constitution of the Committee of the Judiciary, United States Senate on S. 1335 and S. 2395, 98th Congress, Second Session, April 3, 1984.
- Ralph Blumenthal, "New Case of Nazi Criminal Used as Spy by U.S. Is Under Study," *New York Times*, January 9, 1984.
- *NBC Nightly News*, February 1, 1984.
- Union Internationale de la Résistance et de la Déportation (U.I.R.D.), "Liste des Crimes Retenus a Charge De Verbelen Robertus par le Conseil de Guerre de la Province du Brabant (7ème Chambre flamande) Le 14 Octobre 1947," unpublished manuscript.

5. As a starting point for further information on the von Braun story, and other Nazi engineers who followed a similar path, see the web site "Dora and the V2: Slave Labor in the

Space Age" from the Department of History of the University of Alabama at Huntsville, http://www.dora.uah.edu/engineers.html.

6. Dingledine's visit is noted in Rene Cobaux, "Sauvetage des aviateurs allies en 1944: la bonne planque de Gondregnies," *Le Courrier de l'Escaut*, July 28, 1994. Nora Lee's visit with Street is recorded in her files.

7. The final resting place of the *Wolverine* was located by Monsieur Louis Darbé as discussed in the endnotes of Chapter 4.

8. Recorded in the Missing Air Crew report.

9. Information provided by Bernard Deherder.

10. The information in this section was based on conversations with César Van Herreweghen and Maurice Leclerq and a visit to the latter's home.

11. In August of 2014, as this book was in the final stages of production, both Maurice Leclerq and Bernard Deherder passed away within days of each other. The museum is called Maquistory.

12. Obituary of Andrée de Jongh, *The Telegraph*, October 18, 2007.

13. "Anne Brusselmans was een bijzonder moedige vrouw," *Het Belang Van Limburgh*, January 22, 1987.

14. The story of the Phantom Train can be found in "Belgium: The Ghost Train," *Time*, February 8, 1945. Accessible via http://www.time.com/time/magazine/article/0,9171,797049,00.html. Cobaux (note 5) discusses the Lepoivre's arrest.

15. www.evasioncomete.org.

16. See "Le site de l'urbanisme et de l'environnement à Auderghem," http://www.urba.be/Rues/nl_rues_t.htm and www.evasioncomete.org.

17. Unless otherwise noted, all of the information about the Sorensen family below is from interviews with and documents in the possession of Jerry's cousins Darwin Sorensen and Evelyn (Sorensen) Whyte, Jerry's nephew DeLoy Larsen and his niece Claudette (Larsen) Lundt. It is also drawn from the unpublished family

manuscript: "The John Cope Dean and Elizabeth Howard Dean Family of Woodruff, Utah and Groveland, Idaho," compiled by Deanne Yancey Driscoll of Blackfoot, Idaho.

18. This letter is in Jerry's Individual Deceased Personnel File of the U.S. Department of the Army.

19. Unless otherwise indicated, all of the information about Mac in this section is drawn from an interview and records in the possession of his daughter, Janine Park, and from many interviews with and records in the possession of Jenny Abeels.

20. The letter is in the records of Nora Lee Morton.

21. Unless otherwise indicated, all of the information about Jenny in this section is from multiple interviews and records in the possession of Jenny Abeels.

22. Interview with Nora Lee Morton.

23. The information about Jenny's first job came from two of Jenny's co-workers at Air Traffic Control Services, Madame Jill Vandenbroeck and Madame Monique Duroisin.

24. The information in this paragraph is from interviews with Jenny Abeels, Claudette Lundt, and the Morton family.

25. The information about Jenny's visit to Texas and her relationship with the Morton family in the preceding two paragraphs is based on interviews with Nora Lee Morton and her sons.

26. All of the information about Nora Lee in this section is from interviews with Nora Lee, Jim Ed Morton, Jones Morton, Jed Morton and records in the possession of Nora Lee.

27. As recounted in Chapter 8, while Jerry was staying with the Abeels family he wrote a note to his family back home that he asked to be delivered to them in the event that he did not make it home from the war. Before packing up her box, Nora Lee wrote on the envelope of that note the following, "Everything is as Gerald meant it to be. For God, his country & himself."

28. The strangers from Belgium were Laura Hoffman and the author.

Bibliography

"Albert Dares the Kaiser." *New York Times*, August 15, 1914.

Ambrose, Steven. *The Wild Blue: The Men and Boys Who Flew the B-24s Over Germany*. New York: Simon & Schuster, 2001.

Amendments to the Freedom of Information Act: Hearings on S. 1335 and S. 2395 Before the Subcommittee on the Constitution, Committee on the Judiciary, United States Senate. 98th Cong. (April 3, 1984). Serial J-98–108.

Anderson, Clifton E. *History of the College of Agriculture at the University of Idaho*. Undated, but probably 1989. Accessible via www.cals.uidaho.edu/centennial/history/CAgH_04.pdf.

Andrieux, M. Guy. "Le Maquis de St.-Marcoult." *Revue Trimestrielle du Relais des Patriotes*, No. 3 (1997), p. 2.

"Anne Brusselmans was een bijzonderlijke vrouw." *Het Belgang Van Limburg*, January 22, 1987.

Arrington, Leonard J. "Idaho and the Great Depression." *Idaho Yesterdays* 13 (Summer 1969).

Arrington, Leonard J., and Davis Bitton. *The Mormon Experience: A History of the Latter-day Saints*. Chicago: University of Illinois Press, 1992.

Aviation Cadet Regulations, Santa Ana Army Air Base. Printed at Headquarters, Army Air Force West Coast Training Center, Santa Ana, California.

Aviation Cadet Training for the Army Air Forces. U.S. Army Air Force, 1943.

"Belgium: The Ghost Train," *Time*, February 8, 1945. www.time.com/time/magazine/article/0,9171,797049,00.html.

Bernard, Henri. *L'Armée Secrète, 1940–1944*. Paris-Gembloux: Editions Duculot, 1986.

Berten, André. "Souvenirs d'un agent parachutiste." From a private collection, details of publication unknown.

Blumenthal, Ralph. "New Case of Nazi Criminal Used as Spy by U.S. is Under Study." *New York Times*, January 9, 1984.

Bodson, Herman. *Agent for the Resistance: A Belgian Saboteur in World War II*. College Station: Texas A&M University Press, 1994.

Bodson, Herman. *Downed Allied Airmen and Evasion of Capture: The Role of Local Resistance Networks in World War II*. Jefferson, NC: McFarland, 1995.

Bond, Brian. *France and Belgium, 1939–1940*. London: Davis-Poynter, 1975.

"Borger History." City of Borger. http://www.ci.borger.tx.us/history.htm.

Brand Whitlock, Joseph. *Belgium*. New York: D. Appleton, 1919.

Brokaw, Tom. *The Greatest Generation*. New York: Delta Books, 1998.

Brusselmans, Anne. *Rendez-Vous 127: The Diary of Madame Brusselmans, M.B.E.* Trans. Denis Hornsey. London: Ernest Benn, 1954.

Campaign of the Belgian Army in May 1940. http://home.scarlet.be/vdmeiren/The%20Campaign%20of%20the%20Belgian%20army%20in%20May%201940.html (last accessed October 20, 2013).

Carreras, Albert, and Cailla Josephson. "Growing at the Production Frontier: European Aggregrate Growth, 1870–1914." Working paper, October 2009, Universitat Pompeu Fabra, Department of Economics and Business. www.econ.

upf.edu/docs/papers/downloads/1179.pdf.

Clark, George B. *The American Expeditionary Force in World War I: A Statistical History, 1917–1919.* Jefferson, NC: McFarland, 2013.

Cobaux, Réné. "Sauvetage des aviateurs allies en 1944: la bonne planque de Gendregnies." *Le Courrier de l'Escaut* (July 28, 1944).

Community of Auderghem. Web site on the street names of Auderghem, 193 Tedesco. www.urba.be.

Conway, Martin. *Collaboration in Belgium: Léon Degrelle and the Rexist Movement.* London: Yale University Press, 1993.

Cook, Tim. "'Against God-inspired conscience': the perception of gas warfare as a weapon of mass destruction." *War and Society* 18, pp. 47–69.

Correll, John T. "Daylight Precision Bombing." *Air Force Magazine* 91 (10), October 2008. www.airforcemag.com/MagazineArchive/Pages/2008/October%202008/1008daylight.aspx.

Crawford, Raymond, George Crawford, and Fred Crawford. *Three Crawford Brothers: The WW II Memoirs of Three Pilots.* Bloomington IN: AuthorHouse, 2008.

Debruyne, Emmanuel. *La guerre secrète des espions belges, 1940–1944.* Brussels: Racine, 2008.

De Ridder Files, Yvonne. *The Quest for Freedom: A Story of Belgian Resistance in World War II.* Santa Barbara, CA: Narrative Press, 1991.

Dickon, Chris. *The Foreign Burial of American War Dead.* Jefferson, NC: McFarland, 2011.

Doctrine and Covenants, Church of Jesus Christ of Latter-day Saints.

Doherty, Robert E., and Geoffrey D. Ward. *Snetterton Falcons II: The 96th Bomb Group in World War II.* Dallas: Taylor, 1996.

Door, Robert F., and Thomas D. Jones. *Hell Hawks: The Untold Story of the American Fliers Who Savaged Hitler's Wehrmacht.* Minneapolis: Zenith Press, 2008.

Driscoll, Deanne Yancey. "The John Cope Dean and Elizabeth Howard Dean Family of Woodruff, Utah and Groveland, Idaho." Unpublished manuscript, date unknown.

Eisner, Peter. *The Freedom Line.* New York: HarperCollins, 2004.

Fell, Edgar Tremlett. *History of the Seventh Division United States Army, 1917–1919.* Philadelphia: H. Moore, 1927.

Fitzgerald, Timothy L. "United States Army Air Force Enlisted Aircrew Gunnery Training for Heavy Bombers in World War II." Student paper. AFEHRI File 100.048, 1996.

Fletcher, Eugene. *The Lucky Bastard Club: A B-17 Pilot in Training and in Combat, 1943–1945.* Seattle: University of Washington Press, 1992.

Freeman, Roger. *Airfields of the Eighth Then and Now.* Essex, UK: Battle of Britain International, 1978.

Garfield, Brian. *The Thousand-mile War: World War II and the Aleutians.* Fairbanks: University of Alaska Press, 1995.

Gem of the Mountains. Vol. 40. University of Idaho yearbook, 1942.

Gérard, Hervé. *La Résistance Belge Face au Nazisme (1940–1945).* Braine l'Alleud: J.M. Collet, 1995.

"German Dead 5000 in 3 Days," *New York Times,* August 9, 1914.

Gilbert, Martin. *The Second World War: A Complete History.* New York: Henry Holt, 1989.

Hale, Betty, ed. *The History of Bannock County 1893–1993.* Logan, Utah: Herff Jones, 1993.

Hamelius, Paul. *The Siege of Liège: A Personal Narrative.* London: T. Werner Laurie, 1914.

Hickman, Homer H., Jr. *Torpedo Junction.* Annapolis: United States Naval Institute Press, 1989.

Hinsencamp, Maurice. *Le Groupe de Sabotage Marshal.* Aalst: Agora Uitgeverscentrum, 2010.

Historical Studies Branch, USAF Historical Division, "Combat Crew Rotation: World War II and Korean War," unpublished manuscript prepared for the

Aerospace Studies Institute, Air University, Maxwell Air Force Base, January 1968. Accessed via www.afhra.af.mil/shared/media/document/AFD-080424-048.pdf.

Hurt, R. Douglas. *The Great Plains During World War II.* Lincoln: University of Nebraska Press, 2008.

Individual Deceased Personnel File (IDPF) for Gerald E. Sorensen. United States Department of the Army.

Initial Selection of Candidates for Pilot, Bombardier, and Navigator Training. Report prepared by assistant chief of air staff, Intelligence, Historical Division. November 1943.

Jablonski, Edward. *Flying Fortress.* Garden City, NY: Doubleday, 1965.

Johnston, Bill. "Student Cooperatives at the University of Idaho." *The Improvement Era*, January 1942.

Jones, Edgar, Ian Palmer, and Simon Wessely. "Enduring beliefs about effects of gassing in war: qualitative study." *BMJ* 335, December 22–27, 2007, pp. 1313–1315.

Keegan, John. *The First World War.* London: Pimlico, 1999.

Leonard, Barry, ed. *Army Air Forces in World War II, Volume Six: Men and Planes.* Washington, D.C.: Government Printing Office, 1983.

Liddle Hart, B.H. *History of the First World War.* London: Papermac, 1992.

Limestone County. Texas State Historical Association. www.tshaonline.org/handbook/online/articles/hcl09.

Lyr, Rene. *Nos Héros Morts Pour La Patries, L'Epopée Belge de 1914 à 1918.* Brussels: Société Anonyme Belge d'Imprimerie, 1920.

Macay, Ron. *The Last Blitz: Operation Steinbock, the Luftwaffe's Last Blitz on Britain, January to May 1944.* Surrey, UK: Red Kite Books, 2010.

Margerison, Russell. *Boys at War.* London: Northway, 2009.

McArthur, Charles W. *Operational Analysis in the U.S. Army Eighth Air Force in World War II.* American Mathematical Society, 1991.

McMillan, Kelsey. "AAF Aerial Gunner Training." Bomber Legends eMagazine, Vol. 2, No. 2. Accessible via www.bomberlegends.com/pdf/BL_Mag_v2-2-GunneryTrain.pdf.

Ministry of Defense of the Kingdom of Belgium. *Livre d'Or de la Resistance Belge.* Brussels: Les Editions Leclercq, 1949.

Missing Air Crew Reports (MACR) #4237 and #3339. United States Archives, www.archives.gov.

Moore, Bob, ed. *Resistance in Western Europe.* Oxford: Berg, 2000.

National Archives. Electronic Army Serial Number Merged File, ca. 1938–1946 (Enlistment Records), www.archives.gov.

National Archives. Prisoners of War Data File, 12/7/1941–11/19/1946. www.archives.gov.

NBC Nightly News. February 1, 1984.

Neave, Airay. *Little Cyclone.* London: Coronet Books, 1973.

Nerinckx, Emile P. "Comment Vecut et Mourut un Aviateur Américain en Belgique Occupée Sorensen Gerald." Unpublished manuscript, April 27, 1947.

"New Case of Nazi Criminal Used as Spy by the U.S. Is Under Study." *New York Times*, January 9, 1984.

Nichol, John, and Tony Rennell. *The Last Escape: The Untold Story of Allied Prisoners of War in Germany 1941–1945.* London: Penguin Books, 2003.

"Nos héros de la seconde guerre mondiale." 3 vols. Unpublished manuscript of the Syndicat d'Initiative de Silly 2012.

The Official History of the Fifth Division USA: During the period of its organization and operations in the European world war, 1917–1919. The Red Diamond (Meuse) Division. N.p.: Society of the Fifth Division, 1919.

Pocatellian. Yearbook of Pocatello High School for 1937 and 1938.

Pre-flight Training in the AAF, 1939–1944. Army Air Forces Historical Studies, No. 48. Army Air Force Historical Office Headquarters, 1946.

Punches, Joel. "B-17 Flight Log (5 Sept–21 Feb 1944)." Unpublished manuscript.

www.csobeech.com/files/B17FlightLog.
pdf (last accessed October 20, 2013).

Rémy [G. Renault Roulier]. *Le 18e Jour: La Tragedie de Leopold III, Roi des Belges.* Paris: Editions France-Empire, 1976.

Robert, Max. "La résistance pendant la guerre 40/45—Groupement de l'Armée Secrète." Unpublished manuscript, date unknown.

Rostad, Mary, with Susan T. Hessel. *Squirrel Is Alive: A Teenager in the Belgian Resistance and French Underground.* La Crosse, WI: Viterbo University, 2012.

Schrijvers, Peter. *Liberators: The Allies and Belgian Society, 1944–1945.* Cambridge: Cambridge University Press, 2009.

Sher, Neil M., Aron A. Golberg, and Elizabeth White. "Robert Jan Verbelen and the United States Government." A report to the assistant attorney general, Criminal Division, U.S. Department of Justice, June 16, 1988.

Sorensen, Gerald E. "A Day from the Diary." Unpublished manuscript, 1944.

Strachan, Hew. *The First World War, Volume I: To Arms.* New York: Oxford University Press, 2003.

Tasnier, Brevet Lt. Col., and Brevet Major R. Van Overstraeten. *La Belgique et La Guerre, Vol. III: Les Operations Militaires.* Brussels: Henri Bertels, 1923.

Tuchman, Barbara W. *The Guns of August.* New York: Macmillan, 1962.

Union Internationale de la Résistance et de la Déportation (U.I.R.D.) "Liste des Crimes Retenus a Charge de Verbelen Robertus par le Conseil de Guerre de la Province du Brabant (7ème Chambre flamande) le 14 Octobre 1947." Unpublished manuscript.

Van der Essen, Léon. *The Invasion and the War in Belgium: From Liège to the Yser.* London: Adelphi Terrace, 1917.

Van Herreweghen, César. "Ce Heros de l'Ombre, Souvenez-Vous." Unpublished manuscript, date unknown.

Watterson, Sylvia. "Habib Always Held His Cards Close to His Chest." *The Spokesman Review,* August 9, 1982.

Watry, Charles A. *Washout! The Aviation Cadet Story.* Carlsbad CA: California Aero Press, 1983.

Wells, Mark K. *Courage and Air Warfare: The Allied Aircrew Experience in the Second World War.* London: Frank Cass, 1995.

Index

Numbers in **bold italics** indicate pages with photographs.

Aalst, Belgium 130
Abeels, Arthur 1, 98, 110–119, 121, 123, 126, 127, 128–149, 151, 153, 154, 155, 165, 171–181, 184–190, 202, 204, 208, 212–213
Abeels, Clémy 1, 98, 113–114, 115, 117, 121, 123, 124, 125, 128–149, *138*, 151, 153, 166, 171–174, 184–190, 202, 204, *205*, 208
Abeels, Isidore 110
Abeels, Roger 1–8, *114*, 115, 119–121, 123, 126–149, *148*, 151, *152*, 153, 154, 158–168, 169–176, 184, 186, 187, 188, 194, 195, 201, 202, 203, 204, 205–206, 208, 209, 211–213, 217, 219
Abeels, Janine *see* Abeels, Jenny
Abeels, Jenny xii, 1, 3, 4, 115, 121–122, 123, 124, 125, 126–127, 128–149, *138*, *148*, 153, 154, 165, 166, 171–182, *175*, 184–190, *189*, 202–203, 204–209, *205*, *208*, 210
ABMC *see* American Battle Monuments Commission
Adam, Émile 94
Adenauer, Konrad 216
Advanced Flight School 30
aerial gunners 30, 34, 48, 56, 58, 59–60, 77, 78, 79, 81
Albert I 106, 108, 109, 113, 116
Algoet, Pat 185
Allard, Léon xi, 196
Almeria, Christopher xi
Alsace, France 177
Amarillo, Texas 54–57, 182, 183, 207, 209, 210
Amarillo Army Airfield 47, 56–57, 58
Amarillo Business College 55
American Battle Monuments Commission xi, 3, 180, 181, 222
American Overseas Memorial Day Association Belgium xi, 3, 221–222, *208*
Amiens, France 88
Anderlecht, Belgium 110, 134, 151
Andrieux, André 155
anti-aircraft artillery *see* flak
Antwerp, Belgium 106, 185
AOMDA *see* American Overseas Memorial Day Association Belgium

Ardennes American Cemetery xi, 180, 221, 222
Arendonk, Belgium 124
Armée Secrète see Secret Army
armistice 50, 111, 117, 122
Association des Anciens Combattants de Ganshoren see Ganshoren Veterans Association
Ath, Belgium 167
Atheneum Léon Lépage 114
Attleborough, England 74
Aubel, Belgium 180
Auderghem, Belgium 98
Austria 106, 193–194
Aviation Cadet Program x, 29–48, 56, 60
Aviation Cadet Qualifying Examination 30–31

B-17 Flying Fortress: in battle 78–79; crew positions 68–71, 88; technical specifications 67, 76; tour of duty 75–76; training of crew 56, 59–63, 72; weather 59–60, 62, 79–80
B-24 Liberator 124
B-26 C Invader 203
Baby Blitz 74
Baby Shoes 124
ball turret gunner 67, 70–71, 80–81, 82–83
Bangor, Maine 72, 73
Bannock County Agriculture Extension Service 199
Barber of Seville 185
Basic Flight School 30, 45–47
Basilica (Belgian National) 142, 174, 187
Battle of Liège 109–110
Battle of the Bulge 177
Bayonne, France 88
BBC Radio 104, 118, 129, 157, 162
Bean, L.M 40
Belgian Army 100, 103, 104, 116–117, 155
Belgian Legion 103, 155
Belgian National Movement 101
Belgische Legioen see Belgian Legion
Belgische Nationale Beweging see Belgian National Movement

Bell, Christie xi
Bénis 123, *140*
Berlin, Germany 81
Big Bertha 109, 111
Bilbao, Spain 89
Binger, Betty 47
Black Brigades 100
black market 130–131, 132
Black Thursday 74, 77
Blackfoot, Idaho 11, 14, 60
blitzkrieg 116, 118, 121, 155
Bois d'Enfers, France 81
Bolland, André 102
bombardier 29–34, 62, 67, 69, 77, 79, 84
Borger, Texas 54–55, 65
Borger High School 55
Botanique 125
Bouhon, Major 187
Bovingdon, England 74
Boy Scouts of America 22–23
Brain-le-Comte, Belgium 155
Braswell, Maurice x, 72
Brazley, Robert x
Brent, André 166, 167, 169, 170, 172
Brichard, Jean-Pierre 97
British Army 109, 116, 117, 132, 150, 170, 171, 192, 198
Bruges, Belgium 116, 157, 185
Brunswick (Braunschweig), Germany 80
Brusselmans, Anne 91, 97, 98, 124, 126, 136, 150, 185, 196
Brussels, Belgium 88, 89, 93, 94, 96, 97, 98, 100, 110, 113, 114, 116, 121, 122, 125, 130, 131, 134, 136, 147, 150, 154, 158, 163, 167, 170, 171, 175, 177, 184, 185, 196, 197, 206
Buchenwald Concentration Camp 193, 198

Cal-Aero Flight Academy 39–45, *42*, 45
California Air National Guard 40
Callister, Marion 65
Camp Bragg 50
Camp Hill, Pennsylvania 204
Canadian Army 150
Catholic Church 92, 113, 121, 124, 144–145, 186, 201
Catholic Youth Association 114
Cellens family 119, 133, 142–143,
Champa, Vito A. 69, *77*, 78, 84, 88, 93, 191–192
Chant des Partisans 195
Charleroi, Belgium 102, 151
Charles (Regent) 190
Charlotte of Luxembourg 117
Cherniss, Harold 177, 199
Chevalier, Marie-Christine xi
Cheyenne Modification Center 77

Chicago, Illinois 183
Christmas 36, 63
Church of Christ 52, 55, 57, 65, 186, 209
Church of Jesus Christ of Latter-Day Saints ix–x, 14–18, 20, 22–23, 26–27, 28, 36, 37, 64, 65, 71, 75, 135, 144, 174, 186, 199, 200–201
clandestine press 99, 102–103, 118, 120
Claser, Charles 103, 104
Classification Center 30, 32–34, 36, 56
Clébau 113, 131
Clermont Ferrand, France 81
Cold War 8, 194, 218
Colin, Jean 166, 169
collaborators 93, 101, 119, 123, 131, 132–133, 134, 145, 151
Comar, James 88–89
Combat Crew Staging Center 66, 72
Comet Line xii, 88, 89–91, 92, 93, 94, 97, 98, 123, 124, 130, 131, 132, 134, 135–136, 140, 147, 150–151, 184, 191, 192, 196–198
Commemorative Air Force x
communists 101–102, 155, 193, 216–217
Congo 106, 156, 161, 187, 196
Congress Column 122, 185
conscription: labor 102, 118, 120, 150, 151, 163; military 31, 58, 110, 118
Constitution (Belgium) 106
Coorevits, Sandrin x–xi, 3
co-pilot 68
Cracklow, Cécile 121, 126
Cracklow, Daniel 121
Croix de Guerre 187, 190, 213
Cross of the National Federation of Combatants of Belgium 187, 190
Culot, Gustav 155
Cuvelier, Col. 187

D–Day 129
Darbay, Louis xi
Davison, Michigan 203
Dean, Arthur 89
Dean, Jean Cope 18–19
De Clercq, Willy 223*n*4
De Coen, Jacques 98
Decroës, Richard 166, 169
de Fraiteur, Raoul 190
Degauquier, Albert 155
Deherder, Bernard xi, 196
de Jongh, Andrée 88–89, 196
De Keyser, Olivier 120
Delvigne, Madame 119, 126
demerits *see* gigs
De Stobbilier, Marie 97, 151
De Vos, Lea xi
De Zitter, Prosper 231*ch*10*n*2

Dick, Brian xi
Dickon, Chris x
Dijon, France 77
Dinant, Belgium 158
Dingledine, Lt. Eugene 68, 69, 72, 73, **77**, 81, 82, 84, 86, 93, 94, 192–194
Dodo 41
Dora Concentration Camp 194
Douglas DC-4 190
Dow Army Airfield 72
Drew Army Airfield 61, 62–63, 72
Duhainaut, Ghislain 166, 169
Dumas, Texas 3, 207, 210
Dunkerque, France 88, 116
Duquennoy, Roger xi
Durez, Monsieur 92
Dusart, Col. Charles 110
Dyer, Col. Harvey E. 46

18th Division (German) 116
18th Replacement Wing 61
8th Air Force 76
Eisenhower, Gen. Dwight D. 196
llème Regiment de Ligne see 11th Line Infantry Regiment
11th Combat Crew Replacement Center 74
11th Line Infantry Regiment (Belgium) 110
11th Mixed Brigade (Belgium) 110
Elvenden Hall, England 74
Emile André School 115
Enghien, Belgium 153, 155, 170, 171, 172, 187, 195
England 65, 74, 76, 88, 91, 94, 120, 121, 124, 133, 139, 141, 162, 174, 176, 184, 197
Englebin, Oswald 151
English Channel 84, 116
l'Espinette 92, 93, **95**, 135, 154
Etterbeek, Belgium 97, 98
European Theater of Operations 73
European Union 4, 8, 216, 217, 219, 223n4
EVA group 99
Evere, Belgium 206
Expo 58 206

Facer, George 200
Facer, Sharlene 200
Fallingbostel, Germany 192
fencing club *see La Rapière*
Fidelio 101
5th Field Artillery Brigade 49
5th Infantry Division 49, 50
Fillée, Bertha 97, 98, 126, 185
1st Army 50
1st Gordon Highlanders (UK) 88
flak 63, 77, 78–79, 83–84, 124, 203
Flanders 100–101, 106, 180, 193, 221–222

Flanders Field American Cemetery xi, 180, 221, 222
flight engineer 69, 84, 124
Flint, Michigan 124, 177, 201, 203
Ford, Charles 183
Foreign Office 89
Forsyth, Frank 167, 171, 172, 173, 174, 176
Fort Breendonk, Belgium 198
Fort Douglas, Utah 31
Fort Evegnée, Belgium 110
Fort Fléron, Belgium 110
Fort Hall Indian Reservation, Idaho 11
4-H Club 27
448th Bomber Group 124
Fourmanoir, Monsieur 154, 187
Fourth of July 57, 141
Fowler, Doris 61
France 106, 107, 108, 116
Franco, Generalissimo Franciso 89
Franco-Prussian War 106
Frapelle, France 49
Free University of Brussels 100
French Army 49, 108, 109, 117
Friedrickshaven, Germany 77
Front d'Indépendance see Independence Front

Ganshoren, Belgium 1, 3, 98, 100, 113, 114, 115, 116, 123, 126, 154, 172, 173, 180, 181, 182, 185, 187, 190, 194, 204, 212
Ganshoren Veterans Association 113, 116, 173
Geheim Leger see Secret Army
Geneva Convention 105
Georgette 174, 176, 184–185
German Army 49–50, 107, 109, 116–117, 118, 150, 155, 157, 163, 168
Germany 107, 108, 115, 116
Gestapo 90, 92, 96, 98, 119, 121, 124, 125, 126, 134, 143, 150, 151, 153, 156, 160, 161, 163, 191, 198
Gewapende Partizanen see Partisans
Ghent, Belgium 157, 185
Ghislain, Félix 156
Ghiste, Ann xi
gigs 38, 41
Glass, John R. 69, **77**, 78, 84, 88, 93, 191–192
Gold Star Flying Award 44
Gondregnies, Belgium 92, 153, 154
Goose Bay, Canada 73
Goris, Monsieur 151
Gover, Raymond 204
government-in-exile 99, 102, 103, 104, 105, 117, 155
Grand Canyon 207

Grand Duchess of Luxembourg *see* Charlotte
Grand-Place 173, 185
Great Depression 20, 53, 54, 57
Green, William 199
Greenland 73
Groesbeck, Texas 50, 51
Gross-Tychow, Pomerania 191–192
ground loop 44, 46, 48
Group G 100, 155, 192
Groupement Générale de Sabotage see
    Group G
Groveland, Idaho ix, 19, 20, 65, 200
Gryspeirt, Odette **96**, 97, 98, 123, 124–126,
    129–130, 134, 135, 151, 185, 197
Guérisse, Albert 99
Guides 115, 129
gunnery school 59–60
Gustrow, Germany 111

Hainault, Belgium 158
Hale, Arden 65
Hall, Mr. 40, 41, **43**
Hamelet, France 88
Hamm, Germany 77
Hannequin, Alcide 229*ch7n*3
Hasselt, Belgium 110
Hatch, Hugh 200
hazing 38–39, 40, 45, 63
Henri Chapelle American Cemetery xi,
    180, 221, 222
Herstal, Belgium 110
Himmler, Heinrich 151, 193
Hitler, Adolf 117, 213
Hoffman, Bruce x
Hoffman, Laura xiii
Hoffman, Lowell x
Hoffman, Ruth x
Hokanson, Melba 200
Hospital de Bavière 111
Hotel Bannock 66
Hôtel Bedford 174, 177
Hôtel de la Courronne 111
Hôtel Metropole 171, 173, 174, 176, 191
House Insurance Company 55
Howard, Elizabeth 18–19
Howe, Everett 75, 81
Hunter Army Airfield 66, 72
Hürtgen Forest 177
Husson, Maurice xi, 227*ch5n*4
Hutchinson, Lester 70, **77**, 78, 84, 93, **96**,
    97, 191

Idaho House x, 25–27
Ieper, Belgium 116
Independence Front 99–103, 118, 120, 128,
    145, 153, 155, 173, 198

Industrial Revolution 106
initial point of attack 69
Ixelles, Belgium 97, 113

Jamison, Kent x
Japan 28, 60, 203
Jette, Belgium 121
Jewish Defense Committee 102
Jour-J 105, 162, 163, 167

Kaiser *see* Wilhelm II
Kasango, Congo 156
Kearns Army Airfield 61
Keesling, Robyn x
King of the Belgians *see* Albert I, Charles
    (Regent), Léopold III
Kiss, Irma 201, 205
Koekelberg, Belgium 97, 114, 142, 151
Korean War 203–204, 209
Krijkamp, Constance 110

Labliau, Belgium 163
Lady Moe 75
Laeken Belgium 117
Lamda Delta Sigma 27–28
Lancaster bomber 162
Lanquesaint, Belgium xi, 85–86, 88, 194–
    195
Lapeer, Michigan 124
Larsen, Claudette ix, 200, 207
Larsen, Deloy ix, 200
Larsen, Dianne 200
Larsen, Donald 200
Larsen, Gerald 200
Larsen, Gwen 200
Larsen, Henry 200
Larsen, Jeanette 200
Larsen, Kent 207
Larsen, Leo 21, 200
Larsen, Mette Marie 18–19
Larsen, Pete x
Larsen, Sandra 200
Larsen, Sharon 200
Las Vegas, Nevada 59, 75
Las Vegas Army Airfield 58–60
Last Post 173, 187, 188
Lauenberg, Germany 192
Lavaside Canal 13
Lavaside School 13, 14
Leclercq, Georges 100
Leclercq, Lucien 100
Leclerq, Maurice xi, 196
Légion Belge see Belgian Legion
Lemaire, Emile 160
Leman, General Gérard 110
LeMay, Curtis 74

Leopold III 115, 117, 118
Lepoivre, Carmen 92
Lepoivre, Charles 92, 94, *95*, 153, 154, 156, 187, 197–198
Lepoivre, Lucie 92, 94, 187, 197–198
Lepoivre, Marcel 92, *95*, 187, 197–198
Lepoivre, Sylvie 92, 154, 156, 187, 197–198
Le Roeulx, France 163
Leurquin, Major 158
Leuven, Beglium 112, 151
Lewis, Alfred 51
Lewis, Chester 51
Lewis, Clyde 49–56, 64–65
Lewis, Clyde, Jr. 51
Lewis, Dolly 50–51
Lewis, Nannie Mae 50–55, 64–65, 190
Lewis, Nora Lee xii, 3, 48, 49, 51, 54–58, *55*, 61–66, *64*, 72, 75, 135–136, *137*, 161, 171, 172, 174, 176–*189*, 190, 194, 198, 201–202, 203, 205, 207–208, 209–211, 212, 213
Lewis, Tracy 51
La Libre Belgique 99, 120
Liège, Beglium 106, 109, 110, 111, 113
Ligne Comète see Comet Line
Lille, France 163
Limbourg-Stirum, Countess 124
Limestone County, Texas 49, 50, 51, 54
Limey, France 50
Liverpool, England 49
Lloyd, E. 40
Lloyd's Bank 173
Locus, François 134
London, United Kingdom 74, 103, 184
Long Beach, California 41
Lorraine 49
Lovelace, Frank 61
Luc group 100, 155
Luftwaffe 74, 116, 117
Luxembourg 50, 83, 162
Lys River 116

MacConnell, Lt. James 69, *77*, 84, 88, 93, 191–192
Maechelson, Beverly 47
Mannekin Pis 185
Mannheim, Germany 111
Maquis de Saint Marcoult xi, 104, 154–168, 169–171, 188, 195–196
maquisards 156, 163, *164*, 165
Marc group *see Luc* group
Marcq-lez-Enghien, Belgium 4, 167–168, 169–170, 178, 187–188, *189*, 194
Masnuy, Belgium 157
Mauthausen Concentration Camp 196
McGill, Frieda 203–204, 205
McManaman, Bernard 124, 126–127, 128–

149, *138*, *139*, *140*, *148*, 151, *152*, 153, 154, 156, 158–168, 169, 171–*175*, 176, 177, 178, 201–204, 205, 206, 207, 208
McManaman, Lorena 203, 207
Meadows, Claud 75, 81
Mechelen, Belgium 197
Medal of Freedom 196
Medal of the Armed Resistance 187, 190
Member of the British Empire 196
Menen, Belgium 116
Merced, California 46
Merced Army Airfield 45–48, 56
The Merry Widow 122
Metz, France 82, 84
Meysmans, Jean-Louis 192, 194
Micheroux, Belgium 110
MICKEY device 80
Middelkerke, Belgium 117
Milices Patriotiques see Patriotic Militias
milk run 80
Milmort, Belgium 110
The Miracle Tribe 75
Mons, Belgium 157
Moore, Lt. Col. 187
Mormon *see* Church of Jesus Christ of Latter Day Saints
Morse Code 60
Morton, Darwin L. 210
Morton, James E. 210
Morton, Jim Ed xii, 209–210
Morton, Nora Lee *see* Lewis, Nora Lee
Morton, William J. xii, 210
Moseley, Major Corliss C. (C.C.) 40, 44
Mounier, Madeleine 97, 98
Mouvement National Belge see Belgian National Movement
munitions 59
Muraille, Austin xiii
Murdock, Wayne 61
Musselman, Lt. Everett 124
Mussolini, Benito 123

Namur, Belgium 106, 158
NATO *see* North Atlantic Treaty Organization
navigator 29–34, 62, 67, 69, 77, 79
Nazis 1, 2, 5, 6, 7, 37, 73, 88, 90, 91, 92, 93, 101, 103, 105, 116–119, 121–123, 125, 130, 131, 133–135, 142, 145, 150, 151, 153, 156, 157, 158, 160, 162–164, 167, 168, 170, 171, 176, 191–195, 197–198, 201, 212, 213, 217, 218
NBC Television 194
Nerinckx, Emile 155–163, 166, 167, 185, 187–188, 195, 196
Netherlands 106, 110

Neuengamme Concentation Camp 158
Neupré, Belgium 180, 221
neutrality 106–107, 108, 116
New Orleans, Louisiana 61–62, 63, 66, 183
New Year's Eve 37, 39
New York City 183, 190, 194
New York Times 194
Nienberg, Germany 124
19th Field Artillery Regiment 49
96th Bomb Group 74–87
90th Infantry Division 50
9th Service Command Induction Center 31
Nipper, Willy 133
Norden bombsight 79
North Africa Shuttle Mission 74
North Atlantic Transport Command 72
North Atlantic Treaty Organization 2, 4, 8, 9, 217, 218–219, 223n4

Onafhankelijkheidsfront see Independence Front
Ontario Army Air Base *see* Cal-Aero Flight Academy
Operation Market Garden 177
Opwijk, Belgium 192
Order of Leopold II 190

P-47 Thunderbolt 167
Palo Duro Canyon, Texas 207
parachute drop 157, 162–163, 164
Parchim, Germany 111
Paris, France 150, 162, 163, 166
Park, Janine xii, 203–204, 209
Partisans 101–102, 163–164
Partisans Armées see Partisans
Pat O'Leary group 99
Pathfinder 80
Patriotic Militias 102, 119
Pearl Harbor 7, 28, 29
Perreboom, Joseph 187
Peter Pan 99
Petit, Henri 85–86
Petit, Madelaine xi, 85–86
Peyote, Texas 75
Phantom Train 197–198
Phoenix, Arizona 200
Pierlot, Hubert 105, 117
pilot 29–34, 38–46, 67, 68, 77, 79, 84, 94, 114, 120
Plombières, Belgium 180, 221
Pocatello, Idaho 11, 20, 36, 66, 75, 161, 209, 210
Pocatello High School ix, 22, 23–24
Poelman, Lt. 173
poison gas 50, 52–53, 112
Poland 116

Poncer, Marie-Louise 115, 121–122, 124, 129, 132, 173
Post-Traumatic Stress Disorder 53, 201
POW *see* Prisoner of War
Prairie Hill, Texas 49
Preflight School 30, 36–39
Prestwick, Scotland 73
Primary Flight School 30, 39–45
prisoner of war 73, 78, 79, 85, 105, 111, 112, 139, 145, 176, 192–194
Prohibition 52
propaganda 102–103, 118
Prussia 106
Purple Heart 190
Puvenelle, France 50
Pyrennes Mountains 89

RMS *Queen Elizabeth* 183
Queen of the Netherlands *see* Wilhelmina
Queue-du-Bois, Belgium 111

radar 206
Radio Belgique 104
radio operator 70
railroad (Belgian) *see* SNCB
Ramey, H. 40
La Rapière 114, 123, 173, 204
rationing 130–132
Ravensbruck Concentration Camp 198
Red Cross 170, 171, 172, 173, 192
Réfractaire 102, 121, 151, 163
Refuge Tarin see Maquis de Saint Marcoult
Regensburg, Germany 74
Remagen, Germany 185
"Remember Belgium" 108, 110
Renière, Edouard xii
Resistance: Belgian 1, 2, 3, 4, 6, 88–105, 119, 122, 146, 147, 150–168, 169–170, 173, 187–188, 195–198; French 99, 156
Rexists 119, 151
Reykjavik, Iceland 73
Robert, Max xi, 195
Robinson, Nannie Mae *see* Lewis, Nannie Mae
Rose, Idaho ix, 9, 11, 12, 13, 19, 157
Rotheux, Belgium 222
Royal Air Force 79, 120, 171
Royal Atheneum Koekelberg 114
Royal Military Academy 114
Royal Palace 185

S-phone 162
Sabena 190, 206–207
sabotage 100, 101, 105, 120, 158, 163, 164
Sachsenhausen Concentration Camp 198
safe houses 88, 90, 92, 94, 97–98

Saint Die, France 49
Saint Jean de Luz, France 88
Saint Marcoult, Belgium 92, 156–161
Saint Michael's Cathedral 173, 185
Saint Mihiel, France 50
Saint Petersburg, Florida 63, 135, 161
Salt Lake City, Utah 19, 61, 75, 198–199, 200
Salt Lake City Army Air Base 61
Santa Ana Army Air Base 32–39, *35*, 40
Savannah, Georgia 66
Schmetz, Mathilde 229*ch7n*2
Schotte, Julien 92
Schrader, Ruth 200
Schreyen, Marguerite *96*, 124, 185
Schreyen, Suzette 124
Schreyen, Victor 97, 98, 124, 125, 198
Schutters, Victor 94–96
Schutters, Victor (grandson) xii
Schützstaffel see SS
Schweinfurt, Germany 74
Scotland 73
Secret Army xi, 1, 3, 4, 5, 6, 7, 103–105, 120, 146, 147, 151, 153, 154, 155–168, 172, 173, 177, 187, 188, 195–196, 201, 209, 211, 213; Zone I Sector D *see Maquis de Saint Marcoult*
Secret Intelligence Service 99
Seething, England 124
Selective Service Board 31
Services de Contrôle Aérien, 206
712th Bomber Squadron 124
7th Infantry Division 50
78th Infantry Division 50
Shirey, Harry 75, 81
Siegfried Line 195
Silly, Belgium 85, 93, 154, 155
Singletary, Lt. 40
Smith, Lt. George R. 68, *77*, 84, 93, 94, *95*, 191
Smith, John R. 70, *77*, 78, 80–81, 82, 84, 93–94, 192
Smoes, Alfonse 170
SNCB 94, 197–198
Snetterton Falcons *see* 96th Bomb Group
Snetterton Heath 74–78
SOE *see* Special Operations Executive
Soignies, Belgium 155, 163
Le Soir 102–103
Sorensen, Aletta 11, 21, 200, 207
Sorensen, Arlinda 9, 11, 12, 19, 20, 21
Sorensen, Darwin ix, 9, 11, 13, 200
Sorensen, Ephraim 9, 11, 12, 19, 20, 21, 22, 64, 65, 174, 179, 198–199, 200–201
Sorensen, Evelyn ix, 11, 60, 65, 198, 199, 223*ch1n*1
Sorensen, Harold 11, 76

Sorensen, Luella 9, 11, 12, 19, 20, 21, 64, 65, 174, 179, 186, 190, 198, 199–200, 209, 213
Sorensen, Nephi 9, 11, 12, 13, 19, 20, 21, 60
Sorensen, Niels 18–19
Sorensen, Nora Lee *see* Lewis, Nora Lee
Sorensen, Shirley 20, 21, 200
Sorensen, Thora 11, 21, 24, 199, 200
Sorensen, Veliene 11
Soviet Red Army 192
Soviet Union *see* Union of Soviet Socialist Republics
Special Operations Executive 100, 103, 104, 105, 155, 157, 162, 163, 188, 196
SS 5, 119, 151, 168, 169, 193
Stalag Luft IV 191–192
Standard Nine Scale *see* stanine
Stange, Otto, Jr. 70, *77*, 78, 84, 88, 93, 191–192
stanine 33, 34
Star of David 121
Stearman PT-13B 41, *43*, 44, 45
Steeds Verenigd 100
Street, Lt. Denuncio 69, *77*, 84, 93, 94, *95*, 192–194
Supreme Headquarters Allied Powers Europe 3
Suys, Cyrile 94
Switzerland 111

tail gunner 67, 71, 72, 77, 82
Tampa, Florida 61, 63–64
Taos Indian Reservation 207
Taps 173
Tedesco, Gilbert 98, 198
Texas 207
Thanksgiving 33
Théâtre Royal de la Monnaie 122, 185
Thimister-Clermont, Belgium 131
3rd Air Division 74
3rd Army 193
3rd Army Division (Belgium) 110
3rd Bomber Wing 203
13th Bomber Squadron 203
34th Brigade (German) 110
Thoricourt, Belgium 92
359th Fighter Squadron 167
356th Fighter Group 167
339th Squadron 74
Tollembeek, Belgium 94
Tomas (Basque guide) 89
tour of duty 75–76, 80
Treaty of London 106, 108
Treaty of Versailles 213
Troubleyn, Rob xii
Tubize, Belgium 195
Tuchman, Barbara 110

Tyhee, Idaho ix, 20, 22, 23, 25, 31, 60, 65, 176, 198, 200

Union of Soviet Socialist Republics 101, 194, 216–217, 223*n*3
United Kingdom 106, 108, 116
USAAF *see* United States Army Air Forces
USAF *see* United States Air Force
United States Air Force 3, 29, 201, 203–204
United States Ambassador 3, 182
United States Army 37, 49–50, 51, 132, 150, 173, 174, 177, 181, 192, 193, 195, 199, 209
United States Army Air Forces x, 2, 6, 29, 30, 31, 33, 34, 36, 39, 40, 47, 48, 56, 58, 59, 60, 63, 66, 67, 72, 73, 74, 76, 79, 80, 82, 124, 167, 171, 174, 191, 195
United States Embassy 3, 181, 222
United States Navy 49, 50
United States Senate 194
Université Libre de Bruxelles see Free University of Brussels
University of Idaho 24–29, *25, 26*, 31
Unterseen, Switzerland 111

V1 rocket 74, 81, 89
V2 rocket 74, 194
La Valdalion, France 49
Valenciennes, France 88
Van Delft, Gisbert 92, 156–157, 160, 161, 171, 187
Van Delft, Marie-Anne 156, 160, 175, 187
Van Delft children 156, *159*, 187
van den Stichelen, Major 187
Vandercapellen, Edourad 170
Vanderschueren, Armand 195
Vandezande, General M. 158
Van Haalen, Caspar ix
Van Herreweghen, César xi, 163–*164*, 165, 166, 167, 196
Vanhove, Paul 227*ch*5*n*4
Van Meus, Gustav 170
Veiligheidskorps 151, 193
Venquier, Father 166, 169
Verbelen, Robert 151, 193–194
Victoria Air Terminal 184
Victoria Station 184

Villers-en-Haye, France 50
Vlaams Nationaal Verbond 119, 133
VNV *see Vlaams Nationaal Verbond*
von Bethmann Hollweg, Theobald 108
von Braun, Wernher 194
von Schlieffen plan 107–108, 109, 116
Voordeckers, Father 92
Vosges Mountains 107
Vultee Valiant BT-13 45, 46

Waffen SS see SS
waist gunner 67, 70, 71
Wallonia 100–101, 106, 158
War Department 182
Ward, A.O. 182
Waregem, Belgium 180, 221, 222
wash-outs 30, 32, 34, 38, 39, 41, 44, 46, 47–48, 56, 58, 60
Waterloo, Belgium 98, 185
Wauthoz, Jacques 172, 173
Wehrmacht *see* German Army
Weiland, Frank 167
Welkenraedt, Belgium 180, 221
West Coast Training Command 32
Western Technical Taining Command 56
Western Union 61, 176, 181, 198
White Brigade 100, 101, 119
Whyte, Evelyn *see* Sorensen, Evelyn
Whyte, Kenneth 198, 199, 200–201
Wilhelm II 108, 109, 112
Wilhelmina 117
Wilson, Charles x
Witte Brigade see White Brigade
Wolverine xi, 77, 80, 81, 82–86, 88, 91, 93, 135, 154, 191, 194–195
Woodruff, Utah 19
World War I 49–50, 106–110, 116, 122, 145, 155, 180, 215
Wueron family 134

Yellowstone National Park 143, 161
Yosemite National Park 46–47

Zach, Otto 46–47
Zéro group 100, 155